St. Louis Community College

Forest Park
Florissant Valley
Meramec

Instructional Resources
St. Louis, Missouri

GAYLORD

Women and Laughter

Feminist Issues: Practice, Politics, Theory
Alison Booth and Ann Lane, Editors

Women and Laughter

Frances Gray

University Press of Virginia
Charlottesville

First published 1994 by The Macmillan Press Ltd

First published 1994 in the United States of
America by the University Press of Virginia
Box 3608 University Station
Charlottesville, VA 22903

Library of Congress Cataloging-in-Publication Data
Gray, Frances (Frances B.)
Women and laughter / Frances Gray.
p.   cm. — (Feminist issues)
Includes index.
ISBN 0–8139–1512–0 (cloth) — ISBN 0–8139–1513–9 (pbk.)
1. Women comedians—Great Britain.   2. Women comedians—United
States.   3. Television comedies—Great Britain.   4. Television
comedies—United States.   5. Stand-up comedy—Great Britain.
6. Stand-up comedy—United States.   I. Title.   II. Series: Feminist
issues (Charlottesville, Va.)
PN1590.W64G73   1994
792.7' 028' 082—dc20   93–23400
                                                                          CIP

Printed in China

For my son

Contents

PART III STANDUP AND BE COUNTED

Acknowledgements

I should like to thank the University of Sheffield Research Fund for a grant towards this book; Jo Campling, for seeing it through with such patience; Imogen Donelly (Jimmo), Clare and Johnny Maire, Elizabeth Rees-Morgan (Fizzy Lizzie), Claire Schrader (La Dame de Flamme), Kate Rowland and Linda Smith for illuminating interviews and letters as well as entertainment; my seminar groups of 1991 and 1992 for their insights and continuing interest in women's laughter; Tallyn, my son, for making me laugh; those friends who sat around with me in clubs where women start their sets at 2 am, for the company; Olly Double, PhD and standup comic, for generously sharing his own findings and insights and for disagreeing with me most of the time.

FRANCES GRAY

Introduction: or, Why this book does not exist

Humourless: the cliché 'she lacks a sense of humour' is applied by men to every threatening woman when she does not find the following funny: rape, big breasts, sex with little girls. On the other hand there is no imputation of humourlessness if she does not find impotence, castration and vaginas with teeth humorous. (*The Feminist Dictionary*)

Once, you could be reborn. You became one with the goddess Demeter mourning her daughter Persephone, snatched away to hell for half the year, and you rejoiced with her in the symbolic birth of a holy child, the sight of whom blessed you into eternal life. So secret was this rite that even now we know only the ceremonies which led up to it. The initiates shed all distinctions of sex and status as they washed in the sea, the source of life, and dressed themselves in garments which were ever afterwards holy. They sacrificed pigs, symbols of both decay and fertility. They walked as if in mourning towards a fire so bright it could be seen from miles away, and as their walk drew to an end they crossed a bridge symbolic of the transition from sorrow to joy. On this bridge they encountered the rites known as the *gephyrismoi*: dirty jokes, songs and dances performed by a woman.

The Eleusinian Mysteries: secret rites of the ancient world; there are many, and contradictory, ways of reading them, especially those jokes on the bridge. You might favour, for instance, a romantic – feminist view, one encouraged by the story they commemorate. The goddess, in deepest grief for the rape of her daughter, refused to eat or drink; a lame serving maid, Baubo, staged a little comic show, telling smutty jokes, parodying the pains of pregnancy and birth and finally producing from beneath her skirts Demeter's little son, who leapt into his mother's arms for a surprise kiss; the goddess laughed, took nourishment and went on to recover her daughter for half the year and allow Spring to return to the earth. Thus comedy was born. A story of a lost matriarchal paradise, you might say, a rich female culture in which one woman heals another, and

1

ultimately Nature itself, by inventing comedy, a comedy joyously and benevolently sexual without being sexist. It seems an excellent starting point for an investigation into the possibility of a distinctly female form of laughter.

Or maybe not. Turn from the myth and look at the price tag. Set the rites back, not in their misty origins but in the historical context in which we know they were performed, the so-called Golden Age of Rome. In theory anyone, slave or free, male or female, could participate in the Mysteries as long as they spoke Greek and had never killed. Most slaves or women, however, simply could not afford it. The celebrations of the goddess were enjoyed by the male ruling élite – Cicero, for example, who wrote movingly of his hopes of rebirth while devoting his professional energy to the character assassination of women like Clodia, whose main crime seems to have been sexual independence. Such men could, and did, pay for their wives, mistresses and slaves to go to Eleusis. But once you envisage women as a tolerated minority, invited guests rather than central to the ceremony, those jokes on the bridge sound different. Laughing female sexuality is male-defined as something to be transcended, a last reminder of the base body before the spirit moves on to higher things. In this scenario the role of Baubo is played by a woman not because it celebrates female strength but because it is beneath male dignity.

Baubo is not easy to find today. Images survive from antiquity, little dancing vulvas with funny faces, but only in museums. The remains of the Eleusinian shrine are hemmed in by cement factories, rejected by tourists in favour of the Acropolis, Olympia, Epidauros, the shrines of the man made law, the all-male Games and the exclusively male theatre. If you want a souvenir of comedy in the ancient world for the folks back home you can buy a grinning male mask; or – maybe with a view to embarrassing the recipient – a model of Priapus, a minor god with a gigantic phallus and a grin that might be good-humoured or threatening, attached to a key ring, a toilet roll holder, or an ashtray. A less aggressive Priapic update can be found in gift shops all over the West – Wicked Willie* the cuddly toy penis, complete with a smile and a red nose. You

---

* These little love objects appeared in the wake of the cartoons by Gray Jolliffe to whom the character 'Wicked Willie' is copyright. Willie has appeared in *Cosmopolitan* magazine and in book form (*Man's Best Friend*, Pan Books, London 1984, cartoons by Jolliffe, text by Peter Mayle). Subsequently he has appeared on video and has recently begun marketing a range of novelty items such as wine labels. Any resemblance to Shakespeare's 'Will' or to other Willies or Dicks is presumably coincidental.

may find that he too can arouse mixed responses; but the fact remains that these little pink cylinders are snugly at home in our culture while that other, female, symbol is not. Baubo has disappeared so completely from history that her appearance amid the birthday cards and shiny balloons would shock, disconcert, or, saddest of all, be seen as a symbol of female degradation, not female laughter. We should ask ourselves why.

That's it. For some readers I might as well stop here. Because to discuss, with a straight face, something as transparently non-serious, as just-for-a-giggle as a pink stuffed willy, let alone attempt to relate it to ancient cults, is to prove yet again a truth universally acknowledged: *Women have no sense of humour.* Men, and indeed some women, have been reiterating this ever since the word 'humour' began, about three hundred years ago, to denote a capacity for laughter rather than a bodily fluid. Congreve, an early user, announced in 1695 that 'I have never made any Observation of what I apprehend to be true Humour in Women';[1] John Fisher made a long-overdue study of the nature of standup comedians in 1973; he allotted to women half a single chapter entitled 'Are Women Funny?' His conclusion is that

> great comedians have exploited the funniness of women but it is just not on the cards that George Burns' Gracie Allen, Howerd's plump pianist, the girl that Eric Morecambe experimentally calls 'Sid', would be funny if themselves given total control of the stage, unable as they are to comprehend the laughter they evoke in the presence of their male colleagues.[2]

These look like considered statements, even if one doesn't agree with them. Yet Congreve created some of the best female comic roles ever, tailored to the exact gifts of actresses he knew and respected; Fisher seems entirely capable of perceiving the creative energy of male comedians like Frankie Howerd and Eric Morecambe, often at their funniest when apparently fazed by our laughter. We seem to be dealing here with heads stuck firmly and wilfully in the sand.

Women have no sense of humour. It would not be difficult to disprove. I could choose the short, classic reply: women must have a sense of humour to put up with men. Or I could treat the remark in the pantomime spirit it deserves and yell 'O yes they do!', prolonging the yell into a book of five hundred pages or so with a title like *Hroswitha of Gandersheim to Ruby Wax: A Thousand Years of Women in Comedy.* But while these things are worth doing all they do is provide empirical evidence against the 'truth' at issue; and as we have already seen, empirical evidence seems only to push the most cultivated male intelligence into the ostrich position. What I wish to do at the outset is not to counter the 'truth' but to unearth the assumptions beneath.

Our society puts a high premium on humour. Laughter is supposed to be good for us, 'The Best Medicine', as *Reader's Digest* puts it. We have all heard the story about the dying doctor who cured himself by watching Chaplin movies, all read the sad story of the bereaved king who 'never smiled again'. It is supposed to be international: watch any televised performance of the Moscow State Circus and the commentator will burble, over closeups of children enjoying the clowns, that laughter transcends the barrier of politics. It is vital to romance, or so any magazine running that endlessly recurring feature about 'My Ideal Partner' will have us believe. It has been lauded by employers to the point where you might imagine it holds up the capitalist system single-handed. A survey in 1986 by Hodge-Cronin and Associates found that 98 per cent of chief executives looked for 'a sense of humour' when hiring personnel.[3] Not to laugh is to be less than fully human; this is the clearly spelled out conclusion of the cult novel of the eighties, Eco's *The Name of the Rose*, which centres on an attempt to suppress the lost writings of Aristotle on comedy. It underlay one of the more imaginative and courageous defences of *The Satanic Verses*, Tony Harrison's film *The Blasphemers' Banquet*,[4] which sets a place for Salman Rushdie at supper with Byron and Voltaire, allying freedom of thought and expression with generosity and good living; against these Harrison sets rigidity, meanness, and, yes, a lack of humour, driving his biggest nail in the coffin of repression by quoting the Ayatollah Khomeini, 'There is no fun in Islam.' (It may be worth noting in passing that Eco's only female character is a pathetic and humourless drudge, and that Islam, unlike Mr Harrison, permits mixed banqueting.)

This fetishization of humour has made it difficult to resist its pressures at any given moment. To object to a specific joke, in a specific context, is to be perceived as an enemy of laughter in general. In recent years, however, the question of 'inappropriately directed laughter' has been given more thoughtful consideration, in contexts which might, not long ago, have seemed surprising. For instance, that traditional feature of the British holiday, the seaside talent contest at Torquay, became in 1989 the site of a debate about humour which virtually took over the show and seemed to have a more powerful effect on the audience than any of the acts under consideration; one of the judges, the TV critic Nina Myskow, took exception to material she considered sexist and racist; she was answered by the comedian Bobby Davro. *The Stage*, a paper not noted for its radical approach to entertainment, relays his reply in these terms:

> Bobby . . . made an impassioned plea for a common sense approach, claiming that to label all ethnic material as racist, and all gender related material as sexist, is to perpetuate unnecessary divisions within the community as a whole. Passionately, he added that 'we must be allowed to poke fun at ourselves and each other, if humour is to survive', at which the audience burst into spontaneous and enthusiastic applause.[5]

Passion *and* common sense, who could ask for more? No wonder that it hurts – as it does – to be told you have no sense of humour. Bobby's reply taps into the double nature of our society's investment in the 'survival' of humour. He gets his applause by his use of that word 'we', stressing the social nature of laughter, the cement that binds communities together, but also through his status as a star, that is, an individual, defending a personal taste and style. While we see laughter as social, we also cherish the conviction that each individual's sense of humour is unique, as private and as special as our sexual nature. Humourlessness is thus a double burden, rather like barrenness in the Old Testament, a failure both social and personal. And like barrenness, it's assumed to be primarily a woman's problem.

The fact that the debate took place at all reflects the impact of feminism on the most casual aspects of everyday life. Few members of the audience, probably, were unfamiliar with the terminology used by Nina Myskow, even if they were reluctant to use it themselves. But feminist critics have also evolved more complex ways of analysing the relationship between women and laughter than a straightforward anger at sexist jokes. Feminism has taught us that the personal is political; it has brought into the political arena aspects of our lives traditionally shut out as irrelevant – sexuality, domesticity, family life; and it has taught us to be very suspicious of Bobby's term 'common sense'. 'Common sense' suggests a deep inborn knowledge of The Way Things Are. We don't need to be told what 'race' means, or 'gender'; we, like Bobby, just know. Increasingly however it becomes apparent that these 'natural' and 'inevitable' aspects of our world are ideological constructs, unconscious practices dictated by unconscious assumptions, which paper over the cracks made by divisions of class and race and gender to disguise the structures of power as 'common sense'. We cannot retire into our private selves, those intimate parts of our being from which laughter, sexuality and desire spring, because our private selves are the places on which power builds its base.

'Common sense', for instance, told Tertullian two centuries after Christ that the lusts of woman made her 'the devil's gateway'[6], the Victorians that 'a modest woman seldom desires any sexual gratification for herself'[7] and the prophets of the so-called sexual revolution of the late sixties that 'a woman's inability of having an orgasm [sic] is simply the unconscious refusal to have one, in order to get revenge on the husband'.[8] While these statements may look very different, they share a tacit concern, not to discuss women's attitudes to sex, but to define them in relation to male defined and controlled ideas of sexuality; in all three cases, sex remains something men do *to* women. Sexuality, in short, does not have a single and unchanging meaning to which our 'commonsense' will guide us; its meanings emerge in the course of a power struggle within language; Tertullian, the Victorian paterfamilias, and the sixties trendy male, used different labels for women whose sexual conduct they disapproved of – but all of them assumed that those labels were theirs to give or withhold; and, as Foucault showed, to control the discourse of sexuality is to wield enormous social power, precisely because we feel that our sexuality is part of our individuality, our selfhood; only with the development of feminist terminology was it possible for women to impose their own definitions of sexuality and to shift the ideological ground of the debate.

Like sexuality, laughter has been sometimes highly valued, sometimes denigrated; but like sexuality – indeed *with* sexuality – laughter has been closely bound up with power. So it may come as no surprise to discover that women have not always lacked a sense of humour. Just as cultures in which sex was perceived as evil recognised women as having sexual desires, and cultures which saw sex as a normal healthy sport for chaps developed the concept of female frigidity, just so cultures which did not exalt humour to its current overblown status could attribute it to women. The Bible, for instance, finds a fair number of sins to lay at women's door – but humourlessness is not one of them. The matriarch Sarah cracks one of the few jokes in the sacred canon on overhearing God tell Abraham that she will bear a child: 'Now that I'm used to groaning, I'm to groan with pleasure?'[9] – but humour in the Pentateuch is not a moral quality at all. Christian writers charting the fall of the Roman Empire, such as St Augustine and St John Chrysostom, expatiate on the lust, vanity and frivolity of women; they don't complain that you can't have a laugh with them – rather they imply that you *can*, and that

that is further evidence of their guile. Only when laughter is the sign of the civilised man – as, say, in Congreve's world, where 'wit' is the equivalent of the white hats in early Westerns – do women appear to suffer from a mysterious frigidity of the funny bone.

> Women have not only no humour in themselves but are the cause of the extinction of it in others. This is almost too cruel to be true, but in every way women correspond to and are representative of nature. Is there any humour in nature? A glance at the zoo will answer this question . . . women are the undifferentiated mass of nature from which the contradictions of real and ideal arose and they are the unlaughing at which men laugh.[10]

Like a medieval anchorite fleeing the temptation of female flesh, like a would-be swinger leaving the cold marriage bed for the bright lights, a man of humour would be well justified in the face of such barbarity in leaving the home to set up a movie industry, a club or a TV sitcom from which women would – by their very nature – be excluded, or at least would only enter upon male terms. This passage, written by Reginald Blyth not in Congreve's world but in 1959, is remarkable for two reasons: first, for the way in which it reinforces the present exaltation of 'humour'; his book as a whole trumpets its virtues, slotting it firmly into position in the dualistic universe that has been one of the more successful tricks in the patriarchal book of ideologies – light/darkness, good/evil, man/woman/, culture/ nature, me Tarzan/you Jane, I laugh/you don't; second, for the paranoia hidden in that word 'nature'. Aristotle said that laughter distinguished mankind from the beasts. No-one has bothered to dispute this since. Nor has anyone bothered to reassert the humourlessness of animals with any frequency. Here, however, the idea is dragged out to reinforce the idea of an unchanging 'natural' order. There were once university statutes to prevent women from taking degrees, because it was not 'natural' for them to have an aptitude for learning. Zebras also lack 'natural' aptitude, but it was not necessary to make laws excluding them, because no one was secretly afraid that a zebra might become Senior Wrangler. Women have constantly exploded the idea of themselves as naturally humourless, just as they once had to explode the idea of a 'natural' lack of intelligence. Having entered the universities, they have changed knowledge; and Blyth here flies to 'nature' to shore up his right to define laughter – something that men do to women – lest it too be changed.

We have all at some time been put down – usually in the classroom – with the words, 'I suppose you think that's funny', and – usually in the pub – with the words, 'Can't you take a joke?' While the tone of voice differs in each case, both remarks in their context assume a specific power – that of defining and thus controlling the immediate area of discourse. If the discourse of laughter is removed from a specific to a cultural context it can be seen – in a culture which truly believes that humour is what separates us from the beasts – that to define a joke, to be the class that decides *what is funny*, is to make a massive assumption of power. Small wonder that it has seemed prudent to shut women out of the comic arena altogether. There are five basic and easily learned techniques for doing this.

One: Brevity is the Soul of Wit. Foster the myth that women talk too much. 'Many geese, many turds, many wives, many words', as the proverb charmingly puts it. While statistical data collected in contexts as varied as TV panel games, marital conversations, staff meetings and experimental pairings has continually shown that men both talk more and interrupt more,[11] the legend prevails. To be a *yenta* is, of course, to lack precisely that control over language needed to make a joke, and through it assert one's place on the side of culture and one's mastery of discourse, of Serious Talk. As Liz Lochhead puts it

> Women
> Rabbit rabbit rabbit women
> Tattle and titter
> Women prattle
> Women waffle and witter
> Men Talk. Men Talk.[12]

Two: Mrs Grundy. When faced with women's objections to specific jokes, invoke the spectre of a thin-lipped and humourless prude averse to any form of spontaneity, life, or joy. If the joke in question has a sexual element, the word 'frigid' may be deployed to considerable effect. A real master of the Mrs Grundy technique may even be able to use it in contexts where humour is not actually an issue – in, for example, debates about pornography. Mrs Grundy can be relied upon to induce powerful feelings of both sexual and existential insecurity and at her strongest can divide women against themselves, as I hope to show in the story of Laura Ormiston Chant in Part III.

Three: Wild Untutored Phoenix. Where women are visibly making people laugh, deny the existence of a conscious creative process. In the *commedia dell'arte*, for example, women sometimes achieved considerable power and status, both as leading actresses and company leaders and innovators. Isabella Andreini of the Gelosi troupe was so revered as a performer that when she died in 1604 she was given a church burial, unprecedented for an actress. But these women never wore the masks from which the comic power of the *commedia* performances sprang – Harlequin, Brighella, Pantalone. The mask marked the actor as a figure with power to transform everyday reality into one of his own making. He ceased to be the person we might have seen warming up or shifting scenery and became Harlequin, inspiring in us a respect for both his character and his creativity. The woman, however, stepped on to the stage unmasked, even wearing her own clothes. Her talents – for singing, music, dancing, improvisation – are merely aspects of her 'self' which she displays, as Lesley Ferris points out. Ferris makes it clear that women in a male-controlled theatre, like women in art, have been treated as symbolic objects upon which men may impose meaning, rather than as characters in their own right: 'the more symbolic . . . "woman" becomes, the less she herself is and can be culturally creative'.[13] Her function in the story is to be 'the woman' – or, more often, 'the girl' – not to be Harlequin or Hamlet.

If this is so for performance generally, I would argue that it is especially true of comic performance. Much useful feminist critical work on cinema and theatre has been done on the concept of 'the male gaze' – the way in which women are positioned on stage or screen as objects to be looked at by a spectator who is, or who is forced to adopt the vantage point of, a man. Comedy positions the woman not simply as the object of the male gaze but of the male laugh – not just to-be-looked-at but to-be-laughed-at – doubly removed from creativity. Hence the relentless stereotyping of women into roles which permit them to be looked at, judged, and laughed at as sexual objects: the dumb blonde, the wisecracking tart, the naive virgin, the dragon who doesn't realise she is sexually past it. The resentment of actresses locked in their stereotypes by the entertainment industry has been well documented: 'Cute, cute, cute – the ruination of careers', complained Debbie Reynolds, trapped as the eternal virgin-next-door.[14] Barbara Windsor recalls being fragmented and objectified as 'a body, a bosom and a joke'.[15]

The most famous, and the most sustained fight against the imposition of the stereotype is of course that of Marilyn Monroe. It would be a waste of time to chart this struggle in detail; the ridicule heaped on her for attempting to study with the Actor's Studio, for reading philosophy and attending UCLA, her often-difficult behaviour when engaged in a role she resented and disliked, have been described often. Monroe was constructed both on and off screen as a 'natural' combination of sexuality and innocence; the characters she played slid imperceptibly into the 'self' Hollywood wanted to sell: the sweet dancer in a tough world in *The Prince and The Showgirl*/the vulnerable young woman who posed nude because she needed the money; the gorgeous singer who still 'always gets the fuzzy end of the lollipop' in *Some Like It Hot*/the three-times-married woman who longed for a home and children. The *doubles entendres* she utters in her own persona ('I don't know why you boys are always getting excited about sweater girls. Take away their sweaters and what have they got?') and in character ('My fan is caught in the door', breathes 'The Girl' in *The Seven Year Itch*) allow laughter to spring from a sense of (male) superiority while retaining just sufficient 'knowingness' to invest that laughter with a sense of mutuality and sharing, to give the spectator the sense that he himself is more than just a user of her body, that he is actively desired.

'The people made me a star', Monroe once pointed out, 'no studio, no person, but the people did'.[16] Her demeanour was governed by a sense of responsibility to that fact: if her offstage anonymity was penetrated, she would respond by becoming 'MM'; her makeup on public occasions was deliberately exaggerated, geared to the fans who would struggle to glimpse her across the street. But she never lost sight of the fact that 'MM' was a Hollywood construct, and it is precisely her ability to ironize her Hollywood 'self' which transforms the routine comic lines and business in her films. *The Seven Year Itch*, for instance, codes her every possible way as a symbol of comic sexuality: brassy music underscores her walk; dressed in the same soft and clingy clothes Hollywood favoured for Monroe herself, 'The Girl' is frequently positioned in semi-profile to call attention to her breasts, carefully silhouetting them, for instance, against co-star Tom Ewell's grey suit; posters and stills blitzed the public with the celebrated image of Monroe astride a subway grating, her skirt blowing in the breeze, shot from a variety of angles – images far more revealing than the actual shots used in the film, but which of course colour our perceptions when viewing it. Yet Monroe herself, uttering lines which convey transparent stupidity or straight smuttiness, constantly undercuts the obvious reading of her character, making it seem incongruous. Tom Ewell, as the married man blundering into attempted seduction, puts on a record. 'You look to me like a Rachmaninov sort of a girl,' he tries, perched clumsily on the arm of a chair, twitching and leering ineptly. 'Is this what they call classical music?', wonders The Girl. 'I could tell because there's no vocal.' The sequence can be viewed, without apparent damage to the punchline, as a series of 'stills' or pin-ups – The Girl with eyes closed, listening; The Girl cutely 'thinking'; The Girl trustingly questioning her host; but Monroe's real impact on it springs from the way she is constantly in motion, so that we are never allowed to treat her character so dismissively. While the line is moronic, inviting a superior snigger, Monroe's face is alive with comic possibility. The eyes widen ingenuously, we can track precisely the moment that an idea dawns – but her gaze is so accurately directed at the dangling, twitching Ewell that she seems to be summing up not her response to the music but his predicament as married bumbler with a guilt complex. The line itself she delivers with a crisp, self-possessed inflection that utterly negates the slow brain implied by its overt content and plunges us straight into the subtext. The mouth may be moist, half-open, as if ripe for a kiss, but the eyes continue to take in every detail of the scene, mocking its crudity. It is a delicate act of resistance; it is also deliberate, a series of small comic decisions: Monroe deploys 'Marilyn' with the precise bodily knowledge achieved from her study of Vesalius on anatomy and the sense of parody which, she said, she learned from Mae West's technique of 'mocking her own sexuality'.[17]

Small movements, small gestures; set in a scale against the power of a whole industry they may seem insignificant. But they add up to comic performance, and it is through such details, through seizing comic power as and where they can, that women have been able to create their own meanings and their own laughter within roles constructed as symbols on to which men may – or may not – choose to project comic meaning. Symbols, as Monroe pointed out, are things you clash. 'A sex symbol becomes a thing. I just hate to be a thing.'[18] To be so perceived is all too often the price of being a woman and a comic. As Lesley Ferris writes of an actress who shared Monroe's situation:

> Isabella Andreini, the *inamorata*, enters the stage. She sings, plays the guitar, dances elegantly, and then bursts into a tirade against her faithless lover – an improvised speech in which she parodies both ideas of romantic love and turgid French tragedy. Her energetic, comic performance exudes style, wit, charisma. But she is maskless. She is merely playing herself.[19]

Four: Small Potatoes. Sometimes all else fails. Sometimes you are confronted by female humour which is all-too-apparently conscious and controlled. This is most often the case with women writers who, although safely dead, refuse to be forgotten. The safest course is to construct an alternative label. 'Irony' is a good one, especially if qualified with some 'feminine' adjectives – 'delicious' is a favourite, since there's a clear suggestion of nature rather than culture inherent in it (a cake doesn't have to *try* to be delicious); if the writer is young and attractive, the epithet can be neatly transposed on to her, rendering her a harmless sexual object; for greatest effect, juxtapose to references which have clearly masculine connotations – 'savage indignation', for instance, will always invoke Swift, and the word 'Rabelaisian' is invaluable for comedy that is broad, physical, and butch. Alongside these terms redolent of the all-male tutorial in the tobacco-filled sanctum, 'irony' can be made to look like an embroidered hanky alongside the Sistine Chapel. Jane Austen is a common victim of this kind of misreading. The anger perceived by feminist literary critics as an intrinsic part of her wit goes unremarked and she, and countless writers influenced by her, can be dismissed as what J. B. Priestley called 'Feminine small potatoes'.[20]

Five: Fair is Foul and Foul is Fair. Relabelling does not have to stop here. With practice, female humour can actually be adduced *as itself evidence of humourlessness.* The best example of this is, of course, the biggest cliché of all. The remark no self-proclaimed feminist can avoid is: 'Burned your bra yet darling?' To burn one's bra is, in popular mythology, to be *ipso facto* humourless. Now the women's movement in the seventies did organise demonstrations in which bras, corsets, deodorants and all sorts of things classed by consumerist society as feminine essentials underwent some fairly resentful treatment. And there was a great deal of anger about, which might have found expression in burning (male) figures in effigy; if women had wished to make this form of demonstration, there was no shortage of suitable candidates. To choose to perform the classic act of political anger, the one reserved for Hitler or Stalin, on a bit of wire and elastic, seems to me to argue a lively sense of the incongruous; bra-burning was a cheery recognition that some aspects of women's oppression can be dealt with simply and by our own hands, that male-identified techniques like burning in effigy were aggressive and unnecessary, and that the movement would choose to parody, not copy, them. In short, burning a bra isn't a bit of too-earnest fanaticism but a rather elegant joke. It's of a piece with the techniques used by women protesting outside the US missile base at Greenham Common, many of which display a witty sense of theatre. For instance, the intricate webs they wove around themselves were simultaneously an image of female solidarity and a device for fazing the police in their attempts to haul them away in Black Marias. If a similar incident had taken place in a mixed environment (such as the London to Aldermaston march), the participants would have been portrayed by the press not as ugly sisters but as practical jokers, an example of British goodwill and humour.

One of the oldest English inn signs is *The Silent Woman*; it is, of course, a joke: her head has been cut off. Jokes have always been a way of reducing the opposition to silence. As Linda Woodbridge puts it, witty misogyny provides 'an image of the frustration of women's movements throughout history. Seeking human justice, we find the inhuman face of the Jester'.[21] And while the Jester also denies women the right to create laughter, he has a double power to enforce silence.

Most feminist activity has been centrally concerned with silence, and with its breaking. Areas of oppression have not only to be identified but named, because only through naming can they become part of public knowledge. Women's desires have to be named, because through naming they become achievable. But the breaking of silence can bring its own pain, for one enters most fields of discourse on male terms; some women feel that language itself is 'male', that it can only reinscribe the structures of oppression; even those who do not cannot deny the pain which accompanies the assumption of a public voice. The field of comic discourse is perhaps the most fiercely guarded of all, against female clowns and female critics. It is for this reason that it is as important for women to assume these roles as it is for them to enter fields more apparently vital to the achievement of social change. It is the female clown who perhaps best embodies the idea of Hélène Cixous' punning image of woman as *'une voleuse de langue'*[22] – that is, one who steals the language, and one who also flies with the language. The clever thief is a familiar figure in comedy, from Plautus' cunning slaves to the Trickster tracked by Jung through native American folk tale. Women need to grab the language, and to fly with it, and through laughter to show their authority over it. ('I love language', says Deborah Margolin of the Lesbian theatre company, Split Britches, 'How else can you scream for help?'[23])

To map women's relationship to laughter would be not just a gigantic task but a never-ending one, because that relationship shifts and changes all the time – the more so since women have consciously begun to choose the role of flyer/thief. I have chosen to look at areas which seem to me important, because they form part of the texture of common experience in the English-speaking world. First, there is the field of comic theory; to read many of the 'classic' texts concerning humour – that is, the ones still generally prescribed by university courses on comedy – can be a depressing experience for a woman; misogyny is inscribed into some definitions, and where this is not so there is a bland assumption that the experience of both sexes is identical. If theorizing stopped here, it might not matter; but although most standup comedians or writers of popular comedy will dismiss theory by pointing out that 'Freud never played second house at the Glasgow Empire', most comic practice is informed by some sort of theoretical position, as I hope to show. Second, there is the area of narrative comedy. I intend to concentrate on TV sitcom, partly because it is probably, for most of us, the most common way in which we imbibe comic narrative in our society, but also because it is one of the few comic narrative forms in which women performers have played an important part from its inception, and over which women are now attaining a degree of control. It seems therefore a good site on which to examine the tension between structures that are male-controlled and male-designed and women attempting to work creatively within them. Thirdly, there is the area of standup comedy – the field in which a woman commands the stage, where she stands alone. This is not a new phenomenon, although the media sometimes proclaim the present generation of women comedians as such. But while I discuss earlier generations in order to celebrate them and to investigate the existence of distinct female comic traditions, I would also like to suggest that the woman comic today has the opportunity radically to redefine her relationship to the audience, to become not an invited guest at Baubo's feast but the mistress of it.

Baubo. Astute readers will no doubt have deduced from her presence in my text that I am a white, grammar-school educated academic with a by-no-means-universal preoccupation with the past, a desire to recover some of the history of women, to 'give us back our mothers'. In trying to confront and interpret this disconcerting little figure I become aware of contradictory aspects of my feminism. That myth, that story of women against the forces of winter, darkness and rape, asserts a specifically female culture, a female language that exists outside the male order; it haunts me, sets me looking for a uniquely female laughter, even while I would argue that our ideas of gender are socially constructed, that the laughter women have so far created has been shaped by and in specific structures of power that can and should be changed. Sometimes, too, I am aware that women have created a laughter that has helped to support rather than to destroy those structures – and yet I find myself wanting to celebrate their achievement rather than to attack it. My feminism, like that of many women working in a largely male environment, is in short not a unified position but one which varies within its context. I work within a male-dominated environment, a university. This means that I find myself simultaneously struggling to provide myself and other women with power within the structure and arguing to change the structure itself. Among men I am likely to assert that patriarchy is the root of our oppression – even, in the heat of the moment, that women possess qualities which men cannot aspire to; among women I would argue that gender is not fixed but fluid, that to talk of a 'female' laughter or a 'female' culture is to use a kind of shorthand to indicate the products of an unjust society capable of transformation. It is not easy, this plurality, it is often extremely painful. But many of us live with it, and for me the presence of Baubo in my text is a useful reminder that anarchy and contradiction are, in any area of comic discourse, healthy symptoms. Like most women, I have been brought up to adopt the male gaze and to utter the male laugh. To shift this perspective needs radical theories and radical strategies – alternative comedy, alternative laughter. But we should not allow this to prevent our investigation or our enjoyment of the work of women in the present comic world; we need to take from them our own meanings, our own pleasures. In Baubo's world you laugh, then you can be reborn. Jokes are the bridge.

Part I

Theorizing laughter

1

Theoretical perspectives

'He had yet to learn to be laughed at.' (Jane Austen)

Who's laughing?

Some readers may have a sense of *déjà vu* as they examine this section. When I began this book I imagined discovering, guiltily, how out-of-date my knowledge of comic theory is, that complex and passionate debates by critics of both sexes about the relationship between laughter and gender were so well established that even non-specialists could point me towards the relevant texts. It wasn't like that. I did find exciting work by women which dealt with specific comic practitioners – generally literary practitioners – and offered insights into comic theory on the way. But when it came to discussing and defining 'humour', there seemed to be very little that was new. The students I talked to who were doing courses on 'comedy' seemed to be reading texts which grounded themselves in the same assumptions about gender as those I read as an undergraduate twenty-five years ago; which means that to attend a course on 'comedy' in an academic environment is still to learn a vocabulary that serves to reassert the idea of female humourlessness. Perhaps I should not have been surprised. Regina Barreca suggests that 'feminist criticism has generally avoided the discussion of comedy, perhaps in order to be accepted by conservative critics who found feminist theory comic in and of itself'.[1] Barreca's own 1988 volume, by combining jokes, analysis and comic theory, thus created a significant milestone in political as well as in cultural terms.

A study of laughter may proceed in one of two ways. It can start from the comic stimulus, and inquire why it is funny, what is its value. Philosophers, literary critics and anthropologists have all investigated this territory. Or it can start from the laughter itself, from the person laughing. This tends to be the field of the experimental psychologist or the sociologist. Of course boundaries overlap and one field can throw light on another. However, it seems to be the case that only within the second category do women have an acknowledged separate identity. The 'classic' theories of humour, which I shall examine later in this chapter, sometimes assume that social and class differences have a bearing on the subject, but gender is virtually never mentioned. This is not to say – as I hope to show – that their assumptions are not gendered assumptions.

I have chosen to begin with psychological theories of humour, a field of investigation in which women are accorded a degree of separate identity. This does not imply, however, any kind of awareness of sexual politics on the part of the investigators. What, for instance, are we to make of the following rationale of the choice of subject matter?

> There are only a few basic joke themes, as every entertainer will maintain, and the only theme that seems relatively pure, in the sense that jokes containing this theme tend to be massed in one factor in factor analyses . . . is sex.[2]

A persistent and touching faith in the possibility of a 'neutral' joke, funny in its essence and devoid – despite dealing with a central area of human experience – of emotional overtones, against which varying responses can be mapped, is a feature of many experiments on humour – especially those where gender is the topic under investigation. A good deal of relatively recent work has been concerned with gender responses to humour within groups; the terms in which the results have been framed are interesting. Experiments in which male and female subjects saw jokes and cartoons in groups, for instance, showed that females were more likely to look at the rest of the audience before laughing; this prompted the conclusion that women were 'field dependent' and 'subjective' while men were 'field independent' and 'objective'.[3] Among children tested in groups composed of one clearly identified 'pair' plus another lone child, sometimes sexually mixed, sometimes not, it was found that boys laughed more in the presence of friends while 'girls displayed more interest in the excluded child' and laughed in such a way as to include the excluded child, because 'the prevailing low level of intimacy would have caused them to feel uncomfortable'. It was concluded that 'Their laughter may thus have operated as a psychological tool in the cause of promoting intimacy. Boys, on the other hand, seemed content to experience a relatively low level of intimacy, *perhaps in the interest of enjoying humour to the full.*'[4] The inference, in both cases, seems to be that the 'norm' is an unsullied flow of understanding between the male spectator and a pure substance which one investigator calls 'the humour itself'; this contrasts with the response of the female, at worst a passive creature incapable of independently judging what is funny, at best a well-meaning one who simulates a response rather than rock the boat. If a sexual analogy suggests itself to the reader at this point, it is hardly surprising: the investigators assume the same female stereotype beloved in the fifties by peddlers of the 'vaginal orgasm', that chimerical reward for passively accepting male-defined sexuality.

Different conclusions, of course, could be drawn from this data: for instance, that women might choose to define humour in a different way – not as a phenomenon divorced from its context but as something with an organic relationship to that context; that intimacy is not merely a situation in which they might feel more 'comfortable' laughing but part of the texture of a specifically female humour with its own rules.

The magnitude of the imaginative leap required to frame such a conclusion can be gauged by examining the role allotted to women in a number of experiments pursued throughout the years of the sexual revolution, purporting to examine the relationship between laughter and sexuality. In 1959, for instance, John F. Strickland performed an experiment in which male subjects were shown a series of ten nude photographs of women before being exposed to a number of cartoons.[5] Later experiments observed that male responses to sexual jokes were strongly augmented by the presence of a 'young, very attractive female confederate'[6] and that the behaviour of a woman controlling an experiment on laughter strongly affected the results: if she was 'sexily dressed and flirtatious' the sexual jokes shown to the subjects were rated as funnier than when her behaviour was polite and formal.[7] The role which women are being asked to play here seems suspiciously familiar – that of the handmaid of laughter, not its creator. The 'sexily dressed and flirtatious' lady fulfils the same function as Hill's Angels – pretty girls on *The Benny Hill Show* who scamper about when a comic chase is called for and generally decorate the set; they point up the jokes, like human exclamation marks. Their hallmarks are revealing frocks (or underwear, or bikinis), an expression of perpetual surprise (men are so clever/naughty) and a special way of moving that jiggles as many separate parts of the body as possible while covering the minimum ground. Hill was perhaps the most blatant in his use of them, but shows better known for their experimental approach to humour – *Monty Python's Flying Circus* and *Rowan and Martin's Laugh-In*, both contemporary with the experiments under discussion – have also failed to use actresses like Aimi MacDonald, Goldie Hawn and Carol Cleveland in more original and less demeaning ways. These experiments go further than merely assuming that both humour and sexuality are unchanging essences for men to define and consume; they also reinscribe women on the margins of both as objects for male gratification, a role better fitted to a Mars bar, a cigarette, or a wank.

The 'commonsense' assumption that this is indeed woman's place pervades the conduct of what might have become a series of mirror-image experiments to determine female responses to humour when sexually aroused.[8] The title of one of them, however, gives the game away: *Vital Statistics: Perceived Sexual Attractiveness and Response to Risqué Humour*.[9] It, like the others, purports to discover differences in the responses of women to 'Playboy-type jokes' [sic]. 'Vital Statistics' is a coy term much beloved of the purveyors of soft sexist humour like *Reader's Digest* and suggests that the investigators themselves regard the whole thing as a bit of a laugh. The conclusions, however, have been disseminated beyond the bounds of the original specialist report and repeated in a populist study of psychology and the performing arts published as recently as 1985. This reiterates that

> sexually unattractive women enjoyed jokes in which the female character was depicted as a passive recipient of male interest and attention, while attractive women were more amused by jokes in which the woman was taking sexual initiative or symbolically 'castrating' male characters.[10]

It is evidently worth discovering whether men like to be sexually pleased as part of their experience of laughter; women, it appears, have no 'natural' right to such gratifications and it is more relevant to classify them by their potential for pleasing men even when *their* laughter is supposed to be the focus of attention. It can evidently be assumed that they lack the intelligence to work out that they are being sexually evaluated – 'field dependent' though they are; or perhaps they are so used to being judged as sexual objects that this doesn't matter. I find my imagination casting the exponents of this data in a film called *Carry On, Professor*. While the *Carry On* movies have always considered it their duty to the British film industry to squeeze in as many sexist music hall gags as they possibly can, their plotlines have usually ensured that authority figures of such blatant chauvinism get their comeuppance. Or one might simply write up their data with a slightly different emphasis:

> Women who felt their sexuality disparaged by the experimenters preferred jokes in which men were shown as appreciative and attentive; women who found their sexual interest patronising preferred jokes in which men got what they deserved.

One of the few studies of 'sexual humour' that took pains to define the variety of material contained within this term is an experiment by Chapman and Gadfield in 1976 which tried to discover a relationship between sexual humour and sexist assumptions.[11] It did not tabulate results on a simplistic basis of gender, but treated subjects as complex beings, taking into account their age and relationship with feminism; 'sexual attractiveness' came into play, but subjects were invited to evaluate *themselves*; thus the dishonest classification 'attractive' became the more clearly measurable 'sexually self-confident'. The results, interestingly, did not correlate well with the 'Vital Statistics' data. While cartoons were selected by the investigators, the subjects were invited to classify these by theme (e.g. 'male as sex toy', 'rape', 'male chauvinism') and to indicate whether they perceived any of the material as 'sexist'. It was observed that men and women seemed to enjoy equally cartoons which portrayed intercourse as mutually pleasurable, and that both sexes who claimed feminist sympathies gave them particularly high ratings. The chief gender differences occurred over jokes perceived as hostile to one sex; males laughed more at jokes about rape and female masturbation, rated 'sexist' or 'obscene' by some subjects, but failed to respond to cartoons about male impotence. Perhaps, the most valuable aspect of the experiment as written up, however, is the investigators' clear recognition that the factors underlying male or female laughter are too complex to be reducible to conclusive data. Subjects may laugh at a sexist joke because its structure is cosily familiar, or fail to laugh at a feminist one because it is unconventional; a potentially aggressive line can be accompanied by a grimace or a gesture which softens it and facilitates laughter; a conservative subject may be shocked by the fact that a joke is about sex rather than because it is sexist. However, the work by Cantor, Chapman and Gadfield suggests that an important shift has occurred; some investigators, at least, are prepared to treat both humour and sexuality not as monolithic entities but as constantly changing social constructs.

The seventies also saw gender-based research which concentrated on power relations in laughter without a specifically erotic element, examining the laughter of men and women at jokes which disparage one sex over another. Zillman and Cantor, in 1970,[12] exposed two mixed-sex groups to jokes which differed in only one respect: in one set the man was the butt, in the other the woman. Both sexes evidently laughed more when the woman was shown as the victim; however, the investigators could not decide if this was caused by male 'intolerance of disparagement, from female victimisation, or both'. By 1975, however, Cantor, perhaps prompted by the continued growth of the women's movement, repeated the experiment[13] and was even more reluctant to draw simplistic conclusions. She suggested that one should relate her findings – not in themselves very different from the earlier experiment's – less to 'intrinsic' differences between the sexes than to power differentials. Male lack of laughter at jokes which disparaged men was suggested to be anxiety-based: 'the female in our society seems to take the putdowns of everyday life in her stride, while the male struggles to portray a spotless image of dominance and infallibility. He cannot easily laugh at his own expense. The cost in terms of image seems too high'. Or as Elizabeth Bennet reflected about Mr Darcy, 'He had yet to learn to be laughed at.'

Why laugh?

Once we shift from the question 'who is laughing?' to 'why laugh?' women tend to appear only as footnotes to the discussion. Literary criticism, philosophy and anthropology have developed four basic and inevitably interrelated theories: disparagement, relief, celebration and incongruity.

The oldest, and in many ways the most tenacious, of these is disparagement theory – the idea that laughter is closely allied to scorn. Aristotle, despite writing only a few lines on the subject, is perhaps the most often quoted of all.

> . . . comedy embraces the worse types of men; worse, however, not in the sense that it embraces any and every kind of badness, but in the sense that the ridiculous is a species of ugliness or badness. For the ridiculous consists in some form of error or ugliness that is not painful or injurious.

It is worth clarifying the term 'men'. Comedy in the *Poetics* is opposed to tragedy, and the characters of tragedy, says Aristotle, must be 'good'.

There can, he points out with his usual magnanimity, be 'goodness in every class of person' but if we consider women and slaves, 'the one is possibly an inferior being and the other in general an insignificant one'.[15] This makes them, on the whole, rather unfit characters for tragedy, but would be no obstacle to their providing suitable butts for laughter – indeed, inferiority would give them a head start.

Nearly two thousand years later, Hobbes is still in substantial agreement, although he shifts the ground of the debate a little. It is not so much the misfortune of others that causes the laughter, he suggests, as 'the sudden glory' which 'proceedeth from a sudden conception of some ability in himself that laugheth. Also Men laugh at the infirmities of others, by comparison wherewith their own abilities are set off and illustrated.'[16] In other words the laughter is not caused by the intrinsic ugliness or stupidity of someone else but by our perception of ourselves as superior.

This theory is alive and well and has been vigorously reinforced by a 'scientific' backing which takes as its starting point the 'innate aggression' of 'man'. Arthur Koestler, for example, explains that our nervous system is geared to a more primitive time when our aggression against what we perceive as the abnormal – the foreign, the deformed, the unfortunate, the Other – found straightforward expression.[17] More civilised societies, he suggests, repress the urge towards aggression by channelling it through laughter. Konrad Lorenz also links laughter, scorn and 'innate aggression'. Laughter, which he compares to the triumph ceremony in geese, creates fellow feeling among the mockers and defines the objects of laughter as 'outsiders'. 'Laughter promotes a bond and simultaneously draws a line.' It is, however, a contained aggression, preventing actual physical harm. 'Barking dogs may occasionally bite, but laughing men hardly ever shoot!'[18]

This is good news for any woman who finds herself alone in a crowd of drunken men cracking dirty jokes about her, or for a Jew hearing an anti-Semitic joke in Nazi Germany – at least it would be, if one could entirely throw off the suspicion that laughter, by the very process of bonding the mockers, actually makes it *easier* to shoot, or to rape, or to kill by reinforcing the 'otherness' of the Other. This idea of disparagement as a refined version of a 'natural' aggression depends heavily on what one might call the flint-axe school of history. Because what survives from paleolithic culture has largely been concerned with killing, anthropologists have tended to draw the conclusion that killing was at the centre of stone-age life – performed, of course, by Man, while

Woman meekly produced children as flint-axe fodder until such time as Man became 'civilised'. There is no evidence that the first tools were weapons: they could have been gardening implements, baby slings or sanitary protection – all things that would rot away while a more rarely used weapon would survive to help the fabrication of a myth. The 'aggressiveness' of 'primitive man' is a Darwinian construct by a society in which sex roles have been polarised to a massive degree. There is no evidence about stone age humour; we are never going to discover, scrawled on a cave wall, a line like 'how many paleontologists does it take to change a light bulb?' and we would probably not recognise a paleolithic joke if we heard one. But it is not inconceivable that paleolithic laughter coexisted with both the fighting and nurturing life of its people, a phenomenon which they might choose to employ in aggressive or benevolent fashion.

While many (not all) comedians would repudiate any interest in comic theory, the equation of 'innate aggression' with humour frequently plays a part – disguised as 'common sense' – in interviews when they are on the defensive. Jim Davidson, for example (typical Davidson ad-lib to a woman in the audience: 'Look at that – a drunken nigger wouldn't attack her!') draws a distinction which reflects Koestler's between straightforward and channelled aggression: 'I tend not to do racist jokes. . . . I tend not to insult . . . I take the piss more than insult.'[19] Both Davidson and the notoriously racist Bernard Manning have cited as evidence of their refined approach to the deep-seated aggression of Man the fact that they prefer 'spreading it around' – that is, insulting as many social groups as possible (although white, heterosexual British men seem curiously exempt). The targets, of course, appreciate the refinement. 'If you get a coloured gent in the audience he throws back his head and laughs', says Manning, adding, chillingly, 'if he's got any sense.'[20]

Literary critics have often found themselves in a double bind with regard to Disparagement Theory: while suffering from a sneaky feeling that it works as a way of theorising laughter, they are also anxious to distance themselves from its ethical implications. The result is a body of material concerning 'comedy' – that is, a literary or narrative form rather than the stuff of everyday encounters – which asserts, with Ben Jonson, that 'the moving of laughter is a fault in comedie'[21] or with Philip Sidney that laughter is to be sharply distinguished from delight. 'Delight hath a joy in it either permanent or present; laughter hath only a scornful tickling.'[22] The comedy, as opposed to the mere joke, is accorded a more apparently lofty and educative purpose, defined thus by Northrop Frye:

> The[re] are always people who are in some kind of mental bondage, who are helplessly driven by ruling passions, neurotic compulsions, social rituals and selfishness. The miser, the hypochondriac, the hypocrite, the pedant, the snob: these are humours, people who do not fully know what they are doing, who are slaves to a predictable self-imposed pattern of behaviour. What we call the moral norm is, then, not morality but deliverance from moral bondage. Comedy is designed not to condemn evil, but to ridicule a lack of self-knowledge. It finds the virtues of Malvolio and Angelo as comic as the vices of Shylock.[23]

Comedy, by this definition grounded in the dramatic practice of Jonson, or Molière, is a narrative which exists to reinforce a 'moral norm'. An outsider is still a victim of aggression and disparagement, but this aggression is legitimated because he has 'brought it on himself'. There is a cure – self-knowledge; the outsider can become an insider once more. The laughter which brings down the comic victim is an antibiotic for the body politic. This sounds light years removed from a Jim Davidson joke; in practice, however, both the comic narrative which assumes we will find the miser, the snob or the hypochondriac suitable cases for treatment, and the comedian who makes a racist joke to an audience clearly expecting such jokes are choosing to define and attack an 'out-group' on grounds that are politically constructed. The miser and the snob are not 'universal' or 'natural' figures of fun but exclusive to a society grounded on capital and class, just as the black Englishman is not a 'natural' object of derision. 'Hypochondria' may be a subject for comic chastisement, but society chooses which diseases to call 'real' and which ones to call 'imaginary'; and one of the ways in which women have been cast as the Other since the nineteenth century is through labels like 'hysteric' 'neurasthenic' and 'nymphomaniac'. This in itself might well create a degree of feminist scepticism, a growing conviction that this definition of comedy by the male academy as society's self-healing needs to be carefully scrutinised each time it is in operation, and that the hiving off of 'comedy' from 'laughter' is merely a way of legitimating certain kinds of aggression.

Laughter has also been defined as a species of relief or release, sometimes tied to the bodily functions; Kant located it in the intestine and the diaphragm, Spencer in the muscles, Koestler in the glandular system which produces adrenalin.[24, 25] The classic exponent of the concept of relief was of course Freud. Freud saw society as subject to

various forms of needful repression, involving us in the expenditure of
psychic energy; a joke allows the feelings which are repressed to emerge
into the open in a socially acceptable disguise; thus the energy needed to
maintain the repression is saved, and is discharged in laughter. 'Reason,
critical judgement, suppression: these are the forces (the joke) fights in
succession'.[26] Freud's analysis was tightly tied to its specific cultural
context, right down to a choice of metaphor profoundly reflective of
nineteenth century bourgeoisie in its focus on 'economy in expenditure'
of energy rather than Blake's energy as eternal delight. At one point
Freud compared the psychic processes involved in joking with the setting up of a small business. His selection of 'tendentious jokes' provides
an array of repressions specific to *fin de siècle* Vienna: a joke about a
marriage broker allows the hearer to release his repressed hostility to the
institution of arranged marriages; a joke about a beggar may release the
resentment created by the obligation to assist the less wealthy. This
cultural specificity is equally present, even if less superficially apparent,
in his analysis of sexual humour. A sexual joke, or 'smut', is a way of
calling attention to the fact of sex in a society in which men and women
alike are forbidden to do so – although Freud envisaged the nature of
their sexual drives as different. Men are the 'natural' sexual aggressors,
women 'instinctively' inclined to passive exhibitionism – a construct
which makes inevitable woman's role as the butt, not the maker, of the
joke. 'Smut', as defined by Freud, is primarily directed *at* women; if no
women are present at the recital of smut, their *imagined* presence is
essential. 'A person who laughs at smut that he hears is laughing as
though he were the spectator of an act of sexual aggression.'[27] Smut is
like a physical exposure of sexual difference: it will force a woman to
imagine her own sexual organs, or herself engaged in the sexual act, and
it will make it clear that the teller of the joke is also doing so. She may
respond with sexual excitement, or she may exhibit shame, which is a
repressed admission of it. If so, a third party will enter the transaction.
The male joke-teller, experiencing hostility to the woman, will engage as
ally a second male, in front of whom he will embarrass her. To Freud,
then, 'the woman's inflexibility is therefore the first condition for the
development of smut'.[28] The woman leaves, the listener takes her place,
and the smut becomes a full-fledged joke, the only possible form it can
take in a 'refined' society.

The idea of 'man' as a 'natural' aggressor, and of woman as 'naturally' passive, is implicit throughout Freud's analysis of what he called
'tendentious' jokes; his discussion of other kinds of humour, however, of

'innocent' jokes, suggests that his theory of relief can operate independently of these constructs. 'Innocent' jokes provide a relief that is primarily intellectual; they allow a return to the childhood state in which we are free to play with language, reinventing words, breaking grammatical rules, and disrupting logic, without incurring social disapproval.

By divorcing, in this case, the idea of relief from the idea of innate aggression, Freud implicitly postulated that 'relief' can be taken to apply to *any* imposed social restriction rather than confined to those which he perceived in operation around him. In all the situations in which he described the operation of humour, however, there is a corollary to the idea of relief: that of its temporary nature. Jokes permit a brief holiday from inhibition and logic in order to allow them to be re-imposed with greater effectiveness. The student 'rag', as he experienced it, allows a brief interlude of 'nonsense' precisely because of the everyday rigour of academic work; the period of freedom helps to preserve the academic structure.[29] Certainly relief and the holiday spirit are potentially valuable tools of social control – as valuable, probably, as the idea that some people are 'naturally' the Other against whom we can legitimately target our innate aggression. Whether the temporary relief can turn into the permanent lifting of a burden is something that Freud, concerned with changing our self-perception rather than the social fabric in which it is set, did not necessarily choose to explore; it is, however, a question which women, if no longer willing to accept the role of butt, cannot help but ask.

The same need for interrogation underlies comic theories of celebration. These are basically focused on two related themes. The first concentrates on the pattern of many comic narratives – misfortune followed by a 'happy ending' – and locates its origin in fertility rituals, tracing the word itself back to the Greek *komos*, a festive procession. The nature of this procession is rarely in doubt. 'That Comedy sprang up and took shape in connection with Dionysiac or Phallic ritual has never been doubted,' writes Francis Cornford, going on to expound the essential core of this ritual as 'the expulsion of death, the induction of life.'[30] In dramatic form, this involves the death – or humiliation – of one party and the exaltation of its opposite: the death of winter, the triumph of summer. These are, however, complementary: summer will eventually give way to winter. 'When this is remembered', continues Cornford, 'the contest may take the form of a struggle between the Old and the Young King, ending in the death of the former and the succession of the latter to his throne.'[31] The throne is part of a package deal involving the hand of a princess, whose only part in the drama is to wait passively for the outcome of this Oedipal gunfight at the Phallic Corral.

That phallic ritual existed – exists – cannot be disputed, and it does not stretch credibility to trace a development from the dramatic ceremonies described here to the pattern known as New Comedy in which boy-gets-girl-boy-loses-girl-boy-gets-girl. What remains largely unacknowledged, however, is the process by which this pattern has been naturalised, seen as an unchanging aspect of 'human nature'. But the identification of life as originating in the phallus is not 'natural'; it is the product of a culturally specific understanding of human biology. About three and a half thousand years ago a new discovery permeated the world – the fact of biological paternity. Before that women were perceived as the cause and origin of life; their bodies menstruated with the rhythms of the moon, the lovers they took were witnesses, even sacrifices, to their power. As a logic of cause and effect began to supersede the purely magical and symbolic mode of perception, the relationship between copulation and childbearing became evident and men began to perceive themselves as the true source of life. Not sharers in a process involving both sexes, but as sole creators, authors of being. The penis was the implement by which perfect, tiny human beings were implanted in the female, demoted to the role of privileged flowerpot. The implement itself was of course glorified, in a giddy rise from a piece of vulnerable gristle to a mighty phallus immortalised in stone or bronze. Phallic ritual was part of this glorification process – not a 'natural' manifestation of human joy but a counter-rite to existing ceremonies in which men played a less exalted role.

It could well be argued that the phallic origins of most routine comic plots are so deeply buried as to make these details of purely academic interest. (Although Wicked Willie has now made his first video.) But its reiteration in an academic context does three things: first, it gives intellectual respectability to a dangerous myth – that the penis has a life of its own, leading its owner into various phallic scrapes. This has given rise to viciously un-comic episodes, in the theatre and in life. Second, it firmly inscribes women in the role of comic butt or waiting prize; thirdly, it hijacks a form charged with anarchic possibility and presents it as a rigid celebration of the *status quo*. As Rosalind Miles points out,[32] the so-called fertility rituals centred on the mother goddess were not primarily about making the crops grow. The emphasis was rather on the sexual power and pleasure of the goddess. A comedy linked to this rite, rather than to the Phallus, could abandon its insistence on compulsory marriage and eternal Oedipal conflict for a concentration on the pleasure of the moment. The Phallus could abandon its lonely role as hero and become a penis again, fallible, unpredictable, irritating and cherishable: a creature more akin to Sooty than to Dionysus in all his power.

A less apparently gender-specific form of celebration theory is contained in the idea of comedy as carnival. Carnival exists in rigidly structured societies, such as the feudal world, and its characteristic mode is the reversal of the everyday order. It was often linked to the feasts of the Church – Holy Innocent's Day, or Shrove Tuesday – and contained a strong element of parody, not to say blasphemy. As Bakhtin, the best known exponent of the form, points out, Carnival belonged not to a privileged group of performers, but to the people; their energy forced Church and State into tolerating its existence. While officialdom celebrated stability – the consummated and completed task of Christ in establishing his kingdom – Carnival asserted change and possibility. As Bakhtin puts it:

> People were, so to speak, reborn for new, purely human relations. These truly human relations were not only a fruit of imagination and abstract thought; they were experienced. The utopian ideal and the realistic merged in this carnival experience, unique of its kind. This temporary suspension, both ideal and real, of hierarchical rank created during carnival time a special type of communication impossible in everyday life. This led to the creation of special forms of market-place speech and gesture, frank and free, permitting no distance between those who came in contact with each other and liberating from norms of etiquette and decency imposed at other times.[33]

Celebration is, again, temporary, but the focus is on possibility rather than the triumph of one sex over another; all is anarchy for the duration, an acting out of relief theory over days rather than the duration of a joke – relief from authority, a chance for the oppressed classes to laugh at it and at themselves, a chance to develop relationships outside those permitted by custom.

And yet there is something absent from Bakhtin's description. Nowhere are sexual barriers, as opposed to class barriers, seen as being challenged. The carnival world is one of material pleasures, of food and drink, song and dance and sport, and, inevitably, sexuality. But for the last three and a half thousand years sexuality has meant male sexuality. Women's right to pleasure has certainly been from time to time envisaged; but I can't help wondering what it was like for a lone woman to walk the streets at carnival, and whether in this free communion she had the right to say no; and who looked after the subsequent babies if she didn't. Is the language of Bakhtin, so precise about class, so vague about gender, naturalising women as the enemies of laughter by ignoring the reasons why their conduct in a state of carnival might have been some-what circumspect?

The only theories of laughter that seem to contain no hidden sexual agenda are those relating to incongruity, the perception of which is an intellectual process with no necessary relationship to 'instincts' – whether one perceives these as inborn or socially constructed. According to Incongruity Theory, laughter comes out of a clash of unexpected words or ideas, or, as Arthur Koestler puts it, 'bisociation' between two 'uni-verses of discourse' or 'matrices of thought'. He uses a chessboard analogy: to a non-player, this is a display of pieces on black and white squares, but to a player 'a kind of magnetic field with lines of force indicating . . . possible moves'.[34] When the two 'universes' of player and non-player collide, laughter can arise. Schopenhauer usefully links the laughter of incongruity with the way in which we perceive the world; the rational concepts we use to understand the world are, he argues, imper-fect, and when they collide with the solidity of real objects we realise that the world 'cannot get down to the infinite multifariousness and the fine shades of difference of the concrete'.[35] Kierkegaard pushed the discussion further by pointing out that humour thus tends in the direction of social change: 'The comic apprehension evokes the contradiction or makes it manifest by having in mind the way out, which is why the contradiction is painless. The tragic apprehension sees the contradiction and despairs of a way out.'[36] Incongruity Theory acknowledges that humour is not an unchanging essence but a way of seeing; it is relativist, its potential residing not in things or ideas or people but in the relation-ships between them. As such it will inevitably be culturally determined, and as the position of the sexes shifts and changes, so too, according to this theory, can our perception of what is funny.

However, it is still a matter for debate whether the laughter springing from the perception of incongruity is, like Freud's holiday from the rules of logic and repression, a species of temporary relief, or whether it is an instrument of social change. On the one hand it can be argued that a joke may shatter our view of accepted reality, suddenly de-familiarising a political or social system (such as patriarchy) and allowing us to perceive flaws and incongruities; on the other hand, it might be felt that laughter makes it easier to re-enter the system after the permitted break. Laughter can be subjected to various forms of social control. As Mary Douglas puts it:

social requirements may judge a joke to be in bad taste, risky, too near the bone, improper or irrelevant. Such controls are exerted on behalf of hierarchy as such, or on behalf of values which are judged too precious and to precarious to be exposed to challenge.[37]

Because laughter is a social phenomenon, too, it is easy for the hegemony to impose a definition of humour upon us; as Anton J. Zijderveld points out[38] this is precisely the function of canned laughter on a soundtrack; our understanding of humour is thus also effectively 'canned' for us. (A great deal of academic work on comedy does precisely the same thing in a more direct way.)

The debate, however, is not about an intrinsic property of laughter, but about the ways in which society currently chooses to harness it. Laughter, like nuclear energy, has no opinions, positive or negative, about the *status quo*. What it does have, like nuclear energy, is power, to which we can relate in a number of ways. Its potential as a force for change exists in a direct relationship to the intensity and commitment with which it is used by the forces of change or stasis; in other words, if the stakes are high enough, judgements like 'bad taste' and 'irrelevant' simply lose their force. If feminism is to change all that needs to be changed, therefore, it is essential for women to clarify their relationship to laughter.

Women, in the face of all the odds, have always contrived to create laughter, in private and in public, as artists and as social beings. Feminism, however, has only just begun to engage with laughter as a social force; it is now an urgent matter to provide a body of theory if female laughter is not to continue to be read in the light of definitions which at worst deny its very existence and at best force it into specifically masculine moulds. A considerable amount of work is in progress, on, to use a metaphor from a predominantly male activity, two fronts: raising consciousness of overt or tacit sexism in male humour, and exploring women's comedy in order to become aware of specifically female strategies of laughter. However, the metaphor is only a metaphor, and the division between the two activities is often blurred in practice.

Considerable energy was rightly expended in the seventies in simply exposing the sheer weight of misogyny in the day-to-day humour of newspapers, TV shows and conversation. While this humour is still alive and kicking, it is less and less easy for those who indulge in it to be unaware that it *is* sexist. Examination of misogynist humour has largely shifted its ground to discuss its effects. The playwright Sarah Daniels made a highly controversial intervention into the debate with her play

Masterpieces;[39] this asserted not simply the connection between pornography and violence towards women traced by feminists like Andrea Dworkin and Susan Griffin, but placed pornography itself on a through-line from casual misogynist humour. In the closing moments of the play, the central character, jailed for an attack on a passing male prompted by her fury at viewing a snuff movie, specifically cites 'men who make misogynist jokes' as responsible for the climate in which such movies are made and sold. It was a point which few viewers bothered to take up, preferring to treat the play as a call for censorship.

Other work grounded in the study of woman as the butt of humour have concentrated on her relationship with that role rather than with the effect upon the perpetrator. A recent paper by Estelle Philips chose to examine the reaction of the 'classic' target of Western humour, the mother-in-law – inevitably finding a wider audience at second hand via the national dailies.[40, 41] She described not just the extreme dislike of these jokes by the mothers-in-law she interviewed, but also their sense that they were 'conditioned' by them, constantly evaluating themselves against this negative role model – the only one commonly available to them – to the exclusion of all spontaneity in the relationship. This implies a far more complex dynamic between the teller of a joke and its object than that usually promulgated by Disparagement Theory; there the butt tends to be perceived as 'naturally' inferior and lacking a viewpoint of its own, or, in the more refined critical discourse of comedy, sees the error of its ways and becomes a well-adjusted member of society. The pain Philips describes is precisely that of a woman aware of 'society' as an entity which simultaneously demands her conformity and makes her an outsider.

This humour is, as other feminist studies of male laughter have pointed out, a political act. Norma J. Gravely suggests that if humour is seen as a way of reinforcing social control by promoting the disparagement of certain groups, sexist humour clearly arises out of fear:

> men could perceive women, or the autonomy of women, as a threat to their basic security – their 'power', rightness, importance and position . . . The motivation would be strong enough to counteract any tendency towards assertiveness, independence and autonomy with even stronger controls.

The solution, as Gravely sees it, is for women to acknowledge the political base of sexist jokes and to 'write our own jokes . . . and fight back!'[42] It is important, though, to consider what those jokes might be like. While cracking a few jokes about male incompetence or sexual

inadequacy may be an entertaining revenge for years of silent humiliation, it fails to put the power of laughter securely into women's hands.
Humour remains a male construct which women have borrowed, rather
than a new framework for permanent and joyful change.

Feminist theory has, however, postulated roles for women in society
as it presently exists which implicitly involve them in the construction of
their own distinctive humour. It is most useful in this connection to look
at the discussions of women's relationship to language prompted by
Jacques Lacan's post-structuralist reading of Freud.[43] For Lacan, the
child first feels itself to be part of its mother and indeed of everything it
sees. Its sense of separate selfhood, that moment when it can look in the
mirror and say 'I', comes into being when the father breaks up the union
between mother and child. This break marks the child's entry into
language, into what Lacan calls the Symbolic Order, signified by the
phallus, the sign of the Father's difference from the Mother, which thus
represents to the child both the Law of the Father and the loss that the
child has undergone. For the female child, who does not herself possess
the phallus, her entry into language is thus accompanied by a double loss
and lack.

Julia Kristeva has suggested that this process does involve choice,
and a choice which is as open to the male child as the female. She
maintains that it is possible to choose to identify with the mother, and in
doing so to take up a position that is marginal and hence subversive,
outside the symbolic order and thus undermining its phallocentricity.[44]
This outsider role is, of course, that of the clown or the Fool, the outsider
who never ceases to remind those inside that there is a world elsewhere,
who renders the existing order incongruous by surviving outside it.
Hélène Cixous, briefly discussed in the introduction, also needs to be
read in this context. Once denied full access to language by virtue of
one's sexuality, taking up the role of a 'thief of language', as she
suggests, seems not only a logical option but one which cannot help but
carry in its wake the delight in subversion and mischief that goes with
the Trickster of folklore – all the connotations of the word *voler* in its
double sense of thieving and flight. It is no coincidence that much
feminist scholarship of late has chosen to employ a playful, punning
attitude to language – not in the sense of 'comic relief', jokes to lighten
the discussion of difficult and painful subjects, but to de-familiarize
language itself, to expose the hidden agendas behind words taken for
granted, and thus to underline the revolutionary nature of the subject
matter. Mary Daly, for example, has continued to work towards the

establishment of a feminist theology and philosophy through a language which punningly calls attention to itself by exposing a phallic philology: the rule of the phallus perpetuates 'stag-nation'; women are urged to reclaim their old titles, taking 'Webster' back from the author of the male dictionary and applying it to themselves as the spinners of tales and spells; they re-appropriate the positive meanings of words like Hag and Crone because they have 'served the fathers' sentences long enough'.[45] To seize the Word is to seize not just creativity but creation:

> Wording is one fundamental way of Be-Witching – Sparking women to the insights and actions that change our lives. Wording is an expression of shape-shifting powers, weaving meanings and rhythms, unleashing Original forces/sources. Arranging words to convey their Archaic meanings, Websters release them from the cells of conventional senses.[46]

'Wording', like 'flying', is playing with language and thus asserting a right over it, entering the territory of the joker. For Hélène Cixous part of the process of flying is to 'write the body'.[47] Women, says Cixous, have been driven, violently, from the act of writing, and it is time for them to enter it and in so doing to insert themselves into history as agents of change. To write the body is to perform a double healing – of the split between women and discourse, and the split between women and their own bodies, both brought about by patriarchal control. It is publicly to acknowledge and validate female desire and energy by breaking silence in such a way that language will be irrevocably changed. The change will be inevitable because the relationship of both men and women to the phallus and its connotations of lack will first be changed – a process Cixous herself describes with some humour. She parodies the idea of *Penisneid*, the woman's desire for the thing she lacks:

> If they believe, in order to muster up some self-importance, if they really need to believe that we're dying of desire, that we are this hole fringed with desire for their penis – that's their immemorial business. Undeniably (we verify it at our own expense – but also to our amusement), it's their business to let us know they're getting a hard-on, so that we'll assure them (we the maternal mistresses of their little pocket signifier) that they still can, that it's still there.[48]

This gentle laughter at the phallus makes a new relationship to language possible – and thus all other laughter possible – by dislodging the idea of lack from language. The root of patriarchy's oppression of women, the fear of castration, can and must be overcome, says Cixous, precisely through that first laugh, the laugh of the Medusa. While legend shows her as dark, terrifying, the female abyss into which men will fall if they cease to assert the primacy of the phallus and the subordination of woman who lacks it, her true face is different:

> Too bad for them if they fall apart upon discovering that women aren't men, or that the mother doesn't have one. But isn't this fear convenient for them? Wouldn't the worst be, isn't the worst, in truth, that women aren't castrated, that they have only to stop listening to the Sirens (for the Sirens were men) for history to change its meaning? You have only to look at the Medusa straight on to see her. And she's not deadly. She's beautiful and she's laughing.[49]

For Cixous, the laughter of the Medusa destroys all hierarchies by rendering nonsensical the aggression between father and son that is their basis; in destroying hierarchy it will remove all difference between the margin and the centre. Women will not be outsiders, because the concept of the 'outside' or 'inside' will become meaningless. To write *as* a woman, to write the body, is to commit a public act of anarchy, to enter history. Cixous works out the image in vivid, powerful and erotic terms to adumbrate a new form of writing, a new use of language. A woman who both writes and performs, as so many woman comedians do, is making this image concrete, flesh and blood as well as ink, a lived parable of the possibilities Cixous envisages for the woman's text to 'shatter the framework of institutions . . . blow up the law . . . break up the "truth" with laughter'.[50] And as more and more women establish themselves in the comic arena, they also reveal the other property of Medusa's laughter: its permanence. For Cixous, 'blowing up the law' is not a temporary respite; the Carnival will not pack itself away when Lent begins, but will continually point forward to new possibilities, new changes, new relations. The Trickster, the Flyer/Thief, the Clown, is a role women can, and must, embrace.

Part II

Sitcom: story or spectacle?

Don't expect the idea for your first sitcom series to just pop into your head. It might, but it's more likely to come slowly, in bits and pieces. You'll get a vague notion, perhaps prompted by a piece in a newspaper or magazine. With a little thought this may firm up into a half idea. Work on that. Polish it. Make notes. Perhaps the thought of a particular performer playing the main character will get you excited. 'Or suppose I made it a *woman*! Aha!' (Brian Cooke, *Writing Comedy for Television*, Methuen, 1983)

2

Born in the USA: a story of money and angels

I teach at a university. I bring up a child on my own. The builders have
made a mess of my kitchen. Last week the freezer spontaneously de-
frosted. One of my best friends is pregnant. None of this is of any interest
to the reader. It is, however, the stuff of which situation comedy is made.
Sitcom, like its cousin soap opera, is a uniquely televisual form with a
uniquely televisual role. While other programmes seek to provide a (not
always transparent) window on the public world which we view from
our domestic space, sitcom brings the private space into the private
space. Sitcom is about people like us: personal mistakes and problems
overcome in our everyday interaction with others. If it portrays people
different from us – with, say, jobs in public life, or from the past – the
point will still be to elicit the laughter of recognition: we understand the
feelings of the MP who panics because she is late for a debate, the
cringing courtier who gets the wrong gift for Elizabeth I. Sitcom is a
leveller: everyone's laughably human, when you get to know them. And
you will get to know them; a successful sitcom will run for years, and
subsequently reappear with the status of a 'comedy classic' on both TV
and video. It may well attract better viewing figures this time around;
familiarity is part of its attraction. A well-loved sitcom slips into our
lives as so many of its protagonists did in the nineteen fifties, crying,
'Honey, I'm home!'

While the line itself is history, the structure to which it represented a
password is not. It signalled the transition of a (usually male) character
from the 'public' world, in which he had to earn to survive, controlled by
forces over which he had no real power, to the 'private' one in which he

could 'be himself', where his feelings were taken into account, and problems, springing only from the interaction of private individuals close to one another, happily resolved themselves on an individual basis.

This world picture is not a 'natural' one; it would be meaningless in a society in which, say, cottage industry was the norm. It has been constructed by a system controlled by industrial capital, which buys a segment of a worker's time. Once some time is bought, the so-called 'free' time attains a particular importance. The home becomes a castle because it is the abode of the 'true' self, the 'free' part which can't be bought, which may break out in the workplace but does not 'belong' there. (One reason of course why 'the boss comes to dinner' is such a sitcom staple: it's a massive – and slightly threatening – incongruity to have the symbol of hegemony plumped down on your very own sofa.) This same system consolidated the role of woman that had begun to evolve with the Reformation: the guardian of the private sphere and its values, the nurturer of those 'real selves' which could only flourish when they ceased to be 'hands' and became whole, valued and 'free'; the symbol, by virtue of her confinement to the domestic sphere, of her husband's adequacy in his public role.

It is in her sphere that husband and wife sit down to watch television, and what they watch is a celebration of that sphere: a world of ordinary, TV-watching people like themselves, at home with the family. Sitcom is the only dramatic form that has focused from the outset upon women; at times, in their absence from both drama and current affairs programmes, it has been the *only* televisual space significantly occupied by women. Between 1952 and 1973, for instance, the proportion of female characters in prime-time US drama hovered around the 30 per cent margin – and most of these were cast in the role of faithful secretary or helpless victim. Comedy tended to give better opportunities numerically: the figures here rose to 40 per cent.[1] If, however, all it could do was to confirm them in the role of Angel in the House, it would not be worth discussing. But this celebration of domesticity is not simply drama but commodity. Like its cousin soap opera, named to enshrine its origin in the advertising war between Oxydol and Rinso, sitcom was constructed in the USA to attract consumers – not simply of the sitcom itself, but also of the products advertised in the 'breaks'. It is thus addressed to woman *as consumer*. The way in which she performs this role will have a complex relationship not simply to her role as Domestic Angel but to any other strong images of herself she may entertain, images indeed which may radically conflict.

In sitcom's early days a simple triangular relationship evolved: the sponsor produced a show with a well-loved star, the consumer watched the star and bought the product. In the forties Molly Goldberg, an already well-loved radio matriarch, leaned out of her TV kitchen telling us that 'If Mr Goldberg did not drink Sanka decaffeinated instant coffee I don't know what I'd do – I don't even know if we'd still have a marriage'.[2] By the fifties, Lucille Ball occasionally puffed a Philip Morris in *I Love Lucy* but now the sponsor was only named in a coy insert ('Do you inhale? . . . Philip Morris is the one cigarette brand proved definitely less irritating'[3]) outside the narrative. (No character, though, was permitted to use the word 'lucky', however great their good fortune; Morris saw no point in giving free publicity to their rival Lucky Strike.) But by the 1960s control of programmes shifted from the sponsors to the networks, to whom programmes from production companies were licensed. Rather than producing their own shows, sponsors bought advertising 'slots' on these programmes, those associated with the highest ratings ('Nielsens' as they are known in the USA) being the most expensive. The process of calculating these viewing figures became increasingly precise, so that by the seventies Nielsen could not only gauge the number of viewers for any programme, but could also break these figures down into demographic groups. Thus it became possible to target programmes at sections of society with specific interests and spheres of consumer power. Some stories might well go on reflecting traditional family values to keep the market in breakfast cereal brisk, but demographic research also highlighted a new potential market: young, urban, adult women with well-paid jobs and no children – an attractive new target, and one which had to be reached by a comedy closer to their own experience and concerns.

The seventies thus saw the rise of the independent woman as central figure in both comedy and drama: the thirtyish career girls from the MTM stable; Maude, the liberal middle-aged loudmouth who began by berating Archie Bunker in *All In The Family* and spun off on to her own show; Hotlips Houlihan from *M*A*S*H*, transformed from the humourless shrew of the original movie to a feisty and vulnerable figure with a complex relationship to nursing and to the army.

However, there was also, towards the end of the decade, a reaction against these same heroines as ABC, determined to re-establish itself after some lean Nielsen years, aggressively marketed what the industry labelled 'T&A' – tits and ass – and achieved such success with the show *Charlie's Angels* that even well-established sitcoms found themselves acquiring new characters to introduce the so-called 'jiggle factor': *WKRP in Cincinnati*, for instance, added a 'blonde bombshell' to boost ratings, and 'three broads, one blonde'[4] became, briefly, a standard formula for success.

The life of the Jiggle Factor was mercifully short. Wobbling into the Reagan years it encountered the Coalition for Better Television, headed by the right-wing fundamentalist Jerry Falwell and the prominent anti-feminist Phyllis Schafly; their technique was to mobilise consumer boycotts against companies whose commercials appeared in shows containing 'profanity', 'violence', 'sexual innuendo' and 'skin scenes'.[5] Some companies were indeed scared – both General Foods and Gillette, for instance, withdrew advertising, though from specific episodes, rather than entire shows – and networks began to exercise self-censorship. By the end of 1981 T&A was a dead letter; this might have aroused a little more feminist cheer if members of the Coalition had not also successfully organised consumer blockades of ABC's adaptation of *The Women's Room*, killed off a TV film about a woman with a homosexual friend, and helped convince advertisers to pull out of *Lou Grant*, one of the few prime-time shows to deal with topics like rape and incest, because of the leftish politics of its star Ed Asner.

This increasingly complex and endlessly shifting relationship between sitcom, its creators, and its consumers has, clearly, both positive and negative consequences for a specifically female comedy. It has, at least, ensured women employment as actors, writers and producers, and a substantial presence on the screen. Demographic research has to some extent put the ways in which that presence manifests itself under women's control: if the far right removed one positive image of homosexuality from the screen, a powerful gay lobby removed a clichéd and negative one – the gay Jodie in *Soap*, for instance, lost his limp wrist and came out of the closet with some pride. It is difficult to imagine, in the early nineties, that any network would feel financially safe in offering an offensive and extreme female stereotype for our laughter. There may even be moments when the delicate demographic mechanism indicates certain feminist issues as Flavour of the Month – times, as Erica Jong puts it, when 'women [are] all the rage – as if an entire gender could go in and out of style'.[6]

As far as market forces are concerned, however, an entire gender can go out of style and out of mind if the circumstances are right. The ever-worsening recession, for instance, may have serious consequences for women's economic power over their television image; it is still rare to find a working-class woman given dramatic space – except as victim on police shows – and those gains made so far could be extremely vulnerable; the backlash provoked by AIDS may eventually cause the small gains in the area of lesbian representation to be wiped out; and it would be naive to assume that positive images of women, or even non-negative ones, are now a firmly established norm. Meanwhile, within the *status quo* there are more immediate limits to the subversive potential of female comedy. Most obviously, sitcom's dependence upon a consumer culture for its very existence will almost certainly preclude a laughter which provokes analysis of consumerism itself. The comic heroines who take the air may differ in other areas, but they will live within this culture or be (comically) chastised if they attempt to leave it. Other boundaries are less immediately apparent because they are less firmly fixed, determined by endless and shifting negotiation with the interests of other groups. A situation, for instance, in which an older woman challenges prevailing sexual mores may well be modified at some stage in production in order to avoid offending the conservative churches, and diluted by a subplot involving her children dragged in to pacify young viewers bored by the antics of the older generation. Pilot episodes of any series are routinely tested in front of carefully selected audiences and ground-breaking humour may end up with a cast of better-known, more conventionally attractive actors, overt references to political issues deleted and a new, super-bland signature tune.[7] On the other hand, the collective imagination may be seized, in defiance of all projections and prognostications, by a team of radical and original characters; through affectionate and weekly interaction with them, millions of viewers can be exposed to a different understanding of gender, of women's place, of social and sexual issues. While sitcom must reflect societal values in order to sell the products for which it exists, it can, by provoking laughter, also question them. 'Situation comedy', as Seraphina Bathrick puts it, 'situates us'.[8]

To turn on a television set at the present time is to operate a time machine. Zapping through the channels you encounter newly minted comic figures rubbing shoulders with those from the past; women you could meet today on the subway, women from the fifties in New Look dresses; comedies that can take AIDS as the topic of the week and those in which the joke is that the wife has spent the housekeeping on a fur coat. Television, however, exists not in history but in an endless present. The story about the fur coat may be punctuated by a newsflash about an Animal Rights protest that drags it into the present moment and inevitably invests it with new meanings. With this in mind, I should like to take the reader on an archeological dig through layers of situation comedy, reconstructing as we go a kind of female history: one in which old images can take on new meanings; these meanings may no longer have much to do with laughter – or they may yield new laughter, new pleasures, in that audience still watching, still absorbing into itself that community of strangely dressed TV viewers from the past.

The fifties

> Just think, when little Ricky goes to school and some of his playmates ask who his parents are, just what is he going to say? 'My father is Ricky Ricardo, the internationally known entertainer . . . and then there's my mother, whose name escapes me.'[9]

Lucy Ricardo wasn't a lone voice. A spectre was haunting the West – the Angel in the House, this time with a degree. As the War ended and East and West were grimly polarised on opposite sides of the Iron Curtain, American women were pressed into domesticity to vacate jobs for returning heroes, bump up the depleted population and help to affirm the capitalist construct of the family. The older generation of women hung on to their jobs; for the younger, educated middle class, a problem developed and was articulated for them by Adlai Stevenson, no less, in his Commencement address to Smith College in 1955:

> Once they wrote poetry. Now it's the laundry list. Once they discussed art and philosophy till late into the night. Now they are so tired they fall asleep as soon as the dishes are finished. There is, often, a sense of closing horizons and lost opportunities. They had hoped to play their part in the crises of the age. But what they do is wash the diapers.[10]

But as Stevenson, in common with the majority of the post-war US government, saw it, this wasn't a problem at all. Woman had a unique opportunity to 'inspire in her home a vision of the meaning of life and freedom . . . to help her husband find values that will give purpose to his specialised daily chores'. Sylvia Plath, like all the class of '55, applauded enthusiastically.

TV, too, had reason to applaud. The newly-glorified Angel was useful as a buyer for countless new products designed to make housework more convenient (yet somehow never taking up less of the day) and daytime output was geared to making the home a desirable place to be. Soap operas simultaneously provided an escape into romantic fantasy and glorified their domestic setting. When the man of the house entered his castle and assumed control of the set, comedy allowed him to reestablish the chain of command. The titles made it quite clear who was in charge: *I Married Joan; My Little Margie.* And – of course – *Father Knows Best.* When Father donned his cardigan, any symptom of wifely disorder could be allayed within his moral framework. When, for instance, Mother grew restless enough to run off to a strange part of town, buy a new hat and allow a street artist to paint her, he could reassure the horrified neighbours that he had not only diagnosed her problem but has an instant cure. She feels taken for granted so he takes her to lunch. This brings her back into the established order as neatly as Northrop Frye could wish.[11]

Ten years on, the diagnosis would have been different, less easily resolved in comic form. Mother was clearly an early sufferer from 'the problem that has no name', as Betty Friedan finally described it in 1963.[12] Sitcom conventions precluded more extreme manifestations of this existential pain, the breakdowns and the bleeding blisters described in *The Feminine Mystique*. Patricia Mellencamp has, however, identified the two most popular female stars of the fifties, Lucille Ball and Gracie Allen, as important disruptions to the smooth patriarchal surface. Ball's alter ego, Lucy Ricardo, took a more anarchic stance than Mother's. In the first screened episode of *I Love Lucy* she complained 'Since we said "I do" there are so many things we don't';[13] this, however, wasn't an inarticulate cry from the subconscious but the prelude to action taken in a real context. The premise of *I Love Lucy* was her desire to be a star, to be more than, as her husband Ricky wanted, 'just a wife'. Every week she tried, every week things misfired in a slapstick explosion and she dwindled into a wife.

But, of course, Ball *was* a star. She was a brilliant physical comedian, inventive, graceful and precise. So identified did she become with the character of Lucy Ricardo that it comes as a shock to see her putting her talents to different use in the film she made in her seventies, *Stone Pillow*; in the opening sequence Ball, as a bag lady, peers out of a heaving bin liner, slowly registers what kind of day it is, and grunts 'Well, I'm still here'. She washes at a hydrant, cleans her teeth, and tidies her hair with a facial mobility that simultaneously enjoys the sensuality of the process and sends up the notion of 'femininity'. This character knows, and relishes, her own eccentricity, her status as a 'character'.

Lucy Ricardo, however, couldn't do this. Ball rejected the idea of a show grounded in Hollywood fantasy in favour of something closer to viewers' experience, something 'ordinary':

> I remember saying that if I got a fur collar for my coat, I wanted a whole show
> written about that. I want the smallest wardrobe possible . . . we were middle
> class, we had a typical brownstone apartment in New York, and we had
> problems with the washing-machine and with paying the baby-sitter. We
> always talked about bills and expenses.[14]

Madelyn Pugh, who with Bob Carroll Jnr was responsible for the scripts,
tested out the physical gags; the point was that they should be an
extravagant version of real life, rather than pure fantasy, things that
could happen to a real person rather than comic fantasies achieved
through camera tricks. Ball's determination to ground the show in some
kind of reality, to give the audience figures in a recognisable world with
whom they could identify, rather than stars in a Hollywood neverland,
was innovative at the time and gave *I Love Lucy* warmth and humanity.
Inevitably, however, in the fifties, it meant that as the female half of
a 'realistic' couple her talents would be packaged to look like incompetence.

This was, of course, the chief paradox of the show – that while Lucy
Ricardo was a showbiz no-hoper, Lucille Ball played her with the talent
of a Keaton or a Chaplin. Lucy's incompetence was constantly getting
her into situations which provided scope for displaying comic skill; the
audience longed for the moment when Ricky, narratively the star, would
leave so that Lucy could perform, just for us, the comic turns the story
endlessly denied her ability to do. Often these were shameless about
their vaudeville origins. Lucy boasts to her friends that she knows a lot
of movie stars, and when her bluff is called she resorts to a series of
rather inefficient impersonations; dressed as Harpo Marx, she encounters the real one, and turns herself into his mirror image. They execute a
centuries-old piece of comic business, in which Lucy defies all attempts
to catch her out with sudden movements, all attempts to faze her with
poses too acrobatic to copy. But as they finish the beautifully executed
routine Lucy and Harpo tie themselves into a complicated knot and
embrace like old friends. The frame of the story is shattered – as, given
the paradox at its heart, it often had to be.

This interplay between realism and theatricality, with its consequent
disruption of the conventional family hierarchy, was heightened by
Ball's own star status. As an established movie actress with a popular
radio series to her credit, *My Favorite Husband*, she now had the clout
to make her own demands and the finance to back her own judgement.
One thing she insisted on was playing opposite her real-life husband,
Desi Arnaz. This was a major factor in precipitating the show out of the

Father Knows Best mould. Arnaz was a bandleader, not an actor. A refugee from Batista's Cuba, he had a thick Hispanic accent. To write him into the show meant to create the part of a Cuban bandleader, Ricky Ricardo. This had a marked effect on the sexual politics of the show. While the premise – that a wife should not work and that the husband was the head of the family – remained the same, Ricky's attempts to enforce it were not backed by the dead weight of WASP respectability. While Father pronounced judgement on his wife's problem in the language of the ruling male élite, Ricky often lost control of his wife, his language and his temper, erupting into tirades of Spanish when provoked. He was not settled in a social niche, but struggling to prove himself in a new country and an uncertain profession. Lucy's efforts to make some sort of mark on the world reflected, sometimes parodied, his own: several times she managed to enter his act; she threw custard pies, elbowed out his dancers to do her own manic routines; she got a job from the sponsor of the show of which Ricky was MC as the 'Vitameatavegamin girl' and proceeded to get drunk on the alcohol-based product; she performed an aerial ballet in the background while he sang obliviously on. Her behaviour was, literally, childish – when thwarted she would roar like a two-year-old in a tantrum – and Ricky often treated her as a child; once he even spanked her, to the rhythm of his theme song, 'Babalu'. Once, too, he resorted to slipping her a Mickey Finn. While it's all too apparent that life within his ideology would need a jeroboam of Mother's Little Helpers to render it tolerable, Father would never have done this; it reflects a promising instability in the father–child relationship between Ricky and Lucy. This was further disrupted by the presence of their neighbours, Fred and Ethel, who provided each of them with a potential partner in crime. It made it easy for Ricky, as well as Lucy, to descend to a childish level to 'turn the tables on the girls'. When Lucy and Ethel announced their intention to go to a nightclub with other men, Ricky called an escort agency and fixed up blind dates for himself and Fred; these naturally turned out to be Lucy and Ethel disguised as a pair of manic hillbillies; Ricky twigged and turned into a mad Don Juan; both couples vied madly for the overacting honours. Thus the series remained balanced between a comedy of superiority, with Lucy punished for childish rebellion, and the more equal comedy of shared play.

The popularity of *I Love Lucy* blurred the boundaries between Lucy Ricardo and Lucille Ball. When Ball became pregnant, so did Lucy, although the actual *word* was forbidden by the censor. When the coyly titled 'Lucy is Enceinte' episode was played before its live audience

Ricky/Desi was overcome with tears as he sang 'We're Having a Baby' to his wife. The birth of the Ricardo baby beat the Eisenhower inaugural in the Trendex ratings, as the network deftly showed the pre-recorded episode to coincide with the actual arrival of Desiderio Alberto Arnaz IV in January 1953. When Ball was summoned before the House Un-American Activities Committee to account for her registration as a Communist in 1936, her explanation, that she did it to please her grand-father, was accepted with relative ease – it was the sort of thing Lucy might do. The audience of the night, assured by Desi that 'the only thing that's red about Lucy is her hair',[15] were instantly on her side. (Other stars of family sitcom, like Jean Muir of *The Aldrich Family*, had their careers ruined on far more slender evidence.)

One could, in fact, slip any moment during *I Love Lucy* from respond-ing to the tribulations of a 'real' woman to an awareness of her as a star. This, as much as the set-pieces straight from vaudeville, serves to fore-ground the paradox of Ball's talent and Lucy's incompetence; it is this paradox that perhaps accounts for the continuing popularity of the show. The embarrassment that I feel, along with many women, at the narrative structure which relentlessly punishes Lucy for her presumption, is con-tinually modified by the way in which it opens up into a different kind of style which permits the demonstration of comic skill. The dialogue, the positioning of the actors, even the camera work shifts between two modes. This can be clearly seen in one of the most inventive slapstick episodes, *LA AT LAST!*[16] Lucy goes to the Brown Derby to ogle movie stars and manages to hit William Holden with a custard pie. His stricken face closes the show before the commercial break. When she goes home, Ricky has brought Holden to meet her. When Ricky arrives, Lucy is in the bedroom and he goes to fetch her. Here the action moves like a conventionally 'naturalistic' sitcom. Man lays down the law, woman prevaricates. Lucy pretends to be ill, clutching her stomach and com-plaining of a headache. Close-ups of her are matched by close-ups of Ricky. He demands answers: 'Is it your head or is it your stomach?', and she tries to give them: 'It kind of moves around.' She pretends to be shy, sinking on to the bed and hiding her face. He remains upright, the largest figure in the picture. Lucy is, literally, cornered. Then the scene shifts its territory and its balance of power. Ricky and Holden chat over coffee in the sitting room. Lucy emerges. She is wearing a turban, glasses and a large putty nose. The camera now divides its time between close-ups of Lucy and shots of the whole group in which all eyes are focused on her. The nose begins to slip, and she twitches it; she engages in small talk

while desperate to scratch her nose. She finally does so. Holden and
Ricky watch in horror as it bends now left, now right, Lucy's crossed
eyes following its every move; meanwhile, she smiles ingratiatingly like
a host who has run out of Scotch. The men avert their gaze and chat at
the edge of the frame while our eyes are drawn to Lucy making frenzied
adjustments. They talk about the beautiful women cast to play opposite
Ricky as Lucy swivels round, her nose now of Pinnochio proportions.
Shaking, she offers cigarettes. Holden lights hers and catches the tip of
the nose, which bursts into flames. Lucy crosses her eyes, registers the
flames, blows; her eyes bulge, she rises and dunks her nose into the
nearest coffeecup like a heron.

As physical comedy it is executed with tremendous delicacy, each
movement as precise as the jewels in a Swiss watch, and Ball is the star,
clearly acknowledged as such by the camera and the discreetly subordinate positioning of the two men. As such it stands out from the coy
prevarications in the bedroom and from the 'Lucy, would you mind
telling me what's going on?' with which Ricky – as so often – brings us
out of vaudeville and back into narrative. The playful incongruities of
the interlude parody the conventional femininity glamorized by the
media, the more entertainingly because of Ball's own good looks; the
playfulness continues with the absurdity of maintaining a polite front in
the face of evident lunacy and the sheer surrealism of the flaming nose.
Then it gives way to the humiliation of Lucy – here mediated by Holden's
good sportsmanship. He takes the blame for the Brown Derby episode
and kisses Lucy, who gasps 'I KISSED BILL HOLDEN!' and passes
out, the stage-struck zany till the end. The whole sets up tensions rarely
found when male slapstick performers are at work; we are invited to pity
Harry Langdon, admire the stoicism of Keaton or to rejoice in the
subversive triumph of Chaplin's Little Man – but each of these has an
existential integrity denied Lucy as it was denied the sufferers from the
'problem with no name'. Chaplin's hero may be downtrodden by society, but he knows who he is and avoids social or economic thrall to
another individual. The essence of Chaplin is that he is his own man.
Lucy isn't her own woman; her triumphs are always partial, her power
fragmented, her defeats always sanctioned by the narrative. It's understandable that in the world of the eighties Ball chose to play Chaplin's
symbol of existential freedom, a tramp.

Patricia Mellencamp[17] offers an interesting Freudian reading of Lucy.
Picking up Freud's definition of a joke as 'economy of expenditure upon
feeling', she suggests that the feeling 'saved' is one of female anger at

confinement and frustration: the impossible situations raise laughter by 'saving' our feelings about a reality too painful to contemplate. Lucy's own good humour at her weekly return to domesticity is that of the female spectator, aware of the genuine suffering for which that good sportsmanship is a substitute; housework is a bore, and to subvert the convention of contented homemaker by wallpapering over the door or baking a loaf that expands to eight feet long is fun while it lasts, but doesn't change the setup. Sometimes, when the show moves out of the Ricardo apartment and into the world, that reality is all too apparent. When Fred and Ricky agree to swap roles for a week, Lucy and Ethel try to get jobs but find that unskilled workers are not wanted.[18] They end up with far less desirable jobs than their spouses in a candy factory. Conveyer belts rush by; Lucy and Ethel can't keep pace and stuff the excess sweets in their mouths, their clothes. Lucy finds herself dipping sweets in chocolate alongside a morose woman working at high speed; up to the elbows in chocolate, she tries desperately to scratch her nose; a fly bothers her; she lashes out and hits the woman and the scene culminates in a chocolate fight. The morose woman is a real chocolate dipper brought in specially for the show; her skill forms an appropriately comic contrast to Lucy's incompetence, but her expression serves to point up the real unpleasantness of the job: the belt does dictate her day; she really can't scratch her nose. (Reportedly, she didn't find the show funny and her only strong reaction came when Ball clouted her much harder for the cameras than she had at rehearsal.) This is in truth what a woman like Lucy Ricardo, as opposed to Lucille Ball, might expect from working life in the fifties. Real anger at the prospect is contained by the slapstick fight and by the husbands' efforts at homemaking (they starch silk stockings and burn holes in everything they iron). The return to the status quo is marked by a last gag – to make up for the mess in the house, Fred and Ricky buy their wives huge boxes of chocolates.

I Love Lucy's success perhaps arose from its narrative inconsistencies. Imitations that lacked the distancing showbiz framework and the real-life spice of the Desilu team did not remain so long in the public favour. The best of them, *I Married Joan*, started only a year later but ran only three years, despite having a star with a strong radio following and enormous slapstick talent, Joan Davis. But the stories were inserted into a framework that summoned up the patriarchal inflexibilities of *Father Knows Best*. 'I' was a domestic court judge, no less, and each week the story would open with Brad Stevens confronting a couple in difficulties, which he would proceed to solve by relating an anecdote about Joan.

While Davis swung from ladders, got shut into spin dryers and gave operatic recitals in a voice that could swoop from soprano to baritone, her character was not so much a rebel against domesticity, like Lucy, as a conformist who couldn't quite make it. Endlessly contained by Brad's discipline and his framing narrative, her antics couldn't allow us to enjoy her temporary liberation into a different dramatic mode. The comedy yields feminist discomfiture, not feminist laughter.

It is no coincidence that the only other sitcom of the fifties which opens up the possibility of laughter *at* patriarchy as well as *by* patriarchy also featured a woman with an established film and vaudeville background and a high degree of control over the show. The nature of the surprisingly subversive comedy of Gracie Allen is well symbolised by a dance sequence in the RKO movie *Damsel in Distress*. With George Burns, her longtime partner, and Fred Astaire, she dances through a funhouse. She leads them through mazes, over rolling barrels, slides, and a hall of mirrors. The men slip, slither, and play about with fancy steps; Gracie, throughout, dances on with solemn and total concentration, her arms at her sides as if in an Irish reel. She never smiles, she gazes straight ahead, utterly unfazed. It is this sense of Allen as the calm centre of a confusion she has herself generated that made her comedy unique. *The Burns and Allen Show* always leaned on the dualistic premise, man/logical–woman/dizzy. But the highly specific comic styles of the protagonists hilariously sent up the stolid polarities it appeared to endorse.

The apparently unforced and natural comedy of *The Burns and Allen Show* took more than twenty-five years in vaudeville and radio to develop. The first move in the construction of 'Gracie' was almost instantaneous. Burns had hired Allen as a straight to his funny man:

> Gracie fed me a straight line and the audience chuckled. I answered with my topper. Nothing . . . By the time we finished our first show Gracie was getting good laughs with funny lines like 'Oh, how stingy is her father?'[19]

The best responses were to the 'illogical–logic' – the surface clarity that sheathed non-sequiturs and non-sense, as in one of their most famous routines:

George	Do you like to love?
Gracie	No.
George	Do you like to kiss?
Gracie	No.
George	What do you like?
Gracie	Lamb chops.

> *George*   A little girl like you? Could you eat two big lamb chops alone?
> *Gracie*   No. But with potatoes I could.[20]

Allen always delivered her lines with childlike sincerity, as if they made sense, and most importantly, with no apparent awareness of the audience. Vaudeville conventionally depended on interplay between performer and audience; Allen behaved like an actress in the Stanislavski mould in which the touchstone of naturalistic success was to lose awareness of the 'black hole' on the other side of the footlights. Burns retained the vaudeville relationship with the audience but not as funny man mocking straight; he became an intermediary, helping the audience to position the character of Gracie in the comic frame, to make sense of the disjunction between the wacky script and her sweetly authoritative delivery. In one routine they effectively wrote her lines:

> Someone challenged me to think of one thing that Gracie said that made sense . . . and I didn't think that would be a problem. Let's see, in the department store one day a salesgirl said, 'Mrs Burns, if you're looking for Mr Brown you'll find him in ladies' lingerie.' And Gracie said . . . No, that wasn't it. Oh I know, in the butcher shop one day the butcher said, 'Mrs Burns, I have pigs' feet today. . .'[21]

A second major shift in comic style was the decision to abandon boy-and-girl flirtatiousness in their radio show of the forties and act like the married couple they were. This was important because it underscored one of the singular features of Gracie's dizziness: its complete absence of coquetry. She never simpered, or fluttered her eyelashes, or played 'dumb blonde', thus resisting a powerful pressure of tradition. This pressure was still apparent years later, as one can see from the use made of Goldie Hawn in the sixties show, *Rowan and Martin's Laugh-In*. Her mini-skirt and huge false eyelashes encode her as a child and also as a woman trying to be sexy. She makes mistakes and giggles ingratiatingly, as if we were teachers and she an incompetent student. She gives little wriggles of pleasure when engaged in snappy dialogue with the male protagonists, who have the 'consciously' funny lines. Gracie never looked as if she felt inferior to George. Despite her small stature and her soft, childlike voice, she always looked and sounded totally self-possessed. Burns sensed a clear audience demand that he respect her on-stage: 'I couldn't argue with her. And I couldn't touch her. If I had to touch her, I had to do so very delicately.'[22]

The Burns and Allen Show made the transition to television situation comedy in 1950. The structure seldom varied: Gracie would misunderstand a statement or an event and would act on her reading of the situation; everyone else – the mailman, the delivery boy, the neighbours (Blanche and Harry), the regular announcer (Harry VonZell) – would find themselves embroiled in a series of complications. George kept his role as intermediary, talking to us from in his 'den'. Patricia Mellencamp sees this position as one of power, comparing George to the watcher in a panopticon, or an 'analyst's chair behind the couch, unseen, with all scenes visible to his gaze'.[23] But if we identify with George alone we identify with the ordinary, the everyday, and the limited: he can 'see it all' but is denied Gracie's special vision. In an episode of confused identities George sucks up to a nodding dog salesman under the impression he is a famous scientist; meanwhile Gracie's mathematical talent beats the real scientist at gin rummy by three thousand points to twenty-four. 'All right,' says George to us, 'So I'm a dope. You knew who the professor was all the time.' We did, because we trust Gracie, whose character we help to create, to be in the right.

Gracie's logic may be illogical, but it also unanswerable – as the owner of an art gallery discovers when she asks why painters of the nude don't peel the fruit in their pictures. George, Harry and Blanche cannot imitate her twists of thought, while she can sit in (always benevolent) judgement on them:

> *Dave*   I've been wondering, Mrs Burns. How are you going to explain this little repair job to your husband?
>
> *Gracie*   I'll just tell him what happened. I went shopping and bought a blouse and on my way home I stopped to watch them put up the tents and this elephant came along and sat on my fender and smashed it.
>
> *Dave*   He'll never believe it.
>
> *Gracie*   Of course he will. He knows a fender isn't strong enough to hold up an elephant. George is smarter than you think he is.

Gracie ruptures the language of patriarchal common sense, operating in terms of a linguistic and social code more complex and exotic than the everyday. In suburban sitcom a wife is supposed to subscribe to the notion of marital obedience; there is a clear implied understanding about priorities and property. A car, for instance, is male territory; the wife who crashes it – in sitcoms they all do – is supposed to lie and prevaricate like a small child who has kicked a football through a window. Gracie doesn't care what George will say, she is simply concerned to defend him from the charge of illogicality. There are references to George's work, while Gracie stays at home, sometimes performing vaguely domestic tasks which serve primarily to assert that the house is her territory. But the ending of each show, in which the couple do a crosstalk act, always makes it clear she shares control.

This control is most alarmingly – and subversively – apparent at the point when the conventional giddy-wife goes to pieces: the topic of marriage itself. Misunderstanding an overheard conversation, Gracie thinks she is fatally ill; she is regretful, for she has had a happy life, but her first action is to look for a suitable new wife for George. In another episode a friend's wedding sends her into pleasurable reminiscence:

> Gracie   Do you remember when we got married?
> George   Of course I do.
> Gracie   And remember that cute little hotel we went into at Niagara Falls?
> George   I'll never forget it.
> Gracie   Oh. What a thrill. You know, it was the first time I ever tasted Canadian bacon.

What, exactly, are we laughing at? There is an obvious incongruity – we are expecting some routine honeymoon reminiscence, and Gracie's manner encourages us in that expectation: she is happy and excited, she sits close to George and touches his hand, her face takes on an inward look, her hands rest at peace in her lap. But there is another level of incongruity: the remark, in most comic formats, would be a witty put-down of George; Gracie's tone, happy and serene, belies this, and so does George's expression – baffled, but not hurt or even very surprised. Romance itself is being subjected to the most delicate of scrutinies.

Even fidelity did not escape unexamined. In one episode Gracie misreads a remark made by George and thinks that he has become dangerously obsessed by the loss of a five-dollar bill. She consults a psychiatrist, who advises her to give George a shock to take his mind off it. So she threatens him with divorce. Meanwhile George has been having an amusing time: people keep giving him five dollars, pretending to have found the vital bill. 'Don't tell them what's going on', he confides to us, 'and if I get any more money I'll split it with you.' He responds to Gracie's bombshell by remarking to Blanche that Gracie must have found out about their affair – a potentially cruel continuance of the misunderstandings. Here, however, the balance of sexual power shifts. Gracie does not reproach Blanche but commiserates on her luck. 'With all the men in the world you ended up with George and Harry.' When a caller arrives she serenely introduces him to 'Blanche, George's sweetheart.'

In most shows, in *I Love Lucy*, the plot would have involved grief and tears on Gracie's part; if she found out what George was doing, there might have been a determination to 'turn the tables' by *pretending* to accept the affair with Blanche with indifference. But the motivation behind Gracie's serenity is never revealed. She may know George is lying, and be lying in return; she may still think George is unbalanced and be humouring him in a delusion; or she may accept what George says, but not consider it important. Her motivation does not matter, because she can let the apparently disturbing statement be swallowed up in the ocean of her peace. The common sense notions of marriage simply do not seem to matter to Gracie, and in the face of her permanent calm and happiness we are invited to question them too. If George is an analyst, Gracie is like the therapist who refuses to provide solutions and drives the patient back on to his or her own resources, or like a Zen master confronting his pupil with koans. Meaning – like Gracie's lost brother, a running gag on the radio show – is for man to search for and woman to transcend. In 1930 Gracie claimed, 'I've got brains I haven't even used yet'. In the fifties, older and wiser, she could tell George, 'Almost everything I know today I learned by listening to myself when I didn't understand'. The process brought her, in contrast to her sitcom sisters, peace and quiet (no one ever shouted on *Burns and Allen*) and projected an image of marriage unique in its equality and tolerance.

The sixties

Lucie and Gracie were both contained within domestic spaces and small circles of influence; they were both objects of laughter. But they also, because they were created by women who had not only talent but power, put items on the comic agenda denied most of their female contemporaries: female strength and female desire. Gracie always won – the others had to adjust to her logic; Lucy might be humiliated within the narrative – but in order to create space for Ball the slapstick performer, encroaching upon a largely male preserve with total authority, that narrative had to be concerned with Lucy's *desires*. Frustrated they might be, but she was an active, not a reactive, comic. Both stood out in dazzling contrast to the male-constructed wimpesses who in their very wetness embodied the reason for female absence from other television spaces: the cop shows, the newsrooms, the hospital and courtroom dramas.

In the sixties, however, developments took place which should have

made the comedy of untameable womanhood a TV commonplace. More
women entered the workforce. As the decade moved on they became
involved in radical politics, campaigning for civil rights and the end of
the Vietnam war. New contraceptive technologies gave them physical
control over their own fertility. These developments were, however,
adroitly absorbed into the social structure to keep them content in their
place: terms like 'Girl Friday' were coined to disguise disparities on the
wage front; Stokely Carmichael stated that the place of women in the
SNCC was 'prone'; for too many men the Pill removed women's only
reason to say no, and hence their right to do so. Women's anger at the
pseudofeminist gloss on what remained genuine oppression did not erupt
till the end of the decade. Meanwhile, TV offered them a similarly slick
assurance that they were indeed liberated; they could smoke Virginia
Slims and get a little patronising praise: 'You've come a long way,
baby.' Women were important to the medium as the controllers of the
household economy, and it was necessary to remind them of their power
in this sphere while continuing to give the impression that it was their
only sphere.

Hence heroines didn't grow more independent; instead, Father got the
chop. He was, after all, something of an anachronism: a decent individu-
alist from Frank Capra's America, this fellow who chopped logs in his
own backyard, his ideology totally alien to the consumerism that under-
pinned situation comedy. He metamorphosed into 'poor old dad' – a
figure of fun to his children and far less competent than his wife; his
home was a fortress where a tired Organisation Man could hide from
'The Boss', a bogey who reduced him to snivelling terror. This applied
even to men whose professions might be considered the essence of
independence – on *The Dick Van Dyke Show*, for example, Van Dyke,
like George Burns, played a comedy scriptwriter. The showbiz format,
like that of *Burns and Allen*, was often used as a framework for some
Van Dyke set pieces, such as his 'drunk act'. But his character, Rob
Petrie, crucially, was not a freelance; he had a 'boss', who had to be
everlastingly placated; Petrie responded to his servitude by taking smug
pleasure in his wife's misfortunes. (One episode even banished her
physically from the screen while she wailed that her big toe was stuck up
a bathtap.)

The castration of Sitcom Man, in short, provided no opportunity for
a genuinely liberated heroine to make her bow. Sitcom Woman in the
sixties devoted herself instead to preserving his frail ego, to creating the
illusion that his home was still his castle. She joined the cosy conspiracy

constructed by the ads, in which the castle was rendered livable by magical beings – Mister Clean, the butch incarnation of a multi-purpose cleaning fluid; the 'white tornado' that would destroy dirt; the mighty forces at her disposal were, of course, hidden from her husband: a wink to camera and millions of female consumers were let in on the secret that would set them free for lunch with the girls, but not for a full-time career. And into sitcom stepped the woman who had supernatural powers. ABC introduced Samantha, the witch, in 1964; NBC countered in 1966 with Jeannie, who as her name suggests came out of a bottle left over from the Thousand and One Nights; CBS had a Living Doll, a beautiful female robot. All of them could do rather more than the average human being; all of them fell in love, and the result was always the same. He resented her powers, forbade her to use them, and she tried to obey. The only super-being unconfined by domesticity took an escape route tried and trusted since the dawn of the Christian Era: Sally Field, as *The Flying Nun*, kept her relationships platonic; her Mother Superior, although as crusty as Father, understood that a gift was a gift, and nothing to be ashamed of.

For the men, however, a wife with power was a threat. Tony Nelson, male lead in *I Dream Of Jeannie*, was an astronaut, and Darrin, *Bewitched* by Samantha, was an advertising executive. Both men in other words had rather trendy professions, that were both glamorous and well paid. But Tony, when he finally agrees to marry Jeannie, feels compromised by any attempt she makes to provide for them both. 'You are my wife and you're going to have to learn to live on my salary', he solemnly instructs, while Darrin was given to sniffing suspiciously at anything particularly well cooked and inquiring whether it had *really* been prepared in the proper (non-magic, time-consuming, tedious) way.

These weren't, of course, the first men in fiction to marry out of their species. But the premises were new. Old legends, that matched a man with an Undine or a seal-woman or a mermaid or a Lamia, were tragic. If they were narrated from the mortal viewpoint, they were tragic because the hero was *deceived*: enchanted by a beautiful woman, he lost his freedom. She might forbid him to ask certain questions or look at her at certain times, or, like Nimue, cast him into an impotent sleep; at length she would revert to type; at best this would mean her deserting him, resuming a previous identity; at worst, the poor fellow would expire, his mortal soul in grave danger; touch pitch and you are defiled. If these tales focused on the female, they were tragic because to get her man she needed to acquire a soul. Often the price to be paid was horrific, as it was for the Little Mermaid – and often the man would eventually prove faithless, leaving the poor hybrid with no option but to die. She did, however, have the consolation of upward mobility on the chain of being. To be a woman, as opposed to an Undine, is at least one step nearer to being a man.

The legends, from either viewpoint, proceed from the same assumption that female power – especially sexual power – is too dangerous to remain unchecked. This is also inscribed into the stories of Jeannie and Samantha, but squeezed into a comic framework. The first source of comedy is the 'mixed' marriage – assumed to be an incongruity in itself. As the heroines are inavariably white, rather classy, sweetly understanding and utterly willing to give up their independence, the implication would seem to be that any crossing of boundaries in a sexual partnership – racial, class-based, or even intellectual – might also be an aberration. In addition, the concept of the powerful woman as existential threat, not simply to her husband but to society as a whole, makes for a comedy which leans heavily on the farce convention of lies and concealment; the worst thing that can happen to a man, they imply, is to be *seen* to be married to a woman of power. 'If they find out you're a genie I'm a dead duck', complains Tony Nelson, as if NASA were an outpost of Empire and he a subaltern Gone Native, and she leaps back into her bottle or magics herself into tweeds whenever his friends come round. Samantha's secret is too terrible for Darrin to reveal to his family, and as for his boss . . .! It is not the hero's soul which is at stake, nor even his adherence to a moral code, but his position as middle-management clone.

The viewer is certainly prompted to laugh at male prejudice and incompetence, the more so because, of course, they cannot enforce their ban on magic. Darrin's terror of the boss is so abject that he will frequently resort to Samantha to help him out of trouble: he falls in a ditch; she magics his clothes dry and he wows them at the board meeting. Tony crashes the car and meekly goes to jail. Jeannie magics away the bars, and he wants them back. She makes his cell luxurious, and he orders her to put it back the way it was. But when they get to court Jeannie's persistence pays off – she magics an accident which reveals the truth of the situation: the wheelchair 'victim' of the accident is proved to be shamming and Tony can't be sued.

While the stories frequently end with the comic humiliation of the male, they also, however, place the woman of power in a double bind. A staple gag is the incongruity between her 'powers' and her relative domestic incompetence. Tony – always addressed as 'Master' by Jeannie

– hectors and bullies her about money. Failing to understand the concept of the credit card, as any being who pre-dates capitalism by two thousand years might, she overspends; told to economise, she turns off the electricity and water and serves stale bread. Samantha, faced with the arrival of her mother-in-law, uses magic to get the house tidy, protesting that 'I'm doing it for both of us' – but, instead of logically waving a magic wand, she actually does the housework, albeit at quadruple speed. While this process is funnier to watch, underlining her domestic inefficiency endorses the myth that 'clever' women are also impractical. We are invited to feel superior to the women, as well as the men; in fact, there is scope for the male viewer to claw back a good deal of his 'sudden glory' by reflecting that, even with super powers, women still louse up; for the female, her laughter may be muted by the pressure to disprove this myth by becoming Superwoman herself, rather than by demanding a more just apportionment of domestic drudgery.

The narratives construct these women of power as dangerous precisely insofar as they are themselves. As supernatural beings they are as threatening as Nimue or Melusine, and, potentially, as interesting to feminists. They become 'good', in terms of the prevailing ideology, insofar as they deny their own natures – and, narratively, become the incompetent objects of laughter. The credits spell out the nature of their domestic contracts: power is possible only as a cute eccentricity subject to male permission – not unlike women's work outside the home. *I Dream of Jeannie* opens with an oriental dancing girl who becomes a pink cloud and pours herself into a bottle; the bottle retains a woman's face and bats its eyelashes winningly. *Bewitched* starts with the image of a witch flying free on her broomstick to spell out the title in stardust. Then she wiggles her nose – Samantha's trademark 'spell' – and reappears, aproned, in a kitchen. Enter Darrin. She vanishes; a little cat rubs itself against his feet, jumps into his arms, and turns back into Samantha, like a bride being carried over the threshold. A cloud of smoke rises from the frying pan, over which the last credit appears: 'Agnes Moorehead as Endora.'

Endora. In the end, there was not enough latent comic energy in male incompetence or in farce-like attempts to conceal the fact that a wife can have a brain; there was not enough potential for camera magic in a wife who was willing to try, even unsuccessfully, to live without witchcraft. Real comic energy could only come from what the sitcom constructed as dangerous – female power unchecked, genuine, full-blooded magic. While conflict *within* the heroine might undermine the comedy, it could be externalised: the reluctant supernaturals were thus equipped with uncontrollable relatives who could not only drive the mortal husband into a frenzy of shoving them into closets, but who could utter the jibes that a sixties wife should keep under her tongue, and play practical jokes with flying objects, invisibility and transformations. Samantha may have been the central character, but for many female viewers, as the series progressed, the real disruptive comic joy was located in her mother. Endora, Darrin's mother-in-law, literalises the old joke: she really is a witch, a glamorous, acerbic figure of power who answers to no one. Her contempt for Darrin is such that even speaking to him on the phone prompts her to magic sprays of water into his ear, long-distance; her independence is the 'evil' in the story, against which Samantha will define herself by making herself as dependent on Darrin as possible. Significantly, as *Bewitched* moved into the seventies, and as the saga of Jeannie reached a belated conclusion in 1985 with a one-off show *I Dream of Jeannie Fifteen Years Later*, the supernatural relations took up more and more comic space. The husbands threw their weight around a little less: their wives, like Third World countries granted independence only when it is clear they are not a threat, had more visible freedom to make decisions – but still hugged their chains and only used magic to save their men or their marriages, never for pleasure. The relations, however, like zany embodiments of their desires, leaped into the narrative: Sam had a nutty aunt, a sinister father and a cousin Serena – also played by Elizabeth Montgomery – who wasn't above trying to seduce Darrin. Jeannie acquired a sexy sister and a large, black, male cousin with greater power than hers. He finally confronts her with a choice – when Tony's NASA shuttle is in danger, he will save it on condition that Tony loses all memory of their life together. She agrees, but arranges to start her courtship of Tony all over again – what the script might call a 'feminine wile'. All the relations, even the scatty ones, are above 'feminine wiles': they prefer real power. With a nod to the conventions of fairy-tale, they are dark, in contrast to the WASP-princess looks of the heroines – except Endora, carrot-topped like Plath's Lady Lazarus who could 'eat men like air'. Their darkness symbolises sitcom 'evil' – comic anarchy, female lawlessness – all the things that Lucy and Gracie, in a world apparently far more restricted, could unleash without magic help. The reproaches of Endora and Co. to their goody-goody daughters, inserted at the time as the standard jokes about 'the wife's relations', are now readable not as mingy attempts at marriage-wrecking but as healthy reminders that real female power does not reside in the vacuum cleaner.

The seventies

1970 was a key year for feminism. It saw the publication of Germaine Greer's *The Female Eunuch*, Robin Morgan's anthology *Sisterhood is Powerful*, and Shulamith Firestone's *The Dialectic of Sex*. There were strikes at General Electric and the New York Bell Telephone Company at which women workers expressed their sense of betrayal, not only by the management but by the male-dominated unions. There were wage strikes by housewives, marches against the Miss USA contest, the establishment of women's caucuses at major academic institutions. Consciousness-raising groups became a commonly available resource for women. The National Organisation of Women (NOW), set up by Betty Friedan in 1966, began to fragment as some members demanded more radical attitudes to sexuality, class and hierarchy, although the need to push the Equal Rights Constitutional Amendment ensured that US feminists had a project on which many differing energies could continue for a while to find a focus.

None of these events are mentioned in *The Mary Tyler Moore Show*. But for many women it offered concrete images which helped them explore feminist issues, providing a figure they could identify with or question in potentially fruitful ways. Commissioned to attract the new market highlighted by Nielsen's demographic research – middle-class women between 18 and 40 – it did so by celebrating them: the show's values could be summed up in the name of an alternative theatre company founded the same year – It's All Right To Be Woman. The starting point for the show was a deal between Mary Tyler Moore, whose drawing power on *The Dick Van Dyke Show* had begun to outstrip that of Van Dyke, and CBS. Moore and her husband, Grant Tinker, set up their own company, MTM, which allowed them a considerable degree of control, and the show evolved through careful negotiation. Moore's original intention was to plug a gap in situation comedy: there were families, and there were widows, but the subject of divorce had been left well alone. CBS, however, were not happy to break controversial new ground, and 'Mary Richards' became a woman of thirty starting a new career.

The focus on a single woman, however conservative the reasons behind it, was to prove an asset in a decade in which the number of single women in the USA between 25 and 34 rose by 111 per cent; it also meant that Mary was squarely established as the heroine of her own life rather than defined by the absence of a man. Divorce implied economic dependence rather than the meaningful choice of a career, and a Life in

Pieces which had to be Picked Up, letting the past determine the present. The first episode was structured so that Mary, followed to Minneapolis by her former fiancé, was given the option of renewing their relationship, but suddenly realised, not without pain, his real emotional inadequacies. As he leaves he utters a hackneyed farewell, 'Take care of yourself' – but she has already imposed her own meaning on this cliché and replies shakily, 'I think that's what I just did.'[24]

Mary's story is thus, from the outset, defined by the question in the title song, 'How Will You Make It On Your Own?' It is accompanied by a picture sequence of Mary in Minneapolis, a city new to her and to most of her viewers; she is smiling, and at the end of the sequence she throws her hat joyously into the air. 'Making It' is a broad goal which implies the construction of a whole, independent lifestyle. This was a new premise for sitcom, in which women rarely made choices, as opposed to getting into scrapes from which they were then rescued, like Marlo Thomas' scatty actress on ABC's *That Girl*, which ran for several years alongside the adventures of Mary Richards. MTM demanded, and got, an unusually large permanent cast, because Mary had to be shown both at work and in the home she was making for herself. There were two permanent settings, her apartment and the newsroom where she worked as Associate Producer. There were two sets of supporting characters: the apartment building – a converted nineteenth century house – had an attic tenant, a Jewish New Yorker, also single (Rhoda), and a downstairs landlady, Phyllis, with a doctor husband and a small girl. The newsroom had a middle-aged boss with a drink problem, Lou Grant, a vain male-chauvinist anchorman, Ted Baxter, and a writer, Murray Slaughter. These features placed the main storylines in the area of friendship rather than romance. Mary might date men, but their roles were limited – to a single episode or even to an awkward goodbye at the door interrupted by one of the permanent characters. The comedy sprang from the interaction between characters rather than knockabout or jokes. An article in *The Village Voice* more than a decade later saw this as MTM's major contribution to the shape of situation comedy:

> On even the best pre-MTM sitcoms, with few exceptions, the personalities and interplay were machine-designed mostly to generate the maximum number of generic jokes . . . After MTM even the most mechanical sitcoms had to pay lip service to the idea of the sitcom as a series of little epiphanies.[25]

These 'little epiphanies' work differently for male and female characters. For the men, they are revelations of vulnerability, with Mary as the catalyst that permits their expression. Ted Baxter, all vanity and flashing teeth, frequently reveals cracks in his ego which Mary will help to patch, as when she discovers him spending his vacation alone at home, sending postcards about his 'wonderful time'. Lou drops the grouchy mask to express unexpected depths of affection: in one episode typical of MTM's gentle comedy, Mary runs to the Ladies' in a fit of tears; Lou bumbles after her, growling at its other surprised patrons to get out; attempting to dry her tears, he pulls the roller towel off the wall and ends up framed by it like the MGM lion. Mary's own 'epiphanies' – and to some extent Rhoda's – are concerned less with unexpected vulnerability – for she never expects to be other than vulnerable – than with situating herself more clearly in her new world. The politics of the workplace and the family, both central areas of discussion in the women's movement, are not treated in *The Mary Tyler Moore Show* as 'issues' to be resolved in a single episode, but as *processes*, a series of shifts and changes which play a large part in the continuing existential growth of 'Mary', both as the fictional character 'making it on her own' and as the character constructed by an audience in sympathy with those aims. As Jane Feuer puts it in a pioneering study of Moore, MTM and the genre:

> For the generation of women who came of age with Mary and Rhoda, these characters seemed 'real' in a way no other TV character ever had. Of course the 'realism' of any fictional character is an illusion of sorts. A round character seems more 'real' than a flat one simply because 'roundness' is produced by multiplying the number of traits ascribed to the character . . . But what many in the 'quality' audience felt for Mary and Rhoda went beyond a mere quantitative depth. Their 'roundness' was also a cultural construct. The MTM women caught the cultural moment for the emerging 'new woman' in a way that provided a point of identification for the mass audience as well. The MTM women read as warm, lovable TV characters or as representations of a new kind of femininity.[26]

Mary explores all the familial roles at one remove, as it were. A visit by Rhoda's mother, Ida, comically expounds love and guilt, or what Rhoda calls 'Bronx love'.[27] Mary scoffs at Rhoda's family tensions until she agrees to put Ida up for the night and Ida tries to force money on her, money which she will feel guilty for taking and guilty for refusing. Ida chases Mary round the apartment, stuffing notes in her dressing gown pocket. Ida was never simply a figure of fun, however, and by 1976, in the spinoff series *Rhoda*, mother and daughter were able to recognise for themselves the tensions between love and dependency. As Rhoda faced divorce, Ida offered to stay with her, and then added, 'That would have been good for me, but not for you, huh?' and Rhoda, understanding Ida's own need at this time and the real affection behind the offer, told her 'Stick around, Ma.'[28]

Similarly Mary's interaction with Bess, Phyllis' daughter, allows her to play mother. Phyllis asks Mary to explain 'the facts of life' to Bess, and Mary is less and less able to pass the buck as characters narrate their own or their parents' failure to tackle the issue, in comic terms that are only a slight distortion of common experience. 'I thought I had to swim up the Columbia River', says Rhoda. Bess is primarily interested, not in the mechanical details but in the relationship between love and sex: 'If you love someone, do you . . .?' Mary's discomfiture is comic, but her frankness in acknowledging that 'there is a difference' in turn renders Phyllis' attempt to build on her groundwork – 'I'll make it sound spiritual and ethical . . . almost true'[29] – ridiculous. The viewer is permitted to draw her own meanings from the comedy: the new sexual mores tentatively propounded here by Mary can be seen as instrumental in shaping the pleasant heroine herself; or they can be rejected in favour of Phyllis' more conservative line.

Mary's friendships also permit her to examine marriage. Phyllis, at the tail end of the generation suffering from Friedan's problem without a name, provides, at their first meeting, a comically bitter account of the traditional fairy tale, gone sour but still seductive:

> I'm married and I know about marriage. I know how beautiful it can be if you look at it realistically . . . I mean *realistically* . . . face the fact that it means a certain amount of sacrificing . . . unselfishness . . . denying your own ego . . . sublimating . . . accommodating . . . *surrendering*.[30]

In this first episode, Lou Grant also provides an image of conventional marriage: after giving her the job he turns up drunk at Mary's apartment:

Lou   Well, I was just in the neighbourhood . . . visiting one of my favourite spas *(beat)* My wife left today. She's gonna be away for a solid month . . .

Mary (almost sotto) Now I know why you're here. Oh yes, Miss Associate Producer . . . he told you he'd find something for you to do. Oh yes! You sure didn't get the job because of your personality.

Lou   You know, you've got a great caboose.

Mary (continuing to herself) That's it! You got the job because of your great caboose!

Lou   . . . . But not as good as my wife's.

Mary turns and look at him with surprise

Lou (loud and mawkish) You know, she's only left today and I miss her already! I'm gonna go write her a letter. Do you have a typewriter?

The reversal of our expectations, and Mary's, is both comic and touching, a mixture which prevails as Lou sticks around, a gooseberry in the middle of what proves to be the final showdown between Mary and her lover. His presence, laboriously pecking on the typewriter, ironises the sentiments of the ex-lovers. But it also provides Mary with an image of marriage from a world she is no longer part of, in which the man and the woman have clearly defined, and unequal, roles. Eventually Lou himself becomes part of Mary's world as his own marriage ends.

But if there were roles to be explored, Mary and Rhoda also had to deal with the social pressures exerted on their own position as single women over thirty. The power of these pressures is ironically summed up in a remark by the original writing-producing team, James Brooks and Alan Burns. Both felt it necessary to explain, within the narrative, why Mary was not married:

> It tells you a little bit about our own lack of awareness of the women's movement at the time . . . but our feeling was that if a girl was over thirty and unmarried there had to be an explanation for such a freak of nature as that.[31]

But the women writers employed by Brooks and Burns – MTM was to employ record numbers of female writers, many of whom eventually collected Emmy awards – had a shrewder grasp of sexual politics. Mary's dates are a source of comic bathos: the beautiful man she fancies from afar turns out to be woodenly stolid; the exciting teacher at journalism class assures her 'I've gone out with C students before'.[32] The effect is funny rather than sad because Moore projects self-sufficiency, not loneliness. Seraphina Bathrick also identifies a sharper comic edge which is concerned with the way Mary is perceived by society. She and Rhoda join a club for the newly divorced in order to qualify for a discount trip to Paris, only to discover that it is full of unhappy people who prefer the label divorcee to the 'stigma' of singleness. When she complains to Rhoda 'I could discover the secret of immortality, and still they'd say, "look at that single girl, discovering the secret of immortality"',[33] it is a neat wisecrack but also a bitter truth; as Bathrick points out, that word 'girl' gives it away – 'no effort of imagination or humane work can provide a meaningful identity in the face of this *lack*'.[34] If this sounds far-fetched, one might turn to the *TV Guide* article which introduced *The Mary Tyler Moore Show* to the public. It is at pains to construct an image of Moore as a happily married woman, an untrained actress who happens to be lucky enough to fit into her husband's new show because 'I'm not a comedienne, I react funny.'[35]

Mary's own mode of behaviour in her social space, however, is that of a woman in control, one who acts rather than reacts. Her apartment is decorated with a large, fancy letter 'M'. Her arrangement of the furniture allows groups of friends to gather and allows her free movement across its length; it is the arrangement of a person drawing sustenance from friendships, not from coupled intimacy or family life. Mary often mediates between Phyllis and Rhoda, or Phyllis and Bess, but her relationships with them are not grounded on power. At her male-dominated workplace, power and hierarchy are evident, and her relationship with them is complex. She is a facilitator; she can reprove Lou sharply when his temper gets the better of him. In one of the show's typical sight-gags we see Ted shutting his raincoat in the door while making a dramatic exit, and it is the merciful Mary who quietly releases him. Mary reproduces the impact of the influx of women into the workforce in her decade, what has been called its 'feminisation': a greater emphasis on flexibility and interpersonal skills, a loosening of hierarchical constraints and a tacit permission to admit the emotional strains that social and working lives may impose on each other. Her career also reflects the less progressive aspects of women's entry into the workforce. There is a fine line, for instance, between the things she does for Lou in friendship and those he demands from her as a boss. 'Get me a date', he says, peremptorily, when she has been urging him to start his life over after his divorce. And there is an even finer line between the career failures experienced by Mary in the usual sitcom pattern – like all the permanent characters, she often overreaches herself and is pulled back into line – and the failures that spring from her position as token woman. An episode called *Fire One, Fire Two*[36] comically explores – but never resolves – many of these tensions. Mary has organised a birthday lunch for Ted at which the service is appalling. Mary complains, and feels a little guilty when told that Randi, the waitress, will be sacked. 'It's a dog-eat-dog world,' 'says Rhoda, but when Mary admires her cooking adds, with mock relief, 'I wouldn't want you to have me fired.'

The next day Lou is conducting interviews for a new secretary; Mary is testy about Lou's main criterion for rejecting candidates – 'When she walked out of here, I didn't watch her.' However, she persuades him to pick the candidate she wants by pointing out 'she has the necessary skills . . . and I'm sure she qualifies, well, you know . . .' The candidate is, of course, Randi. Lou saddles Mary with the responsibility for the choice; of course she chooses Randi, and of course Randi is a disaster. Not only is she inefficient, but she ruthlessly exploits Mary, who finds that she has assumed Randi's workload as well as her own. Lou finally agrees to fire her – 'I'm a much better fire-er than you are', he tells Mary. Mary glares, but finds herself adding 'You know, Mr. Grant, maybe she could improve if I . . .' and Lou gives her a triumphant QED look. Mary is trapped in a web of conflict: given responsibilities outside her usual sphere, she messes them up – but it is also clear that Lou, who has just confessed to being 'what you'd call a male chauvinist pig', has set her up. It's a comic moment, but it enshrines a dilemma the series never quite resolves.

Mary's farewell speech in the last show articulated the energies that largely governed it:

> I just wanted you to know that sometimes I get concerned about being a career woman. I get to thinking my job is too important, and I tell myself that the people I work with are just the people I work with, and not my family. And last night I thought, 'What is a family anyway? They're just people who make you feel less alone and really loved'. And that's what you've done for me. Thank you for being my family.[37]

The newsroom 'family' could sometimes get oppressive: Lou could behave like a heavy father and Mary acted as Big Sister to Ted and Murray, who never seemed to outgrow the need for one. And, as in family sitcom, members who sought to break out were clawed back: Ted fought an election, and failed; Mary flirted with another network, but didn't take the job. As a woman, Mary was particularly vulnerable to the pecking order. But the show also made comic and affectionate use of the fact that this family had chosen to be together; Phyllis' shrill praise of her 'open' marriage often seemed hollow in a way that Mary's relationship with Rhoda did not. Work did provide a place of friendship and acceptance that validated Mary's choice to 'make it on her own'. While the show's apparent lack of political direction contrasted with the comedy pioneered by Norman Lear, which tackled specific issues in programmes like *All In The Family*, it did run long enough to chart the growing confidence of one woman in herself and her choices. She was, admittedly, a white, heterosexual and middle-class woman, and one gifted with the enormous advantage of physical attractiveness. It is a measure of MTM's residual timidity that when Rhoda got her own show, Valerie Harper lost two stone in weight and became, literally, Mary-shaped rather than letting Rhoda remain her plump and abrasive self. But the story of Mary Richards established in situation comedy an enduring image of the alternative family as a valid community, one rich in possibility for female development and growth.

The eighties and after

Many of the heady possibilities glimpsed in the sixties and seventies were to collapse under the impact of the New Right: the Equal Rights Amendment ratification failed, AIDS panic began to undermine the new sexual mores, and the nuclear family was asserted as the central pillar of American society. In practice, however, the single woman, the gay couple, the lone parent, refused to disappear. The idea of the workplace as an alternative 'home' for a 'family' drawn together by shared tasks, friendship and economic interdependency was rapidly to become a sitcom staple. The balance of gender, in terms of numbers and of prominence of character, varied considerably. *Taxi*, for instance, featured only one regular female character; *Cheers*, set in a Boston bar, had a predominantly male selection of customers, but the staff, whose stories featured more strongly, consisted of two men and two women, a balance that was maintained through several changes of cast. The 'alternative' could even spin off from the literal 'family', as Lisa Bonet's own show about a young girl in a predominantly black college, *Different World*, spun off from the family-orientated *Cosby Show* to become the only sitcom centred on a black woman. Increasingly, however, American sitcom is beginning to exploit the idea of the all-woman community.

Some of these show specific alternatives to the nuclear family. *Kate and Allie*, for example, created in 1984 by Linda Sherry, was first screened as part of CBS's attempt to woo the consumer power of working women with a weekly night of shows specifically targeted at them. It shows two divorced women in their late thirties pooling resources in a New York apartment. Much of the comedy derives from their differences: Allie is conservative, believes in beige, and saved herself for her wedding night, while Kate is a career woman and former campus radical with a hedonistic approach to sex. Its technique, however, differs considerably both from comedy of incompatibility like *The Odd Couple*, which grounded each episode in a comic quarrel between dissimilar men forced to become flatmates, and from the comic staple of the unlikely heterosexual pair fighting to conceal mutual attraction. The laughter instead arises from the fact that despite two sets of life experience and information which the women can bring to bear on their situation as single parents, they are both short on easy answers. When her daughter Jennie is wondering whether to sleep with her boyfriend, Allie consults Kate:

Kate   What did your mother say to you?
Allie   Somehow I don't think Jennie'd believe she'd go blind.

While their different histories do not provide instant solutions, the show constantly reinforces the idea that the partnership between the women is itself a valid form of parenting. One frequently exploited comic riff is that of consultation between the two women at an inappropriate moment: Allie may ring Kate at work, or yell for her in the middle of a romantic dinner between Kate and a new lover. While the scenes get the laughs, they also make the friends' priorities, and the nature of this alternative family, clear: the children, not the bond between them, are the real focus.

Visually the sets often remind us that this shared parenting develops and changes the old style. We see much more of their living space than that of more conventional sitcom couples, and it is used differently. The centre is the kitchen, where the 'family' gathers, but they are often nibbling takeaways from a box rather than seated round a lovingly prepared table. As the series progresses, the kitchen becomes the centre of a catering business, and professional and private life form a messy mix. Bedrooms provide private spaces, but these are not kept inviolate. Kate and Allie perch on each other's beds to discuss their days, and the two daughters share a room. The children, indeed, also serve as a resource for each other: Jennie talks about her boyfriend with Kate's daughter Emma first, rather than Allie. Both girls share the parenting of Allie's young son Chip.

In one episode, Kate and Allie pretend to be a gay couple in order to avoid a rent increase levied against single people. By the rules of sitcom logic, it is of course inevitable that their landlady should be herself gay; the episode squeezed the maximum number of comic embarrassments from the situation, allowing them to hector the landlady on tolerance, before forcing them to admit that honesty was the best policy and finally dancing the night away together at a gay disco. It did also, however, allow the submerged possibility in their relationship gently to break the surface. The closing image of Kate and Allie dancing also reinforced the idea of the permanent validity of this alternative family; they were behaving just like a married couple on a night out.

The episode symbolised in many ways the process that is going on for Kate and Allie, and for the viewers, throughout the series, which is one of negotiation in a new world. Neither character has a clear political analysis of their situation (although in one episode Kate relives her student radical days at the college where Allie is now studying). Both, however, are aware of day-to-day sexism (as when Emma is sexually harassed at her part-time waitressing job) and both are engaged in redefining themselves in a world where feminism is an issue. As Pat

Dowell points out, 'a push-me, pull-you movement is constantly taking place, as two women work out how far to go in social, sexual and political terms'.[38] Often they both – especially Allie – articulate a conservative position but without the thumping assurance of rightness that accompanied the pronouncements of Father in the fifties. Allie, for instance, tells her daughter that seventeen is too young to make love but she also admits that she herself no longer believes in a 'Mr Right', the one and only sexual partner for whom she felt obliged to wait. She tells Jennie that if she intends to go ahead she will help her arrange for contraception and 'send the bill to your father'. The laugh line helps to underline the tensions in Allie's own situation; the placing of this little sermon at the end of the episode implies the 'rightness' of Allie's stance – she is allowed to sum up a position constructed as 'ours'. But our laughter is double edged: the remark is funny because it brings pragmatism into the realm of ethics, but also because Allie's status – as a woman still reluctantly dependent on a man she no longer likes – hardly qualifies her as a source of sexual advice. When Jenny says that she will 'think' rather than accepting Allie's doctrine wholesale, space is opened up for another point of view, even if as an audience we are steered away from it. The 'push-me, pull-you' strategy works at the level of the audience as well as for Kate and Allie; as they negotiate their way in the world of developing feminism the show negotiates with us. We are not politicised by it, but we are aware of a new set of criteria confronting even the most cautious. Our laughter may come from immediate empathy, if we have reached a similar stage in our own negotiations; or from a more distanced recognition if we ourselves have a more developed political position. The recognition of the children as this new family's priority – over romance, career, or the relationship between the adults – implies the validation of more radical structures that TV comedy is too timid to explore in more overt ways: if Kate and Allie *were* gay, it suggests, their play-it-by-ear parenting would not be any less successful.

Designing Women (created by Linda Bloodworth-Thomason in 1987) constructs an extended family cemented by ties of both blood and career; in an Atlanta firm of interior designers, two partners, Julia and Suzanne, are sisters, the other two, Mary Jo and Charlene, are friends. These four comprise the centre of a larger 'family' which includes their children, ex-spouses, current lovers, and their black male gofer, Anthony. Their key position in this 'family' which straddles both the personal and political, and their regional pride in a state which coined the ideal of 'Southern Womanhood', suggests that one of the series' priorities is to explore 'what women can achieve' rather than 'how women cope'; the partners have already 'made it' in terms of wealth, success and a lifestyle which satisfies them. What they go on to do is to establish their own values in the community – values which might be termed humanist–liberal–feminist. One episode spelt these out clearly: Julia, the most politically articulate partner, becomes infuriated by a member of the local Board of Commissioners who calls for compulsory school prayer and compulsory recitation of the Pledge of Allegiance in schools. She is persuaded to stand against him in a forthcoming election, and in a public debate with him on local television she loses her temper:

> We are probably the most uneducated, under-read and illiterate nation in the Western Hemisphere, which makes it all the more puzzling to me why the biggest question in your small mind is whether or not little Johnnie is going to recite the pledge of allegiance every morning . . . I am sick and tired of being made to feel that if I am not a member of a little family with two point four children that goes just to Jerry Falwell's church and puts their hands over their hearts every morning that I am unpatriotic and un-American . . . yes I am a liberal but I am also a Christian and I get down on my knees and pray everyday, on my own turf, in my own time, and one of the things I pray for, Mr. Brickett, is that people with power will get good sense and people with good sense will get power and that the rest of us will be blessed with the patience and the sense to survive the people like you in the meantime.

The episode ends with a closeup of the banner headline BRICKETT WINS BY A LANDSLIDE. This is typical of the way in which politics operate within the series: episodes are frequently engineered to elicit a vigorous tirade from one of the women on behalf of tolerance; the energy it liberates is the source of the laughter; clearly we are expected to empathise with, and enjoy, both the content and the fact that a woman is allowed so much linguistic space and freedom, but the tirade is usually undercut, so that we also laugh at its situational incongruity. Here the instant punchline renders Julia's passion comically redundant.

Tirades are also rendered comic – although not invalidated – because of their relationship with the character who utters them. Suzanne is the most reactionary of the four women: the high point of her career was on the beauty queen circuit some years back. She is the most conventionally 'feminine' and politically the most naively rightwing. Naturally, then, it is Suzanne who finds herself snowbound with Anthony in a hotel room. Throughout the episode she slowly abandons her sexist and racist scruples about spending a (chaste) night alone with a black man, and the episode concludes with them in bed together with Suzanne hoping nobody ever finds out. Suzanne's climb-down is genuinely funny because it is a climb-down from a position she only holds in theory; in practice she loves and respects Anthony. Similarly it's Suzanne, the person least likely to think out a liberal position in theory, who rounds on a neighbour waxing Pharisaical about a mutual friend with AIDS: 'If God was giving out sexually transmitted diseases as a punishment for sleeping around then you'd be at the free clinic all the time'. In an episode which examines the case for women priests, Suzanne's image of God proves the converse of the Christian Feminist position, but her reasons for retaining the traditional Father hardly support patriarchy: 'If God was a woman it'd be men going round in high heels, taking Mydol and having their upper lips waxed.'

On the other hand, Julia and Mary Jo, the characters who often do express a considered, liberal–bourgeois–feminist position, find themselves exploring the attitudes of a Suzanne. Mary Jo briefly considers having plastic surgery on her breasts; trying out some false breasts, she finds herself acting like a parody of Suzanne, claiming 'These things are power!'. When Suzanne enters Mary Jo's daughter for a beauty contest, Mary Jo finds herself making nasty remarks about the other girls, and Julia rounds on a beauty queen who has been doing the same thing to Suzanne:

> You probably didn't know that Suzanne was the only contestant in Georgia pageant history to sweep every category except congeniality. And that's not something the women in my family aspire to anyway. Or that when she walked down the runway in her swimsuit, five contestants quit on the spot. Or that when she emerged from the isolation booth to answer the question 'What would you do to prevent war', she spoke so eloquently of patriotism, battle-fields and diamond tiaras, grown men wept . . . Suzanne wasn't just any Miss Georgia. She was The Miss Georgia. She didn't just twirl a baton. That baton was on fire . . . and when she threw that baton into the air, it flew higher, further, faster than any baton has ever flown before, hitting a transformer and showering the darkened arena with sparks. And when it finally did come down, Marjorie, my sister caught that baton and twelve thousand people jumped to their feet for sixteen and half minutes of uninterrupted, thunderous ovation, as flames illuminated her tear-stained face.

Julia, small, fiery and casually dressed, suddenly becomes Suzanne the Southern Belle with an intensity that arouses laughter; but it also permits us, and her, to explore the beauty-queen position, and to find in it a magic and a pleasure in one's own body that might nourish, not negate, feminism.

The revelations of these secret selves, the liberal Suzanne and the frilly Julia, are the equivalent of *Kate and Allie*'s 'push-me-pull-you' negotiations. Here, however, they take place among the female community alone, developing an energy which is then impacted upon the world as a whole to achieve change. These changes are small, personal achievements lodged within a specific narrative; when, for instance, the group is annoyed by the chauvinist jokes and whistles of a group of construction workers, they solve the problem by the simple expedient of telling the mens' mothers about their behaviour – hardly a global solution. However, the comedy only makes sense in a world which has already named sexual harrassment as a problem and which has raised the need to provide a definition of 'femininity' which goes beyond the virtues Suzanne *thinks* that she subscribes to. In the decade in which Phyllis Schafly managed to make the words 'liberal' and 'feminist' carry the connotations once reserved for terms like 'Stalinism', to construct a comedy which doesn't simply profess liberal feminism, but actually makes the audience look forward to its expression as a comic climax (the AIDS episode attracted record viewing figures), is an achievement which deserves considerable respect.

A third show centred upon an all-female community, perhaps the most offbeat in its initial premise, is *The Golden Girls*, created by Susan Harris in 1985. The 'girls' are three women in their fifties, Blanche, Rose and Dorothy, and Dorothy's mother Sophia, who share an apartment in Miami Beach. Stylistically the show is much closer to fantasy than *Kate and Allie* or *Designing Women*: the apartment is palatial, the four women are never seen twice in the same stunning designer outfits, and while there are episodes about AIDS and ME, the mundane physical problems of late middle age – varicose veins, hot flushes – never touch the 'girls'. They have jobs, socially useful rather than lucrative, but the money flows effortlessly. Despite their total of more than two hundred years of experience, the characters do not have 'pasts' and 'memories' of the kind that Kate and Allie might draw upon. When they reminisce, their recollections are surreal in nature, reinforcing the stereotyped aspects of their present characters. Rose, for instance, whose stereotype might be termed 'dumb Scandinavian country girl', often gives vent to a comic riff about her village, St Olaf: an early episode has her relating the Great Herring War between the Johansens and the Lindstroms: the former wanted to pickle the herring, while the latter wanted to train them for the circus, a situation the others find it hard to envisage:

> *Dorothy*   Tell me, Rose, did they ever shoot a herring out of a cannon?
> *Rose*   Only once. But they shot him into a tree. After that no herring would do it.

Blanche and Sophia have similar 'riffs': the former might be titled 'Southern Belle' and the latter 'Sicilian Peasant'. They might well be open to accusations of racism, although the characters in these stories are markedly different from the Sicilians or Southerners who actually appear in the narrative from time to time, as visitors, relations and old friends.

Although some episodes in present time also take on a farcical quality – they go off for a peaceful weekend in the country together and discover they've accidentally booked into a nudist camp – their most characteristic activity is to sit round on the sofa and chat; the effect of the outrageous stories of the past is to stress the importance of the present in their lives, and their particular importance to one another; the embraces round the table among the four of them are visible, while those with their 'dates' are not. If we follow one of them on a date outside the home, it generally means that the others will somehow turn it into a joint expedition. Plot, in fact, is rarely important and few of the narratives are memorable. They exist largely to provide topics of conversation. The talk consists very largely of witty insults: Sophia puts down Dorothy because of her lack of sexual success; Dorothy puts down Blanche because of her sexual excess. Rose is not bright enough to think up insults, but will often make an innocent remark that fits: when she suggests putting out the welcome mat for visitors and Dorothy protests they don't have one, Rose innocently suggests they might use the one Dorothy said was next to Blanche's bed. Invariably, though, the verbal backchat is counterpointed with embraces and protestations of friendship. After a visit to a particularly unattractive Home for the Aged, Rose suggests that they promise to look after one other:

> *Blanche*   What the hell, if we do have to go to a nursing home, let's all go together.
> *Rose*   But what happens when there's only one of us left?
> *Sophia*   Don't worry. I can take care of myself.

The laugh line – Sophia is at least eighty – is, of course, evading the issue. But, as audience, we cannot evade it so easily, and this gives the show an edge of poignancy that also serves as its main strength. For, above all, *The Golden Girls* is a festival of smut, and often a specifically female smut.

Susan Harris had previously created, in *Soap*, a female character who was cheerfully promiscuous, Jessica Tate. She was 'Dizzy' in the Gracie Allen mould, with something of Gracie's serenity; the last episode showed her facing a firing squad with a kind of sexy composure. *Soap*, however, continually fell foul of the censor. In *The Golden Girls* Harris found a way to celebrate female sexuality, and middle-aged female sexuality at that, while allowing very little actually to happen. The 'smut' of *The Golden Girls* does not depend on generalised *double entendre*; and it positions the audience rather differently from the way Freud envisaged. Take for example a little exchange during one of the girls' midnight feasts. The cheesecake is nearly gone, they've used up the chocolate sprinkles, and Dorothy remarks that whipped cream would be nice. Blanche responds, 'I'll get it, it's in my bedroom', to which Dorothy sighs, with a sort of deadpan weariness, 'Never mind, Blanche.'

Here the 'first condition' of smut is not, as with Freud, 'the woman's inflexibility'; it is, rather, our knowledge that Blanche is a sexually adventurous woman who likes to boast of the fact; we as viewers construct the situation which we are never going to see. Dorothy's remark is, in a sense, the remark of Freud's male joke-teller; she engages us as the second male, the recipient of the joke, in order to embarrass Blanche. But Blanche is, of course, impossible to embarrass. She is proud of her sexuality, and because both Blanche and Dorothy are middle-aged women, the joke cannot be structured around sexual difference. We are, insofar as the joke constructs a specific audience, treated as middle-aged women ourselves, invited into a celebration of middle-aged female sexuality, while being simultaneously reassured, by the format of the show, that we will not be involved in the acting out of it. *The Golden Girls* is careful to maintain a highly conservative position *vis-à-vis* promiscuity in fact, while celebrating it verbally and in fantasy. For instance, when Blanche's niece comes to stay and uses the visit as a kind of extended orgy, Sophia labels her a 'slut'; while this is a harsh word, we are invited to concur with its import, and the episode concludes with Blanche preaching gently to the girl about self-respect and the danger of sleeping with a man simply because you want to be liked. Verbally, however, we are invited to envisage an unfettered sexuality among the women. When Sophia finds her security clearance questioned – the President is about to visit! – she mutters testily 'one lousy night with Mussolini'. The line depends on our simultaneous acceptance of Sophia as a woman entitled to sleep with whom she chooses, and entitled to enjoy sexual activity into her seventies, and our willingness not to take this remark as a bit of

Sophia's literal history with all the attendant political and personal complications.

What *will* happen to the last Golden Girl? And what *would* happen to her in an alternative family less physically fit and financially secure? All these comedies can only retain their upbeat stance by avoiding certain issues. Each remains, for instance, hermetically sealed in a world which is largely white and middle-class, a world almost untouched by domestic or foreign politics. Their heroines are never going to have to fight for custody of their children, or go on welfare; they may have marched against the Vietnam war in their student days, but won't express an opinion about American policy in the Gulf. They will be polite to other races, but will not intermarry. They will have gay friends, but not gay relationships. They may style themselves feminist, but it will be a depoliticised feminism. Nonetheless, they have placed women in the centre of the comic stage as subjects rather than objects, and they have reconstructed the position of the audience. While we might be invited to laugh at them, we are invited to do so as an audience of women sharing an experience of the world. When the heroines find themselves in comic situations, it is not usually because they are messing up something which, the plot implies, any woman can do – as when Lucy baked an eight-foot exploding loaf; rather, they are finding themselves in situations which exist precisely because the position of women is no longer stable and subordinate, situations which are new and involve trial and error. It was only Ball's witty stylisation of her plight that rescued our laughter from patronage; but when the Golden Girls attempt to buy condoms with the appropriate sang-froid, only to find the chemist bellowing to his assistant for the prices in front of a shopful of people, they are charting new territory and the laughter springs from recognition.

These comedies have, too, established the female community sitcom as a genre in its own right; the theme songs of both *The Golden Girls* and *Kate and Allie* clearly establish the subject as female friendship. The genre co-exists with others which inhabit a pre-feminist world with a few contemporary trimmings. There are still witch-comedies, that take as their basic premise the need to control the witch's power (*Free Spirit* turns witch into housekeeper; *The Charmings* resurrected the mother-in-law as evil witch figure in 1988). Another series that premiered in 1988, *I Married Dora*, began with a more promising situation: Dora is a political refugee who marries her employer to stay in the US. But by the end of the first episode it was clear we'd never hear her political views: the comedy was grounded in her adjustment to the housewife role. As

her new stepchildren threw rice, she protested, 'Now I'll have to vacuum
it up.' Too many sitcoms leave women vacuuming. It is perhaps the
shows grounded in the alternative worlds of female community that
contain the seeds of radical possibility.

3

British sitcom: a rather sad story

British situation comedy is the best in the world. British situation comedy is the worst in the world. Almost any serious discussion of the subject in the early nineties has contained one of these statements, and not a few contain both. The reasons cited for each diagnosis will vary: it's too trendy, or too old-fashioned; it's refreshingly topical, or in the best tradition of British humour; it's underfunded, or it makes ingenious use of its imposed limits. One assumption, however, will remain constant whatever the verdict: it is distinctive, clearly distinguishable from, say, its American counterpart, even if there are similarities of plot and situation.

There is, too, a recognisable 'tradition', a set of working practices and priorities that mark it out. To begin with, it is in the hands of a relatively small number of people. Barry Curtis writes:

> The consortium of skills necessary to produce, and to continue to produce, this effect are relatively rare and a small élite of comedy writers and performers much sought after.[1]

It is also writer-centred: the names of comedy scriptwriters – Galton and Simpson, Marks and Gran, Esmonde and Larbey – are as well-known as its stars. Alan Plater summed up on a *Media Show*: 'The actual heart of our business is one person, one room, one typewriter, one sheet of paper.'[2] It's a romantic image, with overtones of the artist in the garret and the feminist writer in that Room of Her Own to which, these days, no one would dispute her right (would they?), and its attractiveness tends to blind the audience to the realities of the 'business' once the writer leaves the magic room.

Certainly a woman writer cannot take for granted the existence of an administration sympathetic to her concerns. In 1991 the Independent Producers Association found that, in the whole of the sector senior enough to commission programmes at the BBC, only 10 out of 52 were women; in the independent companies, the figures were even worse – 3 out of 80.[3] Male producers have often expressed extreme caution about using women writers. Jill Hyem, for instance, cites a BBC project in 1984, a series of comic playlets with the linking setting of a timeshare flat; the producer commented to her that 'most of the funniest ideas are coming from women',[4] but no woman was subsequently commissioned. Arlene Whitacker, whose sitcom *Sharon and Elsie* ran for two series, suggests that the reason for this caution is social – that women tend not to be admitted to the informal networks that spring up in areas like light entertainment and provide the opportunity to gauge the 'general feel of what is required in terms of current demand from heads of department'.[5]

Consequently, the pressures upon a female writer or producer of sitcom can be enormous. Mandie Fletcher, the first woman producer to infiltrate BBC Light Entertainment, who commissioned Janey Preger's successful series *No Frills* in 1988, found that it was referred to as a 'feminist pilot'[6] as if it were some sort of metonym for female comedy rather than a first sitcom by a writer with a strong track record in drama. In view of all this, it is not perhaps surprising that the programme on which Plater expounded his romantic–élitist view of comic writing showed no female British writers. One sitcom featured, *Fawlty Towers*, was co-authored by a woman, Connie Booth, but she was not interviewed. By contrast, Gail Parent, who learned her skills with MTM and became the first woman writer to win an Emmy in 1973, acted as spokesperson for the American group. It was a group whose collective and collaborative working methods the British contingent found threatening. Maurice Gran, who with his co-writer Laurence Marks has been responsible for several popular and high-status British sitcoms, commented that 'Our perception of ourselves is that we're free agents – the American perception of contract writers is that they're slaves.'[7]

Jane Austen once commented that her chosen literary form had a very low status – it was made to be flung aside with a careless 'O! It is only a novel!' when the hero entered the room. It is, maybe, no coincidence that the industry which treats sitcom as the sole product of a writer's individual vision employs very few women – while the 'slaves' of US sitcom include Madelyn Pugh, Gail Parent, Treva Silverman, and Barbara Gallagher, all of whom were winning awards for their work when British

TV had no comedy written by a woman on the air.

The absence of a female tradition makes it impossible to organise this chapter on the historical lines of the previous one. Instead I shall deal with three distinct though related topics. First I shall look at woman-as-image: at the roles constructed by men in predominantly male discourse, which may or may not offer opportunities for the strategies of resistance. Secondly I shall look at woman-as-writer, concentrating, of necessity, on the work of Carla Lane. Lastly I shall look at woman-as performer; at the ways in which an experienced sitcom star can interact with her various roles. My chosen example, Penelope Keith, is typical, in that her individual style has not only coloured existing roles but has been instrumental in the shaping of new ones.

Domestic dragons and 'Doing it very well'

All in all, Austen might well be advised, if she wanted to write in a popular and comic form about a young woman with her way to make in the world, to emigrate to the USA, where *Pride and Prejudice* might easily become *Lizzy!*, in the tradition of Mary Richards or her descendants Molly Dodd or Murphy Brown. If she chose to stay at home, she could always adopt male disguise and push some of her minor characters forward – for *Pride and Prejudice* does contain, alongside its unacceptable centre about a young woman with a sense of humour, an entirely recognisable British sitcom stereotype, Mr Collins. This vain, pompous social climber with his idiotic tricks of speech and his sublime lack of self-awareness embodies many of the preoccupations of British sitcom: male eccentricity, obsession with class, belief in the nuclear family and a sense that, with all its hardships and injustices, life is what it is and cannot be changed. Austen has obligingly arranged the female constellations around this magnificent oaf in configurations which are instantly recognisable on today's small screen: Lady Catherine, the dragonish aristocrat to whom Collins grovels on every available occasion; and Charlotte Lucas, Elizabeth's best friend, the vital injection of humanity and sense into the gallery of eccentricity – and the nineteenth-century incarnation of the sitcom wife. Elizabeth herself is struck by Charlotte's handling of her role as straight man:

> Elizabeth in the solitude of her chamber had to meditate upon Charlotte's degree of contentment, to understand her address in guiding, and composure

in bearing with her husband, and to acknowledge that it was all done very well.

For most of the lifetime of British sitcom, a woman has had the choice of being a dragon or of 'doing it very well'. Although the roles may involve very different kinds of acting style, they both serve a similar function: they underpin the status quo, providing a commonsense context in which (male) eccentricity and anarchy can bloom. This context can involve their physical presence, or their speaking absence (''er indoors', the dragon wife of Arthur Daley, was as significant a character in the comedy series *Minder* as any of those on screen, although she was neither heard nor seen). A great deal of past and current comedy has emanated from the generation Philip Purser once picturesquely described as the 'lucky spermatozoa' who found a place in the TV womb in the sixties.[8] In keeping with his choice of metaphor, much of it has been predicated on a simultaneous revolt from and need for the figure of the mother/mistress. She symbolises the stasis that is at the heart of British sitcom. US sitcom may involve characters contained by their 'situation' – they do not quit the job or leave the family – but there is none the less an assumption that major problems can be solved, and the 'situation', as we have seen, is often one of change. Mary is making it on her own; Kate and Allie have changed their lives and are exploring the consequences. If the message of American sitcom is 'we can work it out', that of British sitcom is 'you'll never get out'. It is a comedy of entrapment within a rigid and class-based social structure.

Comic transgression of that framework, however, may be achieved (for the duration of each story) by an individuality so strong as to qualify as eccentricity. While he may be judged by the audience against commonsense standards, the eccentric is greatly enjoyed. He (rarely she) is a guarantee that we are at one remove from 'reality', that we are on a holiday from convention. It is no coincidence that the celebration of eccentricity is often at its most vigorous in the absence of women, or in situations where it is possible to ignore them.

British sitcom is often said to have effectively begun in 1956 with the development of a major eccentric in *Hancock's Half-Hour*. Anthony Aloysius Hancock was the joint creation of Tony Hancock and his scriptwriters Alan Galton and Ray Simpson, who were to dominate British situation comedy writing for the next decade or so. Petulant, self-important and desperate for upward mobility, Hancock was so socially inept he alienated men and women alike. His greatest comic moments were soliloquies. He lies around his room with nowhere to go, trying to blow smoke rings and burning his lip, experimenting with different walks and pretending to be a guardsman. Attempts to hook up with society – as when he takes it into his head to produce a son and heir and interviews several women for the purpose over a frozen TV dinner – are disastrous. Only when alone, in fact, is he fully himself and fully available for our pleasure. The narrative depends on our understanding of a 'norm' – involving heterosexual relationships, ultimately marriage – which the character transgresses, from a mixture of personal choice and an inadequacy he will never himself perceive.

Twenty years later Hywel Bennet played another lone eccentric, *Shelley*. As the scourge of the dole queue, sounding off about Mary Whitehouse, advertising and pollution, he seemed Hancock's polar opposite. Their sexual politics, however, were more or less identical. His wife was a weary stooge for his epigrams – until she finally left the series and left him to patronise waitresses, barmaids, and other poorly-paid women. While viewers are certainly invited to consider both Hancock and Shelley as both rude and pathetic, they are clearly also invited to enjoy them. It's hard, however, to imagine a woman in a similar role; such behaviour in sitcom would code her as unable to attract a man, a fate sitcom reserves for minor characters.

Shelley and Hancock get their laughs by railing at an establishment they will never escape, but which benevolently contains their eccentricity. Women are forced by sitcom to *be* the establishment. This is clear from innumerable sitcoms in which female absence is the condition that permits male individuality by liberating them from the confines of the family 'norm'. Far from being the site of the alternative family, the workplace in much British sitcom is precisely the place of male freedom from domesticity: the third-rate public school (*Whacko!*); the monastery (*Oh Brother!*); the rag and bone yard (*Steptoe and Son*); the prison (*Porridge*); the Home Guard (*Dad's Army*); Parliament (*Yes, Minister*) – for forty years all-male communities like this nourished characters who were naive or devious, outrageous or timid, characters who never changed their situation (that was the point) and who were dramatic vehicles full of opportunity; all free to be what they so enjoyably were, precisely because there were no women around to 'spoil things' with common sense. A 'character' can be a character, in all his comic glory, on all-male soil. (As, perhaps, the male creators of sitcom can be in their social networks.)

The relationship between femaleness and 'commonsense' is here tacitly constructed by the viewer, but we are in no doubt about its presence because other sitcoms have taught us. Where women and eccentricity coexist, it is because of an eccentrics' alliance which gives them strength to resist the 'norm': a clear example can be found in the popular series by Roy Clarke, *Last of the Summer Wine*, which started in 1976. It narrates the adventures of three pensioners in rural Yorkshire, the military man Foggy, the thoughtful pessimist Clegg, and the scruffy reprobate Compo. The trio's adventures often involve vigorous physical comedy: they fall in streams, crash cars, scale roofs and otherwise conduct themselves in a manner more suited to young men. This, of course, is the humour of the situation; we laugh at the initial incongruity of old men acting like children, but also with pleasure at their very evident enjoyment of transgressing the expectations laid upon old people. However, it is plain that these geriatric Huck Finns can carry on like this only because they remain outside domesticity. The 'norm' is represented by Ivy, who runs the village café. 'Ivy's very steady,' says Clegg. 'You wouldn't catch her doing anything reckless like being happy.'[9] Ivy is largely confined to the café or the parlour, while the three old bachelors range freely over the wide open spaces. The other woman with whom they have a regular relationship is Nora Batty, with whom Compo says he is in love. His desire for her seems largely masochistic; their characteristic encounters show Nora emerging from her doorway to repel Compo with a broom or whatever comes to hand – clearly part of her attraction, for she will never expect Compo to deliver the sexual/ domestic goods, and can thus satisfy his self-image of free spirit and rebel.

The nagging mother–wife, reducing male energy to domestic tidiness, sexually rapacious or coldly puritanical – both equally frightening, since they imply a sexuality under her own control – is of course a familiar figure, from literature, from comic postcards, cartoons and jokes. She is a comic stereotype as well known as the bragging coward, the trickster, the stereotypes on which the comedy of eccentricity largely depends. The fact that we easily recognise them codes the narrative as comedy. Over the course of a series, male stereotypes become vivid and human, as we pick up little items of information about them. The triumph of, say, Wilfrid Brambell's rag and bone man or Paul Eddington's gormless Prime Minister is that they impose individuality so that we are hardly aware of a typology at work. With female figures, however, it is difficult for this transformation to happen; the available stereotypes are strictly limited to the nag, the spinster and the dumb sex object. All of these

define, rather than transgress, the 'norm', since they all relate at bottom
to the invisible ideal of the family against which the male eccentrics pull.
It is a hard task for a comic actress to win the affection, or attention, of
an audience in the face of these limits. Gaye Tuchman writes:

> Sex-role stereotypes are set portrayals of sex-appropriate appearance, inter-
> ests, skills, behaviour and self-perceptions. They are more stringent than
> guidelines.[10]

There is an undeniable pleasure, however, in the comic skill with
which these thankless stereotypes are portrayed. At least, they offer a
vehicle for the vitality of an authoritative performer; at best they can
open up space for new meanings to accrue to the old typology: Frances
de la Tour, for example, in Eric Chappell's bedsitter comedy *Rising
Damp*. While the comic centre is the grasping, slimy and pretentious
landlord, Rigsby, de la Tour managed to create a genuine eccentric out
of the spinsterish Miss Jones who rented one of the rooms. The text
constructed the broad outlines of the character on conventional lines: she
is prudish in resisting Rigsby's dingy advances, and eternally frustrated
in her novelettish desire for the glamorous African student prince, Philip;
but it also afforded the actress crucial opportunities to dominate the
action in a distinctive style. In one episode, for instance, Miss Jones is
persuaded by Rigsby to impersonate his estranged wife, and creates a
memorable monster from his misogynist description. 'Just loosen your
stays, gel, and have a good nosh', breezes Miss Jones, grabbing the
chance to portray a seaside postcard stereotype.[11] But while the episode
is entertaining as farce it also makes explicit something about Miss Jones
that de la Tour's portrayal had always hinted at: the visible relish with
which she gets stuck into the role, blazing with energy and concentration, underlines the fact that Miss Jones is not a spinster because she is
undesirable: rather she is larger than life, too much for most men to
manage. De la Tour gives her a gawkiness normally associated with
shyness but – allied to the intelligence that is visible in the play-acting,
the sense of irony that is implied by sidelong glances – it becomes the
hallmark of a woman whose intellect has run ahead of her social graces.
Miss Jones is too intelligent to find a fit mate in Rigsby's household, but
her awkward beauty and sense of irony set her to some extent outside the
gloomy parameters of marriage or failure. She is a true original, allowing
new meanings to accrue to an old stereotype and providing a specifically
female pleasure by ironising the reading of herself as a dried-up failure
by her fellow lodgers.

A similar individualising of a well-worn stereotype occurs in *Fawlty Towers*, scripted by a male–female team – unusually so, in the late seventies. This is perhaps the British sitcom that approximates most nearly to the spirit and structure of farce; as such it is more firmly divorced from 'reality' than even the stylised versions presented in *Last Of the Summer Wine* or *Rising Damp*. This gave the writers, John Cleese and Connie Booth, liberty to touch on issues below the stereotype surface of domesticity. Basil Fawlty, the hotelier, is a social climber every bit as obsequious as Mr Collins, but he is also consumed with a self-hatred that finds expression in vicious misanthropy towards the guests. His wife Sybil – 'that golfing puff-adder' as he describes her – gives as good as she gets; when Basil, through his own prurient fault, is caught by Sybil spying on a female guest and tries to bluff his way out, she responds 'Do you seriously imagine a girl like that could be interested in an ageing brilliantined stick insect like you?'[12] Linguistically, the characters are equally rich; physically, they are opposites: Basil is stick-limbed, large, uncoordinated while Sybil is small, brisk, running to fat; he wears a set expression of fierce anxiety, she, one of disdain. The effect is one of carefully balanced physical grotesques like Laurel and Hardy: the couple are a double-act as well as a marital unit. The bonding that this implies perhaps allays some of the potential anxiety aroused by the acknowledgement of real marital hatred on both sides: Basil feels trapped by domesticity, responding with fear and loathing to his wife both as domineering mother and rapacious mistress; Sybil expresses the anger at domestic confinement Patricia Mellancamp finds beneath the good humour of Lucy. However, the couple have a common goal, social mobility; the plots are bound up with their mutual, and mutually self-defeating, efforts at social climbing. Basil grovels to the wrong guests; Sybil affects mannerisms she imagines are sophisticated, a braying laugh and a nasal whine, combined with ruthless public put-downs of Basil; the scorn they feel for each other in the process deflects from their more specifically sexual resentments. *Fawlty Towers* is one of the few sitcoms to allow a female stereotype to act as well as react: Basil's eccentricity is not liberated by Sybil's absence, but by her gadfly presence, and her eccentricity is equally liberated by her hatred of him.

For most actresses the alternative to the nagging mother/wife or the sex object is a character like that of Charlotte Lucas in *Pride and Prejudice*, not herself funny but the staunch support of a husband whose eccentricity is containable within the domestic frame, in a sitcom style which bears a superficially greater resemblance to perceivable 'reality'.

'Doing it very well' involves skills which are maternal rather than those of an equal partner, and the eccentric male basically content in the domestic environment is inevitably, to some degree, infantilised. The absence of actual children from these more 'naturalistic' comedies is remarkably frequent; sometimes the 'children' are young adults, or have left home, re-opening the position of child for father; but not infrequently we are shown a youngish married couple in which the husband is clearly a substitute infant. Some scriptwriters in this vein provide actresses with excellent and well-used opportunities for acting – but seldom comic acting. John Esmonde and Bob Larbey, for example, co-authored several comedies which carried a melancholy subtext. It reached an extreme level in the series *Ever Decreasing Circles*, in which a popular Esmonde and Larbey star, Richard Briers, played a suburban busybody, Martin Bryce. His attempts to organise local charities and clubs were always wrecked on his obsessive orderliness and he was constantly piqued by the effortlessness with which his neighbour could win friends, influence people and achieve social success. His wife, played by Penelope Wilton, was supportive in the Charlotte Lucas vein, but the mutual attraction between her and the golden-boy neighbour became apparent through a delicate tissue of looks and glances and inflections. The comedy practised a considerable amount of brinkmanship as Martin's obsessiveness frequently slipped beyond the bounds of what a 'normal' wife could tolerate. In one episode the couple meet, separately, a psychiatrist at a party, who gently suggests to Ann that she might persuade Martin to seek treatment. In another Ann becomes restless and the problem is averted when she begins an Open University degree. In the final episode, a Christmas special, Ann is pregnant and Martin is offered a better job in another town. As they leave 'the Close' that has hitherto been Martin's life, the atmosphere is charged with suppressed emotion as the never-in-fact lovers part; the situation remains comic if – and it is a big if – we can accept the idea that fatherhood will transform Martin into an adequate husband/lover/partner.

Despite Ann's passivity – would it really take so long for a childless and intelligent woman in the eighties to organise a little education for herself? – Wilton and the scriptwriters did probe an established boundary of sitcom by suggesting that women could also be victims of domesticity; most family sitcoms, as I have suggested, are predicated on the assumption that for the woman monogamy and family are sufficient. Ann challenges this assumption through visibly suppressed pain, Sybil Fawlty through unsuppressed anger, Miss Jones by ironising the role of tragic spinster. None do so with such violence as to shatter totally the comic frame, but all raise questions. If women refuse to provide a tacit standard of normality, what is to become of comedy? If they refuse to neutralise the threat – as their menfolk see it – of female energy and sexuality by becoming mother figures to infantilised men, then the comic structure cannot remain the same. The liberation of men, real or desired, from domestic confines, and the suppression of women within them, can no longer be the only comic order of things.

Women, then, are important in British sitcom as backdrop; their absence is existentially liberating, their presence a reminder of the 'norms' which help the viewer to identify the source of comic incongruity. They are crucial, but they are often denied the possibility of being the source of the comedy. I should like to examine the possibilities that, none the less, have opened up along two fronts.

Female independence or female lack? The work of Carla Lane

To look at situation comedy which may be described as being *about* women, rather than simply having female characters to service the male lead, is to find oneself discussing the work of Carla Lane. While Lane is not the only woman writing comedy, nor the first to do so (Jennifer Philips sold her series *Wink to Me Only* in 1967), she is the only woman writer to have become a 'name' like Galton and Simpson or Esmonde and Larbey. She is said to be the highest-paid comedy writer in the country, attracting viewing figures in the twelve million mark. Paradoxically, this success seems to have made producers shy of nurturing other female talent. On the one hand her distinct style is perceived as a 'norm' of female comic writing; it is all too easy to slip from asking of a script 'Is it as good as Carla Lane?' to 'Is it like Carla Lane?', dismissing work which may interrogate ideas of laughter and gender in different ways. On the other hand Lane herself is often constructed by the media as a kind of wayward eccentric, a one-off talent, the exception that proves the rule about women's lack of comic ability. Interviewers are apt to lay stress on her concern for animal rights, her personal menagerie, her extended family, as if strong individuality were an acceptable substitute for maleness.[13]

Lane entered the world of situation comedy in 1969 with *The Liver Birds* (originally co-written with her friend Myra Taylor), a sitcom centred on two young Liverpool girls sharing a flat – a fairly novel sitcom relationship and a fairly novel location at that time. The series was developed between 1969 and 1978 and Lane went on to write other series, mostly but not exclusively centred on women. Only these will concern us here: *Butterflies*, about a married woman contemplating an affair; *Solo*, about a woman alone after the breakup of an affair; and *The Mistress*, about a woman having an affair with a married man. Lane herself wrote for the *Radio Times*:

> I entered the bewildering world of television just as woman had begun to shake her fragile fist in the face of man. I disappeared into that creative mincer and was so busy trying to emerge still looking and feeling like a woman that I seemed to miss it all. When the handle was finally turned and I fell to the ground clutching my first cheque, I discovered that a new breed of female had grown up around me. They were brave and abandoned: they fought with frightening ferocity for all the things which I had accidentally achieved – equal pay, equal rights and individuality. Moved by their endeavours, I cheered them on as they treated the world to their thin soprano voice. 'A woman's place is *not* in the home', they shrieked. It was convenient for me to agree as I was working in London and my home was in Liverpool, my family had booked in at the local chip shop, my Irish wolfhound had dug a hole in the garden and was sulking in it, the family parrot had hacked its way out of the house and was now living on top of the television aerial.[14]

This is (I hope) a piece of public relations writing rather than a considered statement about the place of feminism in comedy; as such it shouldn't necessarily be taken as the last word on Lane's own position, but it does show clearly the contradictions clustering round the idea of female independence as a comic subject; the *Radio Times* obviously felt that some sort of jokey reassurance was in order. The wolfhound and the parrot reinforce the idea of life as sitcom and sitcom as life – wacky, exasperating and to a large extent 'natural' and inevitable. Women who consciously articulate the need to question the 'inevitable' are both frightened and frightening; they may have a point, but their attempts to think through exactly what that point is are embarrassing – 'thin soprano' and 'shriek' are clichés from the most reactionary popular press. Independence and individuality have to be lucky accidents – for the female writer, giving expression to her own (fortunate) eccentricity, or the female character, pitchforked into becoming the heroine of her own life. A Mary Richards, actively seeking a new life, is a scary prospect, it seems; but if she tumbles into it by mistake, laughter is just possible.

Lane's earliest series managed to skirt many gender issues simply because it showed two young and unmarried girls at a moment when the permissive society hadn't begun to press on sitcom's boundaries. Beryl and Sandra – later Carol and Sandra – were intensely preoccupied with boyfriends and eventual marriage, but both the censor and their own strong religious convictions kept men out of their space on a permanent basis; it meant the absence of the will-they-won't-they titillation that permeated later flat-sharing comedies like *Man About The House*; sexual activity and innuendo were displaced by other events, often with a more original comic potential:

Sandra You mean you've been in his flat – all night?

Carol Yeah, isn't is shocking – I did explain about the non-meat-eating, non-smoking, non-drinking, whiter-than-white friend of mine.

Sandra Have you no thought for others?

Carol Look, who do you think you are, me mam or something? I thought we both left home to escape this sort of thing.

Sandra Your Grandad went out last night.

Carol Good – I'm glad somebody had a good time. And if it's any consolation to you, I didn't do anything I can spend my old age gloating about. We had a candle-lit supper, opened a very noisy bottle of champagne – and the next thing I knew his dog was having pups all over the flat. Dog and pups all doing well – dog owner not doing very well – dog-owner's girlfriend spent the night nursing all nine of them![15]

The girls swop backchat, neck passionately with a series of men without commitment, and interact with each other's families. Increasingly as the series went on, the families gave rise to domestic plots that teetered on the edge of surrealism: Carol's grandfather provokes a family panic that he is lost and is discovered at his wife's grave chatting happily to her; Sandra talks down Carol's brother from a suicidal leap by marshalling the gathering crowd to sing 'You'll Never Walk Alone.'

The Liver Birds were in many ways more eccentric and individual than their male counterparts, Clement and la Frenais' *The Likely Lads*. Lane's later comedies were to confirm, however, a directly inverse relationship between comic individualism and female sexuality. The Liver Birds can be themselves – opinionated and energetic selves if still relatively unformed – precisely because they are unattached, literally possessing the virginity that in earlier times signified power and independence. Once Lane's heroines enter the sphere of sexual activity they enter that of dependency or even addiction. Male absence becomes a threat, a demon to be vanquished rather than empowering, as female absence does for the comic male. The jokes are gallows humour – the princess has kissed the frog. He remains a frog, but she can't get free of him; what remains for her is to bemoan her fate with as much wit as she can muster, never quite coming to terms with life as it is and never quite working out a way to change it.

The Liver Birds was set in a specific city, Liverpool; it is, however, the Liverpool of the sixties, and Lane's final abandonment of the series preceded the recession. A few years later a Liverpool setting would have forced some acknowledgement of contemporary political reality; as jobs disappeared Liverpool became a focus of political anger and resentment. Her later work conformed more closely to what Mick Eaton calls the 'timeless nowness' of British situation comedy – a total lack of specificity about time or place that prevents any interrogation of the political or gendered issues on which it might touch.[16] For the next decade or so, Lane's characters inhabited a well-heeled waste land. This was all the more apparent for being so well photographed: location shots, sure sign of a well-regarded and high-budget series, abound as heroines Ria, Gemma and Max wander through anonymous parks and streets to think out their lives. Classical, rather than contemporary, music backs their musings, coding them as middle-class with 'good taste', while serving further to heighten the timelessness. Geographically the locations are non-specific and this principle extends to the social and economic spheres. Gemma in *Solo* decides to get a job after leaving her boyfriend for his infidelity; she's at once ensconced in a responsible position in social work – this despite what one can only presume is a degree of inexperience on her part and in the face of the newly-elected Tory government's massive cutbacks to the social services. Max, the eponymous Mistress, is financially independent; she runs a flower shop. Her small business-woman status, however, exists to provide her with opportunities to take endless time off and with suitably romantic props rather than giving her a source of interest or concern beyond Luke, her married lover. As for Ria, the earliest of the three (*Butterflies* premiered in 1978), her world is remarkably close to that of *Brief Encounter* in the forties: suburban home, husband and children, and a handsome man with whom she has an unconsummated romance. Ria wears gypsyish clothes and feels that she is 'happily married, but not excitingly married'. One running gag is her inability to produce an edible meal; another is her comically energetic tirades against the family's lack of domestic consideration: they expect meals on time, they leave a mess to be cleared. Her resentment should be undercut by the presence of Ruby, the domestic; Ria herself doesn't *do* very much in the way of work, though Lane chooses to reap no laughs from this point. Ria and her dentist husband Ben have a noisy row when she wants to take a job, but this issue is not constructed in terms of economic independence or personal freedom; the emphasis is on lack of romance and excitement, and these are envisaged – by Ria, by Lane, and therefore by us – in purely erotic terms. The comic pattern of *Butterflies* is a sexual version of the old music hall device of the interrupted monologue.

Wendy Craig, the actress who plays Ria, is associated with 'nice' roles, most of them married women, thus encoding the end of Ria's story: she will, of course, never leave Ben. There are allusions to her 'goodness' by her teenage sons, who have suspicions that something is going on, and even the occasional heart-to-heart with God when Ria drops into the local church. Individual episodes gain their laughter by countering illicit erotic impulses with more orthodox ones, leaving Ria and Leonard in stasis. In one episode, for instance, Leonard is sitting in his car outside Ria's house, trying to persuade his chauffeur to go in and give Ria an invitation to lunch. Inside, Ria tries to seduce her husband, who is examining plaster casts of some teeth.

> *Ria*   We should be romantic, try to get back to where we were . . . who is that?
> *Ben*   Mrs Wainwright before I straightened her teeth.
> *Ria*   Who's that?
> *Ben*   Mrs Wainwright after I straightened her teeth.
> *Ria*   She looks much better. What was I saying?
> *Ben*   Something about being romantic and getting back to where we were . . . I've already analysed it all. What you're trying to say is, let's make love on the settee.

After some wrangling, they do go to make love – Ben, prompted by wistful envy of the teenagers who giggle and grope in the potting shed, masterfully beckons her, clutching a large potted plant. Leonard watches the lights go out. The energy of the scene arises from the juxtaposition of the ordinary and the 'romantic' – false teeth and passion – and from the absurdity of erotic impulses which push the basically decorous characters out of control. Similarly Ria soliloquises about housework:

> Now don't panic. Dishes are a fact of life. Not a very interesting fact, but, nevertheless, a fact. (*She clumsily clears plates from the table and dumps them on the draining board.*)
> When you get married your life takes on three extra dimensions – (*She gets a tray onto which she sweeps all the remaining clutter on the table.*)

housework, kids, dishes. There, you see! You did it! You coped. Instead of having a mess over there, you've got it over here. (*She takes up a bunch of flowers and a vase.*) The cheek of those girls. Filling this house with their thin thighs and their hardly used faces. Threatening my son with their chests. Oh my God, those chests. Mother Nature must have put in a bit of overtime on that lot. And they're so aggressive. (*She grabs a tenderiser and hammers the flower stems viciously.*) No gentleness, no femininity. Where's it all gone? When I was young a woman was a deep, mysterious pool. A man had to dip his toe in first, then wade out carefully and gently. Now they just dive in. They don't even bother to put their swimming trunks on. It's all so unsubtle and disgusting and degrading and WONDERFUL and I'd give anything to be doing it myself, but I've got to . . . and then I've got to . . .
(*As she splutters incoherently the telephone rings. She grabs it and screams 'Shut up!' and slams the receiver down. Cut to a phone box. It is Leonard, looking bemused.*)

On the one side of Ria's moral see-saw there is 'romance' – free expression of sexuality. This is roughly equated with a youth recaptured – all the older characters in *Butterflies* complain about getting older; their resentment of the young springs from the fact that they inhabit a more sexually permissive society. On the other side there is the 'real world' of duty and domesticity. Terry Lovell suggests that

> the highly charged ideal of romantic love is subject to comic deflation against the series' construction of the real-typical of marriage and personal relations, and vice versa. We laugh at the ideal, because it is so far from what we are shown as 'real', and we laugh in turn at the 'real' because it is so far from the 'ideal'.[17]

If romantic love is deflated, however, it is not interrogated. The 'reality' constructed by the series is one in which women remain purely erotic beings whether they opt for 'romance' or not. Ria resents being defined only in relation to the family, not because it is hard work (Ruby will clear up the mess) or because she wants to do something entirely different, but because it is not 'romantic'. When Ben becomes 'romantic' Ria commits herself to his 'reality', going off to make love in a tent he has hired while ignoring Leonard. Comic as this is, played by Geoffrey Palmer with an admirable deadpan irony, it reinforces the fact that Ria has virtually no existence that is not sexual.

The series began a re-run in February 1991, accorded by the *Radio Times* the status of a 'classic'. One episode provoked a *Guardian* comment inviting women to complain about a line in one of Ria's fantasising soliloquies, 'I want to be raped!'[18] This highlights more than the fact that public consciousness about rape had been raised over the previous ten years: it also problematises the questions of 'timelessness' and the 'classic status' of sitcoms which purport to show a 'real' world – that is, the comedy of character rather than the comedy of stereotype. It's a little early to see *Butterflies* as a period piece, and its lack of geographical and social specificity make it more difficult to do so. But Ria's remark attracted no adverse media comments in 1979. The fact that the *Guardian* was confident in inviting complaints in 1991 suggests that the framework of 'reality' in which it operates is beginning to break up. To object to the remark is to have certain expectations of Ria – that while she remains within the overall boundaries of her timeless world she should not be ignorant of major changes in public consciousness. These expectations are prompted by Lane's comic style. The chief source of comic pleasure in her work is that of language – wisecracks, picturesque speech and vivid turns of phrase, and comic 'routines' performed in character, such as Ria's antics with the dishes. We enjoy the articulacy of the characters – but articulacy necessarily implies sensitivity to their own situation. Ria sometimes behaves as if she knows she is in a farce, where characters hide and collide according to the whims of fate; her seduction of Ben and his responses are performed with an enjoyably delicate irony on both sides; and yet, with all this self-awareness, she can still cry 'I want to be raped!'

The same difficulty occurs, oddly, in *Solo*, which purports to be specifically about a woman on her own. Gemma laments in the final episode 'If only the world hadn't changed and shown me things I didn't really want to see,' but the problem of *Solo* is not what Gemma sees but how we are positioned in order to see her. Lane seems to be going out of her way to stress that Gemma, even though she has rejected a man, is sexually 'normal', and a great deal of dramatic time is therefore spent on this 'normality'. Danny appears in numerous episodes, coding Gemma not as truly 'solo', but as a 'woman without a man'. This is reinforced by the fact that Gemma seems to have few friends: the role of confidant is filled by her mother, who disapproves of the breakup and hopes that she is not 'going butch', and by the man upstairs, who becomes a platonic friend only after they have slept together, an incident Gemma regrets. It does, however, serve once again to stress her heterosexuality; at one point we are even afforded a fantasy vision of Gemma and her lover cavorting naked in the park. While Gemma is not Charlotte Lucas, but securely at the centre of the drama, she is relentlessly coded as incomplete. Male absence does not empower her; she is, despite her solitude, primarily an erotic being. The options open to her are still those of the fifties: domesticated sex, illicit sex plus guilt, or virtual non-existence.

The same assumptions inform *The Mistress*. Invited to write more of *Solo*, Lane preferred to break new ground while using the same actress, Felicity Kendal. Despite the fact that Max's behaviour is almost diametrically opposed to Gemma's – she is committing the infidelity against which Gemma took an unforgiving stand – the series is ideologically as conservative as ever. The conservatism does not lie in the (inevitable) closure of the narrative which sends Luke back to his wife and leaves Max alone in a stew of regrets and misery – the narrative admits honestly that people in this situation do suffer and Max can be judged as unsisterly as well as un-Christian. Rather it lies in its refusal to treat Max as a being not exclusively erotic. This is further problematised, as so often with Lane, by the highly literate dialogue. The lines rely on witty incongruity of which the speakers cannot but be conscious: Luke complains of rushing from wife to mistress 'weighed down with guilt, remorse, self-loathing – two dinners, two puddings'. In the final episode, Max, in a fit of rage, has returned all Luke's gifts in a bin liner she dumps on the bonnet of his car; inside the house his wife puts him through the classic interrogation of the woman betrayed, asking if Max is younger, more attractive, almost aware she is parodying Shakespeare's Cleopatra – then deflates her own rhetoric as she looks out the window and adds, 'Does she use yellow bin-bags?'. Kendal has some comic set-pieces: when Luke has been taken ill at her house during an illicit weekend, she goes back to his flat to provide evidence of recent occupation; she performs a kind of parody of a man getting up in the morning, splashing talcum and leaving the top off the toothpaste; she sets up a breakfast which she proceeds to eat and then stages a dramatic collapse, writhing and staggering to the telephone with realistic groans. It is wittily and accurately done, but its knowingness – Max playing up to the farcical situation – problematises the 'timeless' aspect of the series. No one as self-aware as Max can exist without placing her situation in some relationship to feminism and its impact on the present. Max has a genuine friend and confidant with whom these problems could be articulated – Jamie, her assistant in the flower shop. On the surface the presence of Jamie is a progressive sign: he is gay, and shown to be so without resorting to camp stereotype. This is reinforced by imaginative casting: Jamie is played by Paul Copley, a wiry Yorkshireman best known in roles like the revolutionary socialist in Jim Allen's *Days of Hope*. However, Jamie's expressions of sympathy are mediated through humorous complaints about his own sexual life; he is neatly coded as a failure, and therefore does not represent any kind of alternative to the heterosexual monogamy Max helplessly longs for. Jamie is denied dramatic and social equality with Max: when he rings her up at midnight on her birthday, she makes him ring off at once because she is expecting Luke's call; when she has the chance of a day with Luke, he agrees cheerfully to look after the shop. The paradox of the employee giving his boss the day off is not remarked upon: the fact that Max is too *distraite* to be a good employer or a good friend is passed over in silence. In effect, this also negates friendship as a valid alternative for Max. She will be a sexual object or nothing. The last moment of the series has her announcing to Jamie that she is pregnant. At this point, the cut-off is inevitable; she has passed out of the realm of sitcom, where women can only be comic on one, erotic, plane. Lane has said in interview[19] that she sees herself as 'nearly in drama', and that she has been typed as a comic writer by virtue of the dialogue rather than the situations. 'I can't help these funny little lines that come out.' This 'naturalises' the process of writing comedy – she related *Solo* to her own experience of divorce – just as comedy of the kind I have been discussing 'naturalises' the events it depicts. All the writer does, by this definition, is record 'the funny side' of relationships – to recognise, wryly, that Life Is Like That. The interview was specifically designed to celebrate the start of a new series of *Bread*, a family comedy about Liverpudlians coping with unemployment. *Bread* fills a gap in the Lane canon of female role models in that its lynchpin is an older woman at the centre of a family surviving in a hard economic climate. Her centrality, however, legitimates a confinement even more narrow than Ria's. The family survives the world of the dole and the Giro with panache, living on their wits and sometimes transgressing legal boundaries. Lane, however, does not go into social or political detail – indeed, the series opened with Ma Boswell dismissing a canvasser from her door without a mention of party politics, Ma being possibly the only inhabitant, real or fictional, of this painfully politicised city ever to do so. Instead it is implied that the family itself provides a kind of insurance against poverty, and it is incumbent upon the mother to hold it together to work its magic. Mrs Boswell is contrasted with another middle-aged woman, Lilo Lil, a gypsyish creature who seduces the feckless Pa Boswell. Tempted to retaliate in kind when propositioned by a charming and respectable businessman, Ma agonises and remains true, coming to see Lil as a kind of *alter ego* and confirming Lane's analysis of the position of women, trapped in a world in which they are solely defined by their relationship to men.

Role and representation: the work of Penelope Keith

British sitcoms rarely extend beyond a few series of about a dozen episodes apiece; this could be seen to deprive the actor of the chance to show a character growing and changing with the times. However, an actor who attains recognition as part of the pool of talented comedy 'regulars' is able to develop variations on a kind of basic persona. To examine the work of a popular actress over a period of years is a useful way to investigate both the limits imposed by sitcom values on an individual talent and the opportunities available for that talent to press on those limits, even to transcend them.

Penelope Keith has been a part of the pool since the mid-seventies and in any one year it is likely that one will be able to see her in a new or repeated series. As with most actors in the pool, the roles in which she is generally cast have a degree of similarity: one might describe her type as 'authoritative', as against, for example, Wendy Craig's 'scatterbrained' or Felicity Kendal's 'desirable'. One of the chief pleasures of watching Keith's work is to see her constantly producing something new out of dramatic situations designed to exploit this single facet.

Until quite recently, 'authoritative' has been synonymous with 'bossy', and only two kinds of 'bossy' persona have been available to women in British sitcom: working class dragon in apron and curlers or social-climbing dragon overdressed to the nines. These heavily stressed class caricatures allow women the outrageousness and energy of male eccentrics, but deny them their anarchic qualities. As I have suggested, both varieties of dragon ultimately serve to assert the status quo; this is especially true of the snob, since her self-deception that she occupies a more exalted place in the pecking order than she in fact does underlines the desirability of that place. Keith's 1976 sitcom debut in Esmonde and Larbey's *The Good Life* was in a role conforming to the dragon pattern: Margo Leadbetter was pampered, snobbish, bossy, prudish and sexually ungenerous to her weary husband (there were knowing allusions to her 'headaches'). She embodied at its most extreme the reaction of the conservative neighbourhood to Tom Good, a forty-year-old former executive trying to live a self-sufficient life, not in some remote croft but in his smart house in Surbiton.

However, the Leadbetter–Good clash was not constructed in political terms. There were jokes about the Leadbetters' greed for consumer luxuries and the futility of Tom's old job designing toys for cornflake packets; but Tom was presented as a lovable eccentric, not a prototype Greenpeace member. He and his wife Barbara slipped into double-act routines; he performed comic soliloquies to the goat. In this celebration of every man's right to cultivate his garden, the neighbours had to be seen as 'human', rather than as obstacles to social change, and each episode dissolved the current dispute in laughter. This enabled Keith to portray Margo as a credible friend for Barbara – young and attractive rather than a harridan. Her youth gave Margo a dimension of vulnerability; using every opportunity the text permits, Keith makes us aware just how Margo has constructed her lady-of-the-manor persona and how fragile that construct is. Her enunciation is carefully crisp and precise, connoting an expensive education, but the voice sometimes becomes shrill or harsh when she is giving an 'order', as if she needs to stress her social superiority rather than taking it for granted. Her clothes are always expensive and slightly fussy, as if she can't rely on her circle to know just how much they cost. Her body language complements them: she is never wholly at ease but seems to be monitoring the impression she is making. Hence we never see her entirely still: she fiddles with her hair, plumps up cushions. She rarely engages others in eye contact but attends to something else – the letter in her lap, her sewing. While the Goods embrace with enthusiasm, Margo daintily kisses a finger and transfers it to her husband's forehead with the delicacy of a philatelist placing a valuable stamp in an album.

Keith had the smallest role of the permanent quartet but frequently provided the punchline to an episode or sequence. Margo's climbdowns from high horse to humanity were invariably a high spot: in an episode in which bad weather threatened the Goods' harvest, she entered with a flourish as would-be saviour in dazzling new oilskins, egg-yolk yellow from head to foot, and promptly fell on her backside in the mud; the obvious laugh lay in Margo's steely attempt to preserve her dignity: 'If one of you so much as sniggers, I shall go straight back indoors!' More subtle, however, was the genuine uncertainty and confusion with which Keith invested the line: this was not only the simple comedy of superiority – stockbroker meets banana skin – but also of irony: Keith's expression signalled Margo's awareness that the right thing to do, the *Good* thing to do, would be to laugh at herself – and her equal awareness that she dare not take the risk. In a role which in many ways typified the class-based limitations set for comic actresses, Keith's carefully placed ironies showed Margo shutting herself inside a prison of convention even while she signalled a wistful willingness to be rescued (perhaps by a woman of more daring eccentricity than the endlessly lovable Lucas-like Barbara Good).

Like the other successful supporting actors in *The Good Life*, Keith was 'rewarded' with a series of her own, Peter Spence's *To The Manor Born*. The heroine, Audrey fforbes-Hamilton, is a young widow forced by death duties to sell her manor house and live in the keeper's lodge, a situation her imperious nature finds difficult. It is a role clearly designed to echo that of Margo, but Keith stresses the differences, rather than the similarities, between them. Audrey is infinitely more relaxed than Margo: she can sit still, she does not primp and fuss, and she can meet another's gaze with steady assurance. When the occasion calls for it she can attain an unstudied elegance. She moves with accustomed ease in her clothes; her upright carriage in crowd scenes often gives the impression that she is the tallest person present. Her voice is carefully modulated, often a little too crisp but never shrill. She is a genuine aristocrat rather than Margo's frenzied imitation.

Audrey made her bow in the England of Margaret Thatcher, an England in which the aristocratic ideal which she embodied and to which Margo aspired was coming under scrutiny. *To The Manor Born* concentrates on Audrey as a member of a dying order. Like the characters in *Brideshead Revisited*, running concurrently with the first series in a lush production by Granada, she symbolises the new role of aristocracy as spectacle. Combining antiquated rituals of politeness with profound ignorance about the 'real world', they became, for the Tory eighties, objects of superior laughter – but also of nostalgia: always, apparently, 'on the way out', their stately homes falling into disrepair, and yet stubbornly *there*, like dinosaurs refusing to acknowledge the arrival of the Ice Age. It's no coincidence that at this time a number of 'impoverished' stately homes turned themselves into safari parks where tourists could pay to gape at endangered species. Audrey's new poverty is a comic spectacle to the locals as she rides on a bus for the first time or sits majestically in the National Health surgery of the doctor she had always imperiously summoned as a private patient. Her comic chagrin is exacerbated by the fact that the manor house is now occupied by Richard de Vere, supermarket king – the embodiment of the New Tory self-made capitalist. Living as she does in the grounds, she cannot avoid seeing him make changes that affect the fabric of the whole community – or, perhaps, cannot bear to miss seeing them; her irritated nosiness about his activities is a running gag.

Inevitably, *To The Manor Born* is constructed in terms of a battle-of-the-sexes comedy. It is clearly designed to afford viewers a specifically intertextual pleasure like Elizabeth I's in seeing Falstaff in love – the spectacle of 'Margo' getting a gentle comeuppance from a dynamic and sexy man. While the interaction between Audrey and de Vere allows Keith to show dimensions of warmth and flirtatiousness in Audrey that are light years from the uptight Margo, 'comeuppance' is the real object of the exercise. Superficially the comedy looks like an equal struggle: Old Tory values soften capitalist brashness, new energy enlivens aristocratic desuetude. In the final episode, Richard loses all his money and Audrey gets hers back; she can thus marry him on her terms. But the fairytale unlikelihood of this serves to underline the premise of the series as a whole: Audrey can only recover her old home and her old lifestyle through marrying Richard. Despite her managing manner, she is shown as lacking capitalist organisational skills: she tries to market the local honey, for example, but lacks the commercial know-how and ends up raiding the local supermarket for supplies. (Ironically enough, the manor house actually used in the series markets itself with great success as the location of *To the Manor Born*. Tourists buy the honey in droves.) While the attraction between them is mutual, Audrey *needs* Richard, while he is self-sufficient. He will win the lady and the class struggle in a New Tory version of *The Taming of the Shrew*. Keith may be the star, but Audrey is the comic butt, lacking self-knowledge. For the 'happy ending' to take place, she has to accept the 'naturalness' of an alliance between *noblesse oblige* and enlightened money-making. To do this she must throw overboard her preconceptions about de Vere: she constantly expects him to be crass, vulgar and boorish. In fact he is charming, courteous, and recoups his occasional social gaffes with enviable grace. In one episode, for instance, she is approached for money by a tramp who habitually turns up at the Manor at the start of the shooting season. She gives him fifty pence, pontificating about duty to the needy and adding that since the Welfare State 'there aren't enough beggars to go round'. Richard, of course, gives him a reasonable sum – then they both discover that he has been sponging off every house in the district and poaching pheasants to boot.

The laughter at their mutual naiveté patches up the week's quarrel between Audrey and de Vere; it also symbolises the series' attempt to have its political cake and eat it. The country-bred Audrey might be ignorant of Cardboard City, but a successful industrialist like de Vere cannot credibly regard a vagrant as a mere bit of local colour. The plot hovers constantly between the image of de Vere as a realist dragging Audrey into the world of the eighties and that of a fantasy millionaire in an old-fashioned escapist musical. Indeed, we never see him at work. Audrey once discovers him absorbed in his computer which he alleges 'Can do in a few seconds everything that your family has achieved in centuries'. She acidly retorts 'You can programme it to rule India?' – but this aristocratic riposte is undercut when she leaves and we alone see that de Vere has been absorbed in a game of screen tennis. We never learn how he treats his workers, how he stands on the ethics of the grocery business; we see him only at play. The double focus means that he not only wins on political grounds, but also on comic terms; this relaxed playfulness is typical of his comic style: we laugh *with* him. Keith is allowed both physical and verbal jokes. Audrey has a sour-grapes quip for almost every confrontation; she also makes a visual spectacle of herself, as when she pretends to go away on a holiday she cannot in fact afford and finds herself skulking back with her suitcases and clumsily improvising with a sunlamp in her tiny sitting room, imperiously telling her butler to oil her back. But in both cases, we are laughing *at* her.

It is Keith who has the difficult task of regulating the quality of that laughter. A bossy and ignorant woman on a private income is not necessarily going to attract sympathy, and her repeated defeats and eventual surrender could provoke a rather sour kind of mirth. Keith defeats this by giving Audrey a cheery schoolgirl innocence which retains our good will. Audrey may order her friends and servants about unmercifully, she may climb on her high horse with Richard, but she also wears her heart on her sleeve. Keith's shame when she has blundered and alienated de Vere, or her glee when she finally corners him in a game of hide-and-seek, has a scrubbed honesty that disarms. She has a hearty, schoolgirlish laugh and a zestful stride; she can be disdainful, but never looks bored. A rather nice child, in fact, who has been firmly drilled not to take the best cake on the plate and has to watch someone else eat it with a good grace. The plot may have more in common with fifties froth like *The Boy Friend* than the Britain of Margaret Thatcher, but Keith roots her firmly in that froth and gives the series a warmth that its yuppie politics could hardly guarantee.

Keith was the 'star' of *To The Manor Born*. She was also a female star, a fact foregrounded by giving her a woman sidekick in the shape of the dimwitted but loyal Marjorie, played by an actress of considerable comic experience, Angela Thorne. Marjorie was paralleled not by a male confidant for Richard, but by yet another female character – his mother, the brisk embodiment of the East European roots he would like to forget. The energies latent in this mix of female comic talent were, however, largely damped by the series' conservative ideology: all three women, in their different ways, represented 'old values', class or national loyalties that de Vere would ultimately transcend. Together they served to stress that Audrey's role, though both large and authoritative, was not active but reactive. It was inevitable, however, that Keith's 'authoritative' style would eventually be exploited in comedy which paid some sort of attention to the changing status of women by constructing a role in which she was a mover and a shaper.

There isn't a satisfactory term for this kind of sitcom. 'Feminist' would hardly be appropriate since the word itself is frequently employed for laughs. It's enough, for instance, for the newly divorced hero in John Sullivan's 1986 battle-of-the-sexes sitcom *Just Good Friends* to mutter 'The judge was a feminist' for us to understand that he's bankrupted by the settlement. Even an otherwise ground-breaking series like *Girls on Top*, written for and by women, including French and Saunders, made its avowed 'feminist' an ineffectual motormouth in a woolly hat. The liberal–feminist tirades of *Designing Women* would stand out in a British sitcom like party political broadcasts.

If feminism as such is a joke, however, domestic sitcom has begun to acknowledge that women do go out to work, even have careers. This is nevertheless presented as gimmick rather than as accurate reflection of the working community. The working wife is often an excuse for 'role reversal' comedy which pairs her with a domesticated male. Titles like *Holding the Fort, Joint Account, The Upper Hand* imply that the situation constitutes a comic incongruity in itself, rather than an opportunity to explore the settings of work and home as a source of varied situations with comic potential. This in turn naturalises the existence of polarised 'roles' which are 'reversed', and the construction of various kinds of work as hierarchical rather than a collection of equally necessary tasks performable by either sex. George Layton's *Executive Stress* (Thames 1987) taps into these values of role: Caroline Fairchild (Keith), a well-educated wife in her forties, announces one day that now the children are grown up she wants to go back to work. Her husband Donald (Geoffrey Palmer) patronisingly agrees that 'a little job' would be good for her, only to find that she has applied under her maiden name for a job in the publishing firm of which he is sales director, and has landed a post slightly senior to his own. Rather than exploring the tensions inevitable in such a situation, Layton grounds the comedy in a farcical (and unbelievably dated) premise: the firm would never approve of this arrangement and so Caroline and Donald must conceal their marriage. Much of the action centres on elaborate arrangements with cars and telephones to create a myth of separate residences. When an author wants to lunch at Caroline's home, Donald dashes round removing photographs of himself, and slips gloomily into the role of a guest.

The pairing of Keith's 'authoritative' comedy with Geoffrey Palmer's talent for comic peevishness situates the audience in a kind of 'soft feminist' position. We are clearly on Caroline's side – but Palmer, moving from crisply efficient worker to grumpy child at home (we see him building a model of Big Ben out of matchsticks, characteristically complaining that matches aren't what they used to be) provides a gloss on this sympathy: committed he may be in theory to equal rights, but in practice he finds it very hard not to be sole king of the castle. He invites two kinds of laughter: one arising from superiority, but the other from affectionate recognition; this underlines the 'unfamiliarity' of Caroline's situation as constructed by the series. In a society in which many families need two incomes to survive, the working wife is still depicted as comic novelty.

This also, of course, gives Palmer the obvious laughs. Keith, though clearly the protagonist, is lumbered with the part of straight guy; the flatness of Caroline's role robs the series of its real centre, and it is not surprising that *Executive Stress* ran for only one series. Keith's body language, however, cuts across the lines. Caroline becomes a character with a genuine enjoyment of an absurd situation; this enjoyment is clearly rooted in the competence she has attained in her years as homemaker, the occupation most attuned to the absurd; she sews while discussing the latest manuscript, a half-concealed, indulgent grin flashing out equally at Palmer's antics with the matchsticks and his cynical approach to marketing. The episode in which author and executives descend on Caroline's house reaches an inevitable farce climax with the arrival of her son and his new girlfriend. Keith avoids the clichés of panic and makes instead a bravura display of control: she outlines the situation crisply, managing to kiss her son affectionately without stopping the narrative flow; her reassuring body language gives a civil welcome to the unfamiliar girl while deftly plunging her into a situation of total confusion; lies trip smoothly off her tongue as she introduces Geoffrey as a 'colleague' to his own son. Her energy never flags.

Caroline, like Audrey, is a zestful character, and her situation allows her to have fun without the inevitable comeuppance for 'bossiness'. Her 'authoritative' aspect gives credibility to her working status and the effective way she manages her life. (It also arguably perpetuates the Superwoman myth: we never see Palmer mending.) But here it is permitted to co-exist with a relish for anarchy. *Executive Stress* might operate on silly premises, but it has so far been the only Keith vehicle to hint at her potential as disruptive clown.

Alex Shearer's comedy for Thames, *No Job For A Lady*, has so far eschewed the opportunity to do so. Keith's starring role as fledgling Labour MP Jean Price is clearly designed as piquant contrast to her socially up-market roles. Jean is, potentially, a complex comic figure. The title sequence shows the Commons portcullis crashing down behind the credits. As this suggests, much of the comedy is derived from Jean's clashes with male prejudice: one episode shows a Tory MP sweeping majestically past, a crowd of tourists in train, with the remark 'Now that is what we call a woman MP'. Male Tories are mercilessly caricatured throughout, characterised by aristocratic drawls, wilful ignorance of the lives of ordinary people and perpetual readiness to turn a fast buck. When Richard, Jean's pair, pontificates that a man should 'walk in my shoes' before passing judgement, Jean acidly turns to retort 'Handmade, I suppose, Richard?' before striding into the Chamber. But she also has more complex conflicts with the men of her own party. This exchange with a Labour Whip after she has agreed to vote for a Tory-inspired bill about the representation of women on public bodies is typical:

> *Norman*   I mean, it's not as if women were all that badly represented on public bodies.
> *Jean*   Then how come that out of 650 MPs only 40 odd are women?
> *Norman*   Well if you're going to quote meaningless statistics . . .

The plots are structured around Jean's innocence and impatience and their unexpected consequences. Thus her concern for the homeless results in a hard-up family kipping in her spare room, to her husband's annoyance; her support for the Tory bill is not reciprocated when she tries to win support for increased benefits for single parents; her attempt to contact a pusher to prove how easy it is to purchase drugs results in her arrest.

Thus in terms of plot, we are generally expected to laugh *at* Jean. Her heart's in the right place, but she all-too-clearly doesn't know the ropes. In terms of dialogue, however, when she is face to face with the outrageous Richard or some of her more stroppy constituents, we are invited to laugh at her deftness is putting them down. Keith's performance manages to link these disparate comic modes without jarring. Her body language connotes a driving honesty rather than naiveté: engaged in political discussion, she literally leads with her chin; she looks characters straight in the eye, or, if they are talking nonsense, turns away to something else – there are no sidelong glances. If fazed by a remark like Norman's, she won't remain wide-eyed for long, but collects herself as if to stress that she expected no better. She rarely gives a wholehearted laugh or smile. The soundtrack dubs audience laughter at some of Richard's excesses: for instance, he has a bet with Jean that he can live on standard unemployment benefit, but on the second day is dismayed to discover that what he assumed to be a day's allowance is supposed to last a week. Keith, however, only half smiles, as if to underline the fact that Richard may be enjoyable as a caricature, but is nonetheless the instrument of a genuine social policy. Her rare uninhibited grins arise from naughty-schoolgirl jokes, like fatuous nicknames for the opposition – from moments of respite from a tough existence. The overall effect is of humour reined in, of control, and this in turn suggests that Jean has to some extent *chosen* innocence, that she is willing to take a risk and make a fool of herself if she can bring her point home. Within plot frameworks that could undermine Jean, Keith prevents her from looking simply silly, ever.

The prevailing conventions of the series do, however, confine potential feminist comic energy in ways that performance cannot redress. Shearer never takes us into the Chamber. Events typically occur in the lobby, in two very different offices – Jean's untidy cubbyhole and Richard's palatial one aglow with Tiffany lamps – in the bar, in 'surgeries', or in Jean's kitchen. This may well be because Shearer is trying to reflect the working realities of an MP's life, occupied with constituency problems and administration rather than debate. It may be that he wants to offer a contrast to the Marks and Gran satire, *The New Statesman*, which employed a mock-up Commons and a Thatcher soundalike. It does, however, markedly affect our reading of Jean. We see her constantly as an individual, doing her best in the struggle: at home she is shown buttering sandwiches for the homeless or enlisting the support of her husband while he does his domestic chores; in the House she is always occupied while simultaneously engaged in conversation about the issue of the day. A nice woman, in short, who practices what she preaches – but visibly confined to the margins. Because we never see

Jean in debate, we never see her in control of political discourse at the point when policy is made. As an opposition MP, elected in the twelfth year of a record Conservative government, she could hardly be shown triumphantly carrying through a piece of legislation – but any MP is free to make an impact in debate, and thence through the media. While this is denied Jean she is encoded as a nice woman rather than a force for change.

Jean, Margo, Audrey and Caroline seem widely differing roles and Keith explores those differences with considerable skill. They have all, however, been constructed with similar assumptions about roles for strong comic actresses: they operate within tight parameters of socially acceptable behaviour. All four lead lives of blameless sexual conformity; the 'career women' have husbands who may complain, but they never have to fight for the right to work. They do not cope with poverty, with the demands of young children. In fact they have no real reason on the purely personal level to complain or demand change. None of them are unorthodox, or anarchic, or dangerous; none of these roles have been written by a woman. One would like to see Keith afforded these opportunities.

The future

Keith is, of course, one of the lucky ones, in that she has had opportunities to develop a comic style, even within limits. For many actresses this will not prove to be the case. Equity's latest survey on the employment of women[20] points out that actresses – especially those over thirty – have fewer work opportunities in television than men; it lays the responsibility at the door of story editors and producers commissioning series rather than individual writers. Meanwhile the BBC's Comedy Development Unit asserted in 1991 that only 10 per cent of scripts submitted are by women, a figure reiterated by both Thames and LWT before their demise in the franchise auctions later that year. *The Stage* flippantly explains this: 'Perhaps it's because women have tender souls. They can't bear being continually turned down, an irreversible by-product of the business'.[21]

There is, however, a difference between being turned down because you don't yet know the craft and being turned down because what you have to say is unacceptable. In a week chosen at random (28 March to 3 April 1992), not untypically, you could have watched fifteen British sitcoms. All but one featured women; the *Radio Times* listed six women as 'starring', although in two cases they were billed after male stars. Only two were written by women, one of whom was Carla Lane. (Her most recent series, *Screaming*, is about three women who have loved – and lost – the same man.) The other writer, Lisselle Kayla, is new to sitcom, and her series, *Us Girls*, is the BBC's first comedy centring on black women. Kayla's version of family sitcom follows a pattern set in 1987 by Janey Preger in *No Frills* and Penny Croft and Val Hudson in *Life Without George*, in that it redefines 'family'. Mother and daughter live together without men. The maternal grandparents are regular visitors and not infrequently irritants. While sitcom has coped happily enough with father–son tensions brought to fever pitch in series like *Steptoe and Son*, it has rarely acknowledged that a woman can feel frustrated by parental disrespect for her chosen lifestyle, or jealous of her child's more apparently carefree existence. The obverse is also true: rows, in this vertical family structure, can be defused by alliances between different generational groupings, leaving space for expressions of love between women. Kayla's 'family' is a fluid entity, inventing itself as it goes along; monogamy is a choice the characters might make, not a monolithic reference point to which each episode must finally return. It opens up the possibility for volatile and varied comedy.

That is, of course, if it gets the opportunity. While it is still unusual for a woman writer to be given a series at all, it is even more uncommon for her to get a second or third. While it is widely acknowledged that a series may take time to develop, women still seem to be expected to deliver high ratings at the first attempt. Preger, Croft and Hudson, for instance, have not been given the chance to follow up their work of the eighties, although both series attained respectable ratings. There is, however, some hope that more women will be able to explore the craft on a basis not unlike the American system. At least two independent production comedies, Witzend and Alomo, have women as heads of comedy, Heather Peace and Sarah Saw. Alomo has already developed the practice of working on a sitcom with a stable of writers. Notably, Marks and Gran's series *Birds of a Feather*, premiered on BBC 1 in 1989, has developed a situation in which women's input is demonstrably valuable. Sharon and Tracey, the eponymous 'birds', are, like Mary Tyler Moore, wondering how they will make it on their own. Their independence, however, is not chosen: their husbands are serving long prison sentences. The situation explores sibling and class rivalries: Tracey, the 'good' sister, has ended up in nouveau-riche luxury, while Sharon abandons her reeking tower block to live off Tracey. It touches on the economic struggles of women who have suddenly lost their major source of income, on sexual loneliness, and, in Sharon's case, the possibility of missing out on motherhood. The situation can make for easy laughs about female incompetence (they cope with household repairs for the first time) and about class, but it has moments of real courage. One episode, *Baby Come Back*, by Sue Teddern,[22] picked up on a situation from the first series, which showed Sharon having an abortion after a brief fling. Two years later Sharon, whose husband has blamed her for his own infertility, now wants a child and meets the man again. She confesses, he sadistically leads her to expect that the possibility of a relationship is still open, and then produces his wife.

The episode ends on a sentimental note, with Tracey assuring Sharon that there will be other chances and that 'You'll make a great mum' – which it then, not untypically, undercuts by having Tracey scream at her son to turn his stereo down. But it also refuses the formulaic possibilities of this laughter-and-tears mix by gently planting, through a laugh line, a darker note: motherhood does indeed pass some would-be mothers by. Dorian, their snobbish and promiscuous next door neighbour, is one of them:

Sharon If I don't have a baby soon –
Dorian You'll end up a spoilt unfulfilled little madam like me.

Birds of a Feather can be formulaic, sometimes racist, and its central characters are, as usual in sitcom, hostile to the very notion of feminism. Sometimes we're invited to laugh at their own sexism (as when they debate whether their woman plumber is 'lezzie'). But it has the advantage of operating in 'real time': the sisters chart milestones along the road of the twelve-year sentence; they can look back to their older, less independent selves, and forward to a future that may involve their men but will also involve them in careers and decisions of their own. (Sharon in particular has discovered a talent for running her own business.) It has also, vitally, signalled an opportunity for women writers and actresses to work together on potentially challenging subject matter, and shown that women writers and a drop in the ratings are not synonymous.

This is important. Sitcom is slow to reflect new currents in society, and perhaps it will always be. It is interesting that comic actresses with the clout to make high-level choices, such as Victoria Wood and Maureen Lipman, have often opted for a series of single plays, which allows them to use their talents more variously and does not tie the fate of the series to the popularity of a particular character. No female character in a British sitcom has yet been given the dramatic licence of a Hancock or an Old Steptoe to be rude, disruptive, dirty or aggressive; for that matter, no female character has been gay, or poor, or a full-blooded spinster without regrets. Both the theatre and TV drama have nurtured female talent that doesn't need to confine itself to family pieties, and it would be good to see names like Debbie Horsfield and Sarah Daniels filling those half-hour slots.

When I suggested at the beginning of this section that anyone's day-to-day experience is sitcom material, I was of course disingenuous; anyone getting their hands on my life for prime-time comedy would have a deal of tidying up to do. There would be an ex-husband to make an honest woman of me plus an occasional romantic interest to confirm my heterosexuality; I'd have to be a domestic incompetent to make up for the fact that I'm in a job which requires a functioning brain. My accent would go up-market; that of my childminder would go down-market. I might acquire a comic boss, but the forces that actually shape my working conditions would never get a mention (although the word 'ludicrous' comes to mind often enough when current education policies are under discussion, heaven knows). I could guarantee at least one critical response on the following lines:

> Pick a sitcom, any sitcom of the dozen or so currently on offer. Save the obvious fact that it will probably be suicidally dull, you can be fairly certain of two things: (1) at some point a mobile phone will ring and somebody won't be able to find it; (2) one of the characters will be black or gay or all will be women.[23]

That is to say, any attempt to make comedy out of my life – or out of lives far more anarchic and interesting than mine – would be written off as doomed from the start, for it isn't the presence of women, or gays, or people of colour, that is objected to here. It is their position as comic subjects rather than objects. This kind of response leans heavily on nostalgia for an imagined world, in which 'classic' comedies simply grew out of the 'natural' order. Put back the sexism and racism, it seems to say, and the comedy will follow. Assumptions change, however, and even 'classic' comedy can embarrass and anger ten or twenty years on. What does not change is the need for adequate working conditions in which to produce comedy out of those changes. Since 1991, when the independent television franchises were auctioned off with the most perfunctory nod in the direction of broadcasting standards, British television has been under increasing pressure to make commercial interests paramount. It will be all too easy for producers to fall into critical postures like the one above rather than to allow new writers, new comic styles, to develop. Women in sitcom still occupy an uneasy space 'between narrative and spectacle',[24] and future conditions do not look as if they will make it easy for them to progress. Unless, perhaps, women make unprecedented use of consumer power and vote with the Off button.

Part III

Standup and be Counted

All those jokes boys love to tell . . . why d'ya think they call it standup, kid?
(Roseanne Arnold)

4

On the halls: Ms/readings and negotiations

Suddenly . . . he said, 'Esther, have you ever seen a man?'
The way he said it I knew he didn't mean a regular man or a man in general, I knew he meant a man naked.
'No,' I said, 'Only statues.'
'Well, don't you think you would like to see me?'
I didn't know what to say. My mother and my grandmother had started hinting around to me a lot lately about what a fine clean boy Buddy Willard was, coming from such a fine, clean family, and how everybody at church thought he was a model person, so kind to his parents and older people. . . All I'd heard about really was how fine and clean Buddy was and how he was the kind of person a girl should stay fine and clean for . . .
'Well, all right, I guess so,' I said.
I stared at Buddy while he unzipped his chino pants and took them off and put them on a chair and then took off his underpants that were made of something like nylon fishnet.
'They're cool', he said, 'and mother says they wash easily.'
Then he just stood there in front of me and I kept on staring at him. The only thing I could think of was turkey neck . . . and I felt very depressed.[1]

An American woman tells us her history. She has stylised, she has shaped it for laughter, but it is *hers*, not a collection of gags that do not touch the personal. The older women in the audience laugh because they have lived something like it and it is good to have their sometimes-painful experience transformed on the stage; they frequent comedy clubs for this very reason.

Except, of course, that it isn't an extract from a female comedian's set at all but a passage from Sylvia Plath's *The Bell Jar*. When she wrote it thirty years ago, the only place for a narrative like this was on paper;

while male comedians like Lenny Bruce might, just, have essayed the subject matter, the female perspective would have shocked many an audience who could have sat through his explicit – and often misogynist – material with equanimity. My point is not simply that women have always been *capable* of creating gendered comedy in private. Rather I hope to show that through the act of performance itself, through making it 'public' in a way that a written text is not 'public', the meaning of such material is radically transformed.

The first English actresses and playwrights knew what it meant to go public. As Angeline Goreau points out:

> The woman who shared the contents of her mind instead of reserving them for one man was literally, not metaphorically, trading in her sexual property.[2]

Aphra Behn explores the implications of comic performance in her first play, *The Forced Marriage*: a male actor speaks the Prologue:

> Women, those charming victors, in whose eyes
> Lie all their arts and their artilleries,
> Not being contented with the wounds they made,
> Would by new stratagems our lives invade.
>   Beauty alone now goes at too cheap rates
> And therefore they, like wise and politic states,
> Court a new power that may the old supply,
> To keep as well as gain the victory.
>   They'll join the force of wit to beauty new
> And so maintain the right they have in you.[3]

In other words, wit prolongs the woman's power over the man beyond the transitory sexual encounter inspired by her beauty; at least, that's the man's reading of the situation. But the subsequent entry of actresses – still a novelty – implies that he's missed the real point. Subjecting herself to the male laugh and the male gaze, the woman comedian offers her wit *instead* of her body, thus shifting sexual relations with her audience from those of prostitute and client to the slightly more equal plane of tradeswoman and customer. Had English drama retained its vitality, writer–performer partnerships like Behn and her friend Nell Gwynn might have fruitfully pursued these arguments. But the rise of the novel to pre-eminence made it possible to 'go public' without direct exposure to the laugh or the gaze; negotiation took place between a single reader, in a private space, and a novelist who could choose how far to reveal herself – discovering in the process, as 'Currer Bell' did, that hiding behind a neutral pen-name made it hard for your readers to decide whether *Jane Eyre* was good or bad.

For most women, the choice between private and public negotiations was dictated by social and economic circumstances. Brontë and Plath were not 'free' to become comedians; Nell Gwynn and Marie Lloyd used the outlets life offered them. Some women – not all – do now have that choice. Before looking at the work of specific women, however, it is important to look at the risks they incur, since these risks are part of the meaning of their performance. To clarify these we should ask what meanings accrue to the figure of the comedian, the figure who stands apart in a public place and invites our laughter.

While standup comedy as we know it began with the Music Hall of the nineteenth century, the lone joker is a much earlier figure in western culture. We know him as the Joker, the Trickster, or the Fool. The figure of the Fool holds in tension some mutually contradictory qualities. A Fool can be a grown man with the mind of a child, a madman, or a professional counterfeiter of folly; in the Fool all these aspects overlap and blend. The Fool can be deformed, or crippled, and thus relieved of everyday responsibility; and yet he is visible: he does not leave society, but rather forces his presence, and his difference, upon it. He triumphs over our desire to avoid seeing him, flagrantly displaying his folly. Society insists, against all the evidence, on equating madness with stupidity; the Fool seizes the licence given to the stupid and childlike to articulate his often-unique and socially disruptive viewpoint; he will relate with difficulty to what we see as reality because he takes pride in different talents. As Red Skelton put it, 'I've got the sixth sense, but I don't have the other five.'[4] He may be sexually rampant or an unrequited lover. He can be loved, listened to and feared in equal measure.

'He', however, is the operative word. There have been female fools. Mary Tudor, for instance, had a woman fool called Jane, and if medical bills are anything to go by seems to have been solicitous for her welfare, but history has preferred to mythologise her father's fool, Henry VIII's Will Somers. Jane is yet another of those women denied the chance to be part of a female comic tradition. The following extract suggests why that process of suppression takes place. It is describing the figure of 'Mother Folly', an icon of the secular Fool Societies of the Middle Ages:

> [Mother Folly] allows the representation of the feminine within the cult, the Virgin and the Bride of Christ, to be opened to kinds of femininity that are excluded from that representation. Within the cult, selfless maternal compas-

sion is represented, but jealous rage is not; chastity is represented, but whorishness is not; silently contained inner knowledge is represented . . . but mindless chattering is not.[5]

The way in which the female character is constructed through these oppositions reveals a misogyny that can only be hostile to Mother Folly and require her disappearance from the comic canon. The female Fool is a jealous, devouring and terrifying whore as well as a *voleuse de langue*. Female madness has always been constructed as more dangerous to the social order, less containable, than that of the male, because of the fundamental alliance between the ideas of 'woman' and 'madness' inherent in the dualistic concept of the universe. The comic madman expresses topsy-turvy, carnival values, but the female expresses something latent to her sex at all times. The Victorians considered that the menarche, pregnancy and childbirth weakened the mind and opened up the channels for the emergence of insanity. Unless preserved from too much activity of the body or the mind, woman would show herself in her true colours as ravening sexual threat. Photographs from Victorian asylums show women carefully displayed to the rational gaze of the doctor–photographer: before treatment, draggled and beflowered like Ophelia, that more decorous version of Mother Folly; transformed in the 'after' pictures with 'respectable' clothing and a demure downcast look. In this Catch 22 world, women were sexual beings by nature and female sexuality was by definition a form of insanity. (As late as 1958, a woman who had a child out of wedlock could be hospitalised as mentally deficient.) Cixous writes:

The madmens' festival, the savages' wild celebrations, the children's parties: woman is the figure at the centre to which the others refer, for she is, at the same time, both loss and cause, the ruin and the reason. She, once again, is the guilty one.[6]

The guilty one; hence the one most at risk, the one most likely to encounter hostility, violence even. But a figure of power. A disincentive for the female comic: but the best reason to be one.

At present there is, rightly, considerable research devoted to the rediscovery of forgotten names; the female comic presence in music hall and vaudeville has been seen as an early sign of change in the position of nineteenth-century women, evidence of at least a few women who managed to come out on top despite the enormous obstacles to their freedom and independence. It is, however, important to note that the female comic, trailing clouds of the Fool's dangerous sexuality and autonomy, was involved in a complex process of negotiation with her audience. It was a tacit process on both sides: the days when you could, like Aphra Behn, embrace the idea that a player/playwright is perceived in the role of whore, and then briskly redefine it, were gone.

One of the first functions of a woman on the bill – on both sides of the Atlantic – was as a guarantee of 'respectability'. The Music Hall evolved from the impromptu pub entertainments of the early nineteenth century. The clientele for these was almost exclusively male, the only women present being the prostitutes, there as alternative entertainment rather than for their own pleasure. Increasingly, professional entertainers took over from amateurs, purpose-built additions to the buildings were constructed, pubs lost their licences for singing and dancing, privileging the halls, and 'Ladies' Nights' became an institution. The process of 'respectabilising' was completed when Charles Morton built the Canterbury Hall in 1852, with the specific intention of admitting 'the gentler sex' to its 'rational and refining recreations'.[7] Likewise in America the 'concert saloon' that was a feature of most cities offered what was basically 'stag' entertainment, where women at first worked as hostesses, earning commission on the amount of beer they forced down their customers, later as dancers, and, as variety entertainment detached itself from the saloons, as specialist acts.

The woman entertainer thus occupied a highly ambivalent position. Her very *raison d'être* was to make the place fit for decent women, yet everyone 'knew' that she could not be a decent woman herself. As Clement Scott of the *Daily Telegraph* put it, 'It is nearly impossible for a woman to remain pure who adopts the stage as a profession'.[8] This perhaps accounts for the tone of contemporary critics and biographers of the early female stars. While it is not possible to get a clear sense of their comedy – the earliest predated the gramophone, and the recordings of later ones are often misleading, leaving out audience by-play and patter and reducing acts to song pure and simple – these accounts seem to be imposing upon potentially anarchic commentators on the contemporary scene the status of objects for male consumption. There is, for example, considerable use of the 'King Cophetua' trope: stories of social advancement are relished, like that of Bessie Bellwood from rabbit skinner to mistress of a Viscount, or Vesta Tilley from poverty to Lady De Frece, wife of a Conservative MP. Marriage is of course not the only alternative. The female performer can be viewed as a bit of rough, as in Jerome K. Jerome's famous description of Bessie Bellwood:

she was once heckled by a hefty-looking coal-heaver who made it clear that he had no intention of having his drinking disturbed. A slanging match ensued with Bessie declaring her intention of 'wiping down the bloomin' 'all with him and making it respectable'. For over five minutes she let fly, leaving him gasping, dazed and speechless. At the end, she gathered herself together for one supreme effort and hurled at him an insult so bitter with scorn, so sharp with insight into his career and character, so heavy with prophetic curse . . . that strong men held their breath . . . Then she folded her arms and fell silent and the house from floor to ceiling rose and cheered her till there was no more breath left in its lungs.[9]

Heckling – like wolf-whistles and personal remarks yelled in the street – is a way for a man to enjoy the spectacle of a woman's embarrassment. Jerome is, of course, far too refined a gentleman to indulge himself, but, busily inscribing himself into the story as an amused observer of his social inferiors, he finds a way to participate. He acts mock-scared: 'prophetic curse', 'strong men fell silent'; this is the almost-inevitable response of a street heckler to a woman who actively objects. Bellwood becomes a sexual object; her verbal wit disappears to be replaced by Jerome's clever-dick patronage.

If man gives, he also takes away, and a second repeated strain in accounts of these women stresses his power to do so: the myth of the woman who finds success but not true happiness, who is unable to control her life and attaches herself to worthless men. Marie Lloyd's disastrous marriage to a violent man is narrated at length; Jenny Hill's latter years are dwelt on in Harry Hibbert's *Fifty Years Of A Londoner's Life*, in which Hill reminisces about the artificial flower factory where she began work as a child and pathetically tries to make paper flowers with her 'trembling fingers'. As J. S. Bratton points out, this hardly accords with Hill's view of herself: in her diaries she seems opinionated, self-confident and determined to manage her own life, entertaining lavishly and generously; her final poverty had more to do with the hostility of managements to her attempts to control her own career than her own incompetence.[10]

The relentless reporting of the backstage mistakes – real or imagined – of female stars implied that their onstage gifts were probably also beyond their control – that they were 'being themselves', unconsciously funny rather than artists in their own right. The refusal to see them as such meant also that their darker comic insights into the position of women could be dismissed as harmless. One of Hill's songs ran:

> I've been a good woman to you,
> And the neighbours all know that it's true;
> You go to the pub,
> And you blue the kids' grub,
> But I've been a good woman to you.[11]

This is described in H. Chance Newton's *Idols of the Halls* as 'husband-nagging'[12] and a reviewer of the time wrote in similar vein of this 'fine piece of comic acting' as 'a drunken wife, the inconsequential and self-satisfied burden of whose ditty is "I've been a good woman to you" '.[13] Hill's soubriquet, however, was 'The Vital Spark', which suggests an energy more intelligent and incisive than drunken or weepy by-play. Other reviews speak of her as 'sharp', 'outspoken', 'a strong-minded female speaking her mind freely about the men'. Her popularity with women, who formed a substantial part of the audience in the later part of her career – 'women always go to the music hall and seem to appreciate you more than the men do'[14] – suggests that her observational comedy was perceptive rather than glibly dismissive of its objects. For the Chance Newtons of Bohemia, however, as for Jerome, an angry woman made a comic spectacle in herself, and the target of her anger could safely be ignored.

Not content with patronising women performers on the grounds of both sex and class, patriarchy also co-opted them as spokespersons for a sexuality that was male-defined. Nowhere is this more apparent than in accounts of the most famous Music Hall star of them all, Marie Lloyd. Virtually all accounts of Lloyd pay tribute to the accuracy of her observation: the characters in her songs might be children, old women, or smart seductresses, but in each case the props were painstakingly selected, each inflection calculated with precision. But her reviewers also show a tendency to carve her up ideologically so that her talent looks one-sided, much simpler than it was.

For T. S. Eliot, who writes rather movingly that 'I certainly did not realise that her death would strike me as the important event that it was',[15] Lloyd was the embodiment of working class values and vitality, giving dignity to a way of life by expressing it most fully:

> The working man who went to the music-hall and saw Marie Lloyd and joined in the chorus was himself performing part of the act; he was engaged in that collaboration of the audience with the artist which is necessary in all art and most obviously in dramatic art.[16]

Eliot perceives Lloyd purely in terms of class, not of gender; but Lloyd's songs and patter were one of the few places in which the lives of working-class women were documented with accuracy and tenderness, and Eliot's hypothetical man in the audience was perhaps broadening his imaginative sympathy and experience as well as simply identifying with a member of his own class. But when Lloyd *is* discussed in terms of her gender, it's almost invariably in crude terms. In the later stages of her career, she turned more and more to the characters she called her 'drabs' – like the moonlight-flitting lady with her 'old cock linnet', or the riproaring old 'ruin that Cromwell knocked about a bit', who loses her money after 'sitting in the grass with a commercial traveller'. Too many of her admirers ascribe only one motivation for her choice:

> [Marie], realising that she was growing old, determined, with that honesty which has ever been one of her dearest traits, to show herself to her public as she really was. No smart woman of fashion, but an old, grey-faced, tired woman.[17]

Lloyd was only in her early fifties when she began to specialise in this material, and more than capable of being a 'smart woman of fashion'. She liked expensive clothes and wore them with taste and spirit. But the writer is not really interested in 'fashion'; he is taking for granted that a woman performer's chief desire is to be a sexual object; if she fails to be one then she can (courageously) solicit male pity. It's hard to recognise in the 'grey-faced, tired old woman' the star who asserted into her old age that 'A little of what you fancy does yer good'. (By this critic's lights, a 'grey-faced, tired woman' has no right to fancy anything.)

The sexuality of Lloyd as constructed by popular biographers and in the well-known and possibly apocryphal legends is of a specific kind. She is cast in the role of mighty opposite to the forces of prudery and puritanism, a spokeswoman for bawdy joy against the viciously repressive Social Purity Movement. Superficially her career bears this out. She was capable of slick ad-libs: when a banana skin landed onstage she remarked 'If the gentleman who threw this wants his skin back he can collect it after the show'. She liked to have the last word on mild obscenity: when Sir Henry Tozer charged into her dressing room to demand that she change the words of the song 'she sits among the cabbages and peas', she did – to 'she sits among the lettuces and leeks'. And she did fall foul of Laura Ormiston Chant, the chairwoman of the Purity Party. Lloyd was called before the Theatres and Music Halls Committee of the LCC with a view to the censorship of some of her songs. She sang 'Johnny Jones' in tones of angelic purity and without eliciting a single laugh. She then sang 'Come Into the Garden, Maud', larded with winks and nudges and innuendo, triumphantly proving her case that 'It's all in the mind'.

Stories like this are deployed to make the Purity Party's opposition to Lloyd seem petty and spiteful, and Mrs Ormiston Chant has been almost irreparably stigmatised as a vicious prude; several modern accounts of Lloyd, though alive to her complex role in patterns of class interaction, nevertheless dangerously simplify the gender issues in this conflict by labelling Chant 'the Mary Whitehouse of her day'.[18] Mrs Ormiston Chant did try to get the licences of some Halls withdrawn and she conducted a campaign in 1894 to remove the 'Ladies of the Promenade' from the Empire theatre. Opposed by their more influential customers, she only succeeded in prompting the LCC to erect screens around the promenade and the bars, rapidly torn down by an outraged public. Lloyd's opposition to Chant and her championship of the prostitutes tends to be depicted in terms of a victory over censorship and an affirmation of the right of poor women to earn money the only way they could. Chant, a contemporary of Jack the Ripper, was concerned less with censorship than with the consequences for women of the prostitutes' immediate availability to men understandably aroused by what they saw on stage. Inevitably, she can be made to look ridiculous by the argument that Lloyd used to such effect in court, that smut is 'all in the mind'. Nineteenth century convention demanded that women with any pretensions to purity should be sexually ignorant. Chant, by entering a court at all, admitted her ability to read the gestures that were as integral to the performance text as the words or the music. 'He only laughed and went like so –' and 'It would make you feel so funny if you saw them –' left the experienced patron of the Halls in no doubt as to the omitted verb. 'Every little movement', sang Lloyd 'has a meaning of its own.'[19] But by refusing to hide her ignorance of that meaning, Chant became, for the male journalistic population, a hypocrite, a woman who obviously *wanted* what she tried to suppress, and thus a legitimate object of the smutty laughter described by Freud.

However Chant held no brief for ignorance. One of the mainsprings of the Social Purity Movement was the anger of women who had to suffer venereal diseases contracted by their husbands. The Movement's demand that the Halls clean up their acts both inside and out went hand in hand with their campaign to repeal the Contagious Diseases Act of 1860, Parliament's own attempt to address the problem. This Act meant, in effect, that any woman walking the streets alone could be seized by the police as a suspected prostitute and subjected to a forcible examination for venereal infection. Chant was still campaigning in 1922 to prevent children being forced into prostitution; she urged that the age of consent be raised to sixteen, a demand which the House of Commons, no doubt primed with mother-in-law jokes, stigmatised as 'henpecking'. And one of her particular dislikes about Music Hall entertainment in particular has a contemporary ring: in a pamphlet called *Crimes Against Women* (1915) she attacks the idea that domestic violence is a source of humour, drawing an analogy with the way the white races speak of blacks. 'There is something rotten in a judicial system which thinks ill-treating a woman is funny.'[20]

This evidence of a wider concern for women's welfare serves to emphasise that the hostility and mutual incomprehension between Marie Lloyd and Laura Chant was not the 'natural' opposition of prudery and carnival but a socially constructed polarity that undercut the sexual radicalism of both. The Social Purity Movement stressed the right of the woman, at risk from frequent and hazardous childbearing, to refuse sex. Lloyd stressed the right of women to sexual pleasure on the same terms as men, in the persona of the old woman whose husband wanted a fortnight's fun on his own:

> I always 'old with 'avin' it, if you fancy it,
> If you fancy it, that's understood,
> But if that's your blooming gime, I intend to do the sime
> 'Cos a little of what you fancy does yer good.[21]

A song Lloyd sang in her last years, 'The Three Ages of Woman'[22], suggests that her appeal lay in the fact that both sexes could find their own meanings and pleasures in her characters. Deftly moving between impersonating the characters and commenting on them, she compressed a lifetime's experience into a few minutes. The first 'age', the girl of seventeen, sees a man as an idealised object of desire, 'for his trousers are creased and he wears a tall hat', and believes his promises. 'Fancy', Lloyd interjects, 'Chocolate creams and a palace of dreams – I don't think.' The second, at twenty-five, vows she will never marry, but finally does, so lovestruck with a sense of male superiority that 'she really can't think what he's wedding her for' – 'But her ma says 'The dunce, I can tell her in once – I've had some.' Of the last stage, when she 'has to be careful when dressing' and her body needs a few aids to beauty, Lloyd comments:

Great, oh she's great – is the woman of umpty-eight,
A lot she's endured from the thing they call – man,
Still if to live life o'er she began,
Would she live it again, would she play the same game?
Well – rather!

The song is a vehicle for a versatile and sexually attractive performer to display consecutively the erotic appeal of innocence, desire and sophistication. It is a cheerful endorsement of patriarchy's favourite myth – that women always forgive men who sow their wild oats – indeed, prefer them. At the same time, however, it parodies and satirises the woman who allows herself to be emotionally dependent on a man, or who fails to recognise a cheap ploy when she hears it – and against this it celebrates the 'greatness' of the old woman, a person in her own right with enjoyable memories. It can be read as profoundly subversive of the idea that man is the arbiter of women's destiny, yet it also claws back that subversiveness. Lloyd celebrates female desire, spells out its price, and remains ambivalent as to whether that price is fair. This is a more complex relationship with an audience than is often suggested.

Lloyd's popularity and success ensured that she was never personally identified with the 'Ladies of the Promenade', but she was, nevertheless, considered unsuitable entertainment for the Royal Family; and the association of her places of work with prostitution meant that, like Aphra Behn's actresses, she was engaged in the task of transforming the prostitute–client relationship, simultaneously trading on her sex appeal but also, in songs like 'The Three Ages of Woman', defamiliarising it. It may have been all too easy for male patrons to treat Lloyd as a jolly celebrant of the sexual status quo, just as it was easy to brand Laura Chant a hysterical prude. But Lloyd not only provided an image of what a single woman might achieve, she also raised questions about female desire and sexual freedom that the 'legitimate' theatre of her day hardly dared to handle.

As Music Hall mutated into Variety in England, character comedy predominated over songs; later, straightforward joke-telling was to predominate over both, especially in the South. But these changes were superficial. The sexual politics of the popular stage, like those of its 'legitimate' cousin, remained constant. Both, in fact, were grounded in the same subject matter and the same attitude to that subject matter: the family; and neither 'straight' plays nor comedians' jokes questioned society's fundamental assumptions about domesticity. Male performers leaned heavily on 'the wife' and 'the wife's mother' for material; they purported to lament the fact that women were at once economically dependent upon men and domineering in the home, that marriage was the price of sex – which was then made less than blissful by the wife's frigidity or excessive appetite; these assumptions are seen as 'facts of life' rather than as incongruities to be exposed and changed. Women's comedy might dwell on 'the wickedness, the artfulness, the sinfulness of men', but it never undermined the institution of the family. Several women, however, capitalised on this very conservatism, by putting themselves into a familial relationship with the audience. This meant that sexual attractiveness became irrelevant; the performer did not have to relate to the male audience as sexual object and her act could explore different avenues of humour, while she tacitly defined the audience as her family, her protector rather than a potentially hostile force.

Nellie Wallace, for instance, adopted the persona of an ageing spinster, the sort of aunt-figure familiar in every family. The old maid was, of course, a staple target of male comedians, typified, in Max Miller's phrase, as 'a bundle of sour discontent'. Most accounts of Wallace stress her unattractiveness – Willson Disher sees her as 'excit[ing] our sympathy' with her 'protruding teeth and a heart-rending squint';[23] but when she narrated her search for a man (she had a song, 'My mother said always look under the bed'), you knew that, if she did find one, she'd give him hell rather than elevate him into an object of desire:

> Man   I wonder why a woman as intelligent as you troubles to run a club like this.
> Nellie   I'm doing this to forget a man.
> Man   Crossed in love?
> Nellie   No worse – I've been run over.[24]

Wallace – who claimed to have abandoned serious acting after being sneezed off her horse while playing Joan of Arc – wasn't limited, but visibly liberated, by lack of sex appeal; old maids were permitted, indeed expected, to be eccentric, and much of her act consisted of grotesque and surreal clowning. Alec Guinness describes the experience of watching her in 1921 in a sketch in which she deconstructs one of the archetypal images of spinsterhood, the nurse, assisting one of the archetypal images of male nobility, the surgeon:

> Nellie stood by looking very prim, but every now and then she would dive under the sheet and extract with glee and a shout of triumph quite impossible articles – a hotwater bottle, a live chicken, a flat-iron and so on. Finally she inserted, with many wicked looks, a long rubber tube which she blew down.

The body inflated rapidly to huge proportions and then, covered in its sheet, took slowly to the air. Nellie made desperate attempts to catch it, twinkling her boots as she hopped surprisingly high.[25]

He was seven years old at the time, and 'in love with her'. At seven, he was perhaps not in a position to realise that one is supposed to patronise old maids; his response thus picks up most clearly the factor that makes Wallace different from the hated and pitied figures lampooned by male comics – that she is the audience's *own* spinster aunt, whose personality can be relished and enjoyed. Her search for a man does not include the men in the audience, so they are not empowered to reject her – as they do, implicitly, the spinsters of the jokes – because they are family. They may laugh at her failure to get married – she laughs herself – but she is more than her spinsterhood, and her spinsterhood has liberated her from the necessity to modify her anarchic self.

As Variety and Vaudeville moved into the twentieth century the impact of the cinema became apparent. While some stars could find a niche in both, their relationship to the audience was not the same. Instead of being part of a reciprocal exchange of attention and applause, negotiated afresh with each performance, the stars on screen became commodities, glamorous but also available at the flick of a projection switch, and their image was subject to the control of the studio – off screen as well as on. Some strong female comedians were to find their familial relationship with the audience re-presented, mis-re-presented, or not presented at all. Two very different performers, Gracie Fields and Moms Mabley, were to find the process painful in very different ways.

Gracie Fields began singing in the music-halls at the age of ten; an ugly attempted rape precipitated a nervous breakdown in her teens and she left to work, like her mother before her, in the cotton mills of her native Lancashire; she returned to the theatre, however, at her mother's instigation. Up to this point she had been a straight singer, but now took to guying songs she didn't like and began to develop the comic style that was her hallmark; she polished it in revues which toured the north of England and by the 1920s had become a major star; the persona she projected was that of an elder sister, larky, practical and hardworking. She could fool about, pulling faces and turning cartwheels, like a real sister at a party, sharing a good time with the audience. But there was also her voice, and its relationship to the songs she sang. These were precise documents of family life: they described events like marriages and christenings, trips from 'the pop shop to the co-op shop' – that is, from the pawnshop, where every week you took out a loan on your valuables, to the shop built by and for working people to get everything 'from a chop to a prop or a mop or a bottle of ginger pop' and all the other necessities of life. She sang about trying to keep up with the posh neighbours in their grand underclothes:

> Said Dad, 'Aren't you cold in these things Celanese?'
> Said Mother 'I was till I hit on this wheeze,
> I'm wearing my fleecy ones underneath these
> 'Cos we've got to keep up with the Joneses.'[26]

The unspoken theme of many songs was that of disappointment. The twenties and thirties did not encourage high expectations. Two-thirds of the population lived on or below the poverty line; the returning 'heroes' of the First World War found no jobs to come home to and as the thirties wore on the conviction grew that another war was inevitable. When Gracie sang to Walter, the fiancé who would never commit himself, 'It's either the workhouse or you', she wasn't altogether joking; she sang for the women of her generation who would never get married, because the War had decimated the male population, women who would not, on their own, earn a decent wage. The audience wanted her to win Walter; she'd get them to sing his name in the chorus, as if the sheer volume of sound might make up his mind for him:

> I've kept my bottom drawer together
> My bridal gown's as good as new,
> Walter! Walter! lead me to the altar
> And make all my nightmares come true.[27]

All this material was presented in a voice that was always strong and powerful, but which could shift from the music-hall roughness to a pure coloratura. Sometimes it sent up the pretensions of high culture, by applying its beauty to a song about 'the biggest aspidistra in the world' – but it also defamiliarised the culture that the songs described. It made it impossible to exercise the *de-haut-en-bas* attitude of critics like Jerome K. Jerome, because the vocal quality asserted that the disappointment of this comic spinster was also the stuff of tragic opera; on the other hand the opera seemed overblown next to the figure who suddenly seemed to invite our respect rather than our laughter. It made an assertion about the value of a world that was beginning to disappear; the war and the new technology would transform much of Fields' world and the image of Fields herself.

Gracie Fields' elder-sister cheerfulness was co-opted by the media to put over a reassuring message that if the nation pulled together, everything would be all right. Basil Dean's 1934 film *Sing As We Go* showed her as a mill-girl; the film opens with a billboard announcing 'Mill Forced To Shut Down'; it's taken for granted that this is a 'natural' event beyond the control even of the owner; artificial silk is replacing cotton and the man who could help the factory make the switch, Sir William Upton, is on holiday. It would be churlish to inquire why Hugh, the boss, didn't diversify earlier, especially as he's the romantic lead, so Gracie leads the workers out singing. Then, as the unemployed are still urged to do, she literally 'gets on her bike'. She goes to Blackpool to get a seasonal job, and finds work as a maid, a fortune-teller's assistant, a toffee vendor and a 'human spider' in a freak show. Meanwhile Hugh comes to Blackpool to find Upton, but falls in love with Gracie's roommate instead, while Gracie finds Upton herself. Her 'sisterly' quality is thus her tragedy, in romantic terms; Hugh is clearly a more glamorous object of desire than Walter, who'd 'make all your nightmares come true'. On the other hand, it's her good fortune in purely economic terms since it leads Hugh to appoint her welfare worker in charge of all the girls at the newly opened mill; without uttering a word about pay or conditions she marches them back singing, behind a large Union Jack, as the credits roll. The nation didn't need political solutions to its crisis, the film assured you, only a spirit like Gracie's, which you could share for the price of a ticket.

To watch *Sing As We Go* is to get a sense of enormous vitality and delight trapped in a creaking narrative; an audience researcher at the time found that people leaned forward when Fields sang, that they absorbed her energy without much interest in the politics. Indeed most of her best routines can be detached from the storyline: she puts on a false moustache and guys a sentimental song; she tips jelly over a rude customer; she glares at a heckler in her spider costume. It was, however, Gracie as the representative of the status quo, rather than Gracie the artist of deprivation, that the media abused as war finally broke out. Shortly before, she had married Monty Banks, who directed her in *Queen of Hearts*; although he lived in California he was still an Italian citizen, and when Italy entered the war he faced internment if he chose to live in England with Fields. She went with him to America, instructed by Churchill to 'raise some dollars', which she did; but this did not prevent the British press from labelling her a traitor and conducting a campaign of unprecedented viciousness. Churchill actually intervened to halt the most violent attack in the *Eighth Army News*. While other personalities suffered from similar prejudice (Noel Coward was consistently vilified for not doing enough for the war effort) it seems as if Fields was singled out, partly for her popularity but also because of its nature: an elder sister is supposed to put 'duty' before 'love', and she is not supposed to be a sexual being at all; in films Gracie always lost her man to the pretty ingenue. Thus the title of 'Forces' Sweetheart', which had looked set to be hers, went to the blander, middle-class Vera Lynn, depriving wartime propaganda of a comic and unpatronising portrayal of working-class life as its focus. The public, however, seemed more generous than the press. Fields not only raised dollars, she also returned to England to tour factories, shipyards and army camps; it seemed that the audiences were able to respond to her in a more complex way than the press wanted them to. Her talent could transcend both patronage and misrepresentation because it did not finally depend on the delivery of specific lines but on communicable joy. Harry Thompson recalls, 'She could be more happy than anyone else ever could.' However, she lived abroad after the war. A recording of one of her later shows demonstrates both affection and acerbity towards her audience. Amid cheers she declares 'I know this much, I can go into anybody's house in Rochdale and say, "Missus, I'm sorry, I've nowhere to sleep tonight" [*Applause and laughter*] – I know what the answer would be – "Gerraway from here!" '[28]

A vaudeville performer who also used familial strategies – again, to find herself badly treated by the mass media – was Jackie Mabley. Born in 1894, she began working the black vaudeville circuit in her early teens to provide for the child she was expecting, and by the time she was twenty had developed the persona known as 'Moms'. Moms wore a washed-out cotton dress and clumsy shoes; she didn't always bother to put in her false teeth; she addressed her audience as 'children'. Mabley based Moms on her own grandmother; for the rest of her career she was to 'let granny grow'. She became the first woman comic at the prestigious Apollo Theatre, where a recognisable tradition of black entertainment had emerged during the Harlem Renaissance; its songs were emotional, its humour often strongly political. One of her jokes is grounded in the lynch law that haunted black America, a story of two bank robbers, one black, one white. When they are caught, the white man is terrified; the black guy says 'Oh man, we done killed up all them people . . . they gonna hang you, so why don't you face up to it?' 'That's easy for you to say,' says the white man 'You're used to it.'[29] The humour has more bite because it's put in the mouth of a nice old lady who chats amicably about

cooking greens at hog-killing time. It roots the story in familiar surroundings and incorporates it into the texture of black experience; it is
the more chilling because the story is told without indignation, as nothing special. She celebrated geriatric sexuality in women; its subtext was
about women's strength and ability to survive: 'A woman is a woman till
the day she dies, but a man's only a man as long as he can.' And it
acknowledged that in a racist world survival was precarious:

> Love is just like a game of checkers, children. You sure got to know which
> man to move. Cause if you move the wrong man and he jump ya, tear your
> Mason-Dixon line up![30]

Like Gracie Fields, Moms was a figure who could make affection
palpable; live records are punctuated by laughter which goes on for
several seconds at lines which are not in themselves especially comic;
the response is to her enjoyment: despite the smuttiness of much of the
humour, the effect is of an indulgent granny who has at last got the
parents out of the way and is able to indulge herself in an orgy of spoiling
the children. Many black Americans grew up with Moms Mabley's
eternal grandmother – among them Clarice Taylor, best known in the
UK for her work on *The Cosby Show*, who won an Obie for her one-
woman show about Mabley. The spoiling, however, didn't allow the
children to lose sight of poverty and injustice: she lectured them about
the mess the world was in, with faith in their capacity to improve it –
except Richard Nixon. 'Even Old Moms couldn't do nothin' for that man
'cept give him a few licks upside the head.'

As a black artist, however, she had to wait a long time for recognition
by the white public and the largely white-controlled media; much of her
Apollo material was stolen by white comics, who played it in houses that
wouldn't dream of employing her. 'God always gives me some more',
was her only comment. She was seventy before she got TV exposure
throughout America – secured with some difficulty by Harry Belafonte
– and produced a number of bestselling records as a result, although
these might have been even more successful if they had been cut when
her voice was stronger; some of them are extremely hard to follow. She
made a movie, *Amazing Grace*, in 1974, which left all her subversiveness on the cutting room floor and had her mouthing lines like 'we're all
just the dark meat on God's great chicken'.

In an interview in 1975 with the *New York Times*, Moms Mabley told
a reporter 'There was some horrible things done to me. I've played every

state in the union except Mississippi. I won't go there. They ain't ready'.[31] Mabley had survived rape and the murder of her parents and her concept of 'readiness' was in terms of racial politics. In some ways, however, virtually all women comics in vaudeville, music hall and variety have run up against the unready audience. They have had to struggle against the stereotyped images of women on several levels: unless theatres are specifically created for specific audiences, there is a tendency for audience and cast alike to assume the white heterosexual male, conservative in outlook, as the norm. The task of reconstructing that audience, to make it alive to female experience, is an extra burden laid upon women comic performers. Too often, they are then perceived as so different from the 'norm' that it becomes difficult for other women to find role models, to see themselves as part of a tradition. Male comedians who learn from them may be perceived as originals in their own right. Female comic impressionists, for example, are often seen as a modern phenomenon, whereas it was a woman, Florence Desmond, who virtually invented the art and developed techniques – like the party full of famous and incongruously linked people – that are now comic staples. One reason I have dwelt at some length on the careers of women now dead is to affirm that there is indeed a tradition, and one on which women can still draw.

5

Making it on your own: women in the new comic traditions

Take my wife – please! or, Coping with the clubs

Music Hall, or Variety, or Vaudeville, or whatever you want to call it, is dead. Television killed it. All comedians seem to agree on this, even if they agree on nothing else. Throughout the 1950s variety theatres – like cinemas and 'legitimate' playhouses – closed down while families stayed in to watch the box. In the first place, they were still paying for the set and couldn't afford to go out; in the second place, television featured stars; the bill at the local theatre in a small provincial town couldn't begin to compete.

Performers did not, of course, disappear. They adapted and changed. And television did more than knock down the sites of the older tradition of entertainment. It also radically transformed the relationship between the comedian and the audience. High-quality acts in the older tradition still had a place on television – Hylda Baker and Joan Turner were early television favourites. Victoria Wood is, in her use of song, her Northern accent, and her jolly-sister persona a throwback to music hall. But television developed a far more complex relationship with a tradition that had grown up as variety faded, that of club comedy.

Clubs had provided an alternative source of entertainment on both sides of the Atlantic for years. As with Music Hall and Vaudeville, they were originally a place for men to congregate and entertain themselves by a mixture of means ranging from political debates to comic songs. In England the Working Men's Club and Institute Union was devised 'To improve the character and condition of the working classes' by a Unitarian minister, Henry Solly, with the financial backing of a number of wealthy aristocrats.[1] The point was to provide working men with occupations which would keep them off beer and on good terms with employers, from whom they might then be reluctant to demand higher wages. Rapidly, however (largely to do with the ban on beer), the clubs were forced to democratise themselves to survive, and passed into the control of the working men themselves. They became associated with radical politics in the 1880s, but, again running into financial problems, had to turn to the breweries for financial support; entertainment elbowed out politics and the breweries expected an increasing level of control over the clubs. Subsequently, in the 1950s, custom-built clubs were set up, mainly in the North of England, with strong brewery backing. Les Dawson, a comic nurtured by the club tradition, describes these:

> This enterprise meant the takeover of an old cinema; breweries did the fittings in conjunction with the backers; on average these venues could seat about a thousand patrons, so a fair return could be expected with confidence. On the strength of the turnover, top class variety acts were booked and so, for the added sum of twopence on a pint of beer, the customer could have a night out that rivalled anything in Europe.[2]

This indicates clearly the role of the club performer, however talented: not the sole reason for attendance, but one component in 'a night out'. This was a radical shift in the relationship of comedian and public, and it was strongly influenced and reinforced by television. Television made the comedian a commodity obtainable at the flick of a switch, and a commodity, moreover, that competed with other kinds of entertainer – straight actors, soap-opera characters, politicians and ordinary people talking about their experiences as a hostage or their skateboarding dog. All vied for a part of the viewer's attention, which could also be concentrated elsewhere – on food, housework, or a book. The live entertainer in the club worked in the midst of a crowd who had come to drink and talk as well as watch, and who, as the television age wore on, might feel few inhibitions about treating him as if he were not 'live'.

I use the pronoun advisedly, because, as this thumbnail history makes clear, the clubs were set up specifically by and for men; in those under the control of the Club and Institute Union women are still denied full membership, despite forming about a third of the total grass-roots membership on which the CIU depends for audiences. The CIU has voted four times on this issue since the late 70's and continues this policy.[3] Any woman who enters this territory – as spectator or performer – is thus disadvantaged by the rules. She is then further disadvantaged by the fact that she is one of the staple butts of club comedy. While misogynist jokes were nothing new on the Halls, the distinctive style that emerged from the clubs in the 1960s was more extreme. At this point the comedian abandoned the more individualising aspects of costume or dialect and became a figure in smart but anonymous evening dress relating a string of jokes. These had no connecting thread; you could listen to one, ignore another, and still follow the drift of the act. Performers like Bob Hope had already begun to develop this style in Vaudeville, but it came into its own in the world of the clubs, where the concentration of the audience was so diminished. There were no complex sketches or byplay, no expressions of individual eccentricity. These jokes clearly framed themselves as jokes, with stylised openings like 'Did you hear the one about . . .?' While a successful comic could use his own writers to produce exclusive material, most comics used prepackaged jokes with a wide circulation. The point was not radically to change the audience's perceptions but to get a reflex response. A joke need not be new to do this, but it needed to be slick, concentrated and pack a punch, and the best way to do this was to be aggressive. Misogyny, along with racism and homophobia, was an easy way.

Many acts were more interesting and adventurous than this, and many of the more polished comedians had to tone down the most overtly aggressive material when they made it on to television – for TV, partly responsible for the status of the comic as commodity, rapidly absorbed the new style. Shows like Granada's *The Comedians* gave it wider currency and fed back the most successful acts into the more prestigious clubs. For a while, any woman who wanted to work in comedy at all had to come to terms with the club style. The complex negotiations of the halls, in which a woman could adopt a variety of strategies to avoid becoming an object of sexual aggression, were too slow and subtle. Many women never tried. Others did, and do. It is not difficult to get an audition with a local agent; it is not difficult to assemble jokes: books like Robert Orben's *Working Comedian's Gag File* (reputedly patronised by Richard Nixon) circulate widely, and advertisements in papers like *Variety* and *The Stage* offer items like 'Heckler Stoppers', 'Kids' Sayings (Risqué)', and '*Hilarious Ten Page Monologue*, 20 subjects including: Sex aids, Streakers, Size' for a fairly modest outlay; and the fees of even a small club compete favourably with wages on offer to women in many other areas.

The most apparently obvious way for a woman comic to cope with the club style and audiences is to behave as if she were male. I cite the following joke, which I won't attribute, performed at a local CIU club:

> There's a bloke and a woman in a pub, having a drink, sat at a table. And you know the bloke always decides 'e wants to go to the bog, don't he? So there she is, sat on her own, and this man's watchin' 'er. Eventually 'e plucked up courage, and walked up to 'er, and said, 'D'you know love' 'e said, 'I've been looking at thee now for the last two minutes,' 'e said, 'I've decided I'd like to pick thee up, tip thee upside down, rip yer knickers off, fill yer thingy full of Guinness and drink it.' She says, 'I beg yer pardon?' He says, 'I'm telling thee, I'd like to pick thee up, tip thee upside down, rip yer knickers off, fill yer thingy full of Guinness and drink it.' 'Ooo', she says, 'Yer disgusting person, now go away.' So 'e walked off to the bar. Next minute, 'er 'usband comes back. She said, 'You see that man at the bar', she said, ''E just come up to me and insulted me,' she said. ''E told me that 'e'd like to pick me up, tip me upside down, rip me knickers off, fill me thingy full of Guinness, and drink it.' 'E said, 'What man?' She said, 'That man there, at the bar.' 'E says, 'Give over,' he says, ''E couldn't drink five pints of Guinness.'

I didn't want to transcribe this depressing piece in full: it's not original, and readers will have heard more than enough of this stuff to last them a lifetime; nor did I want to pillory an individual woman with a living to earn. However, it seems to me important for two reasons. First, because when I showed it to my students they assured me that it must be ten or twenty years old, and that such jokes are simply not told now; it is necessary to point out that some forms of entertainment have not changed. Second, I feel that it is important to look, not at the aggression in the joke, which we can take as read, but at the trap for the woman performer constructed by the form and content. The rhythm of the joke is typical: repetition of a key phrase – usually, as here, the most 'shocking' – in the mouth of the butt or butts of the joke, then a punchline. Both the first man and the woman are here set up as 'stupid' by their repetition of the key phrase; the husband then comes in and breaks the pattern with the punchline.

Normally, though, this punchline would be in the first person; the joke wouldn't be about 'a man and a woman' but about 'the wife'. The comedian would be unambiguously inviting the men in the audience to share a laughter of aggression grounded in common attitudes. (No doubt 'all in fun'.) The woman comic, however, can't do this. She makes an attempt to narrate the story from a female viewpoint – 'the bloke always decides 'e wants to go to the bog' – but she can't sustain this; her next line humanises the aggressor – 'so 'e plucked up the courage' – and by implication his proposal; we're invited to laugh at the idea of it, not at his fearful or too-macho delivery. By the time the woman in the story speaks, the structure of the joke has clearly designated her the butt, and the line she speaks – 'Oo, you disgusting person' – is clearly designed for a man to utter in falsetto, a stylised female, not a real woman. The joke, in fact, will only work in so far as you forget the teller of it; her femininity will only get in the way.

She therefore has to sacrifice any real attempt at individuality; this puts her at a major disadvantage in terms of marketing. While jokes of this kind are interchangeable between comics, commercial success depends on the comedian's ability to be 'different', to impose some kind of personal style. Male aggression and misogyny can be packaged in a variety of personae: Jim Davidson's cheeky-boy-with-an-edge is markedly different, for instance, from Bernard Manning's middle-aged malevolent dumpling. Both project physical toughness and sexual self-assurance, traits which underpin the attitudes expressed in the jokes that they tell, in very different ways. However, the persona of a woman club comedian is largely constructed by these very same jokes. To look physically threatening, to express enjoyment of sexuality, to be overtly feminist, is to become an object of laughter. To maintain her role as subject, a woman has to endorse patriarchal attitudes while distancing herself from the stereotype role: in short, she has to efface the very 'personality' that is her stock-in-trade. Marti Caine relates the unspoken but rigid taboos:

> She cannot mention Tampax or anything to do with the menstrual cycles and she can't mention fart, for some reason. You're allowed to talk about sex as long as you put it in someone else's mouth . . . 'and he said' or 'my kid said', not 'I said' – it can't be you.

Caine's own comic style is grounded in an alternative strategy by which the woman comedian can negotiate with the club audience, that of self-deprecation. A female comic frequently shares the bill with acts that have an overt intention to be physically attractive to men – strippers especially – and this provides a means to exploit the ways in which she differs from these. Caine dressed like them, but the dress would fall to pieces; she sang similar songs, but would sit on a stool that collapsed in mid-song; she guyed her looks with comments like, 'I've all the family traits – me mum's eyes, me dad's chest'.

Self-deprecation, however, only works if it is clearly perceived to be an *act*. Caine narrates an early gig at which she replaced the stripper:

> I caught sight of myself in the peeling mirror: long thin legs, blue from the
> cold, clashing with the bright pink mini-dress which began at my neck and
> finished at my knickers. The design of the dress robbed me of breasts but
> revealed white angular shoulders which added an extra foot to my thin white
> arms. I looked like a rag doll, and they were expecting Princess Voluptua.
> . . . To survive, a performer has to establish dominance within twenty
> seconds, and already I could feel the pack instinct rising in them. 'Ger 'em
> off!' slurred one, to the amusement of his fellows. 'If it's as big as your
> mouth, you're on' I replied.[5]

The comedian may tacitly acknowledge her inadequacy as sexual object
and consent instead to be an object of laughter, but it is essential that she
is an object and not a victim, and the most self-deprecating performer
will use aggressive material to make her control of the situation clear.
Some, like Caine, do this through interaction with specific individuals in
the audience. For others aggression is an integral part of the act, most
notably for some women who pioneered standup comedy in the post-
vaudeville days in the USA. Phyllis Diller, for instance, who started as
a comedian at the age of thirty-seven and came to prominence around
1961, was explicitly told that she was 'too plain' to be a singer and opted
for deliberate onstage ugliness, shaving her eyebrows and wearing a
fright wig. Self-deprecation for Diller was primarily a 'passport'; she
reversed all the traditional 'family' routines, with stories about her
mother-in-law (Moby Dick) and her husband (Fang). The reversal process, however, is incomplete. It is contained in the *words* of the joke, but
in performance the invitation to laugh at her, not with her, is made plain
by a visual style that states that she is herself the 'nagging wife' of
stereotype.

A similar mixture of self-deprecation and conventional aggression is
characteristic of Joan Rivers, whose career began in earnest at about the
same time. The style she developed was powerfully aggressive, especially against herself. One set opened:

> When a woman reaches a certain age people don't think you're attractive
> . . . and if they don't think you're attractive in my country, America, you're
> just considered yuk, ugly . . . you know, and no one likes ugly women – the
> truth, the truth! – nobody likes you. I was walking in the door today to the
> studio and a man grabs me – I thought, Thank God, somebody likes me – he
> said, 'How are things in Loch Ness?'[6]

The aggression then moves outwards to other targets, mostly women.
Her 'friend' Heidi Abromowitz, about whom she made an entire TV
special, replaces the 'wife' of the male standup comic – 'Kraft named a

spread after her . . . she put mirrors on her own shoes'.[7] Her 'trademark'
comedy consists of bizarre and aggressive one-liners about famous
women: 'Elizabeth Taylor – mosquitoes look at her and scream "Buf-
fet!"' or 'Christina Onassis, the ugliest woman in the world . . . the first
time I ever met her I thought she was wearing a fur coat – she was
wearing a strapless dress'. Rivers' delivery is fast and even angry; she
paces, wags her fingers, prowls the audience and demands of the women
if they have managed to get married: 'Twenty-six? You're no spring
chicken.' Her catchphrase, 'Can we talk?', suggests that she and we are
sharing a moment of honesty.

This invitation, however, does not extend to questioning received
values. It may tap into the resentment the public feel at having celebrities
relentlessly hyped in the media when they are manifestly not as desirable, intelligent or glamorous as the publicity machine would have us
believe, it may tap into a resentment about film stars having too much
money. But it also buys without question into society's obsession with
body images, into a male-defined understanding of femininity. The
Heidi Abromowitz patter may be more deft and literate than the 'take
my wife' routines of the cheap club comic, but it is grounded in his
definition of sexuality. Rivers tells us that Heidi is a 'tramp', but she
doesn't define the word, and therefore cannot re-define it, but simply
endorses the idea that any woman who shows sexual enthusiasm is
automatically fair game.

Self-deprecation as comic strategy has been a cause of feminist un-
ease, and since the beginnings of the women's movement some comedians, like Carol Burnett, have consciously removed it from their acts. It
does, to some extent, challenge the audience's expectations about women:
a self-deprecating routine can say, all right, I'm fat, I'm ugly, I'm a
hopeless cook, a terrible mother and a lousy housewife, but I'm *here*. For
women in the audience this can be in itself a kind of release: in a
nightclub the majority of women who perform are present as the fulfilment of male desire, but here is a figure with whom they can empathise.
Where the jokes against the self are relatively gentle, self-deprecation
can also foreground itself as an obvious strategy: Marti Caine may make
gags about her appearance, but dresses with a luxury that connotes self-
respect; the gawkiness becomes a way of establishing approachability,
of individualising her relationship with the audience. Some of her recent
jokes against her appearance concerned the short crop that had been
necessitated by chemotherapy; it was a touching and courageous use of
her comic style.

On the other hand, self-deprecation can come perilously close to self-hate, as it does in much of Rivers' work; this makes it impossible for the comic to issue a clear challenge to society's expectations of her, because she is tacitly endorsing them. She may disarm the laughter of superiority, and do so with elegance and wit, but she is still validating this laughter and promoting it at the cost of styles less destructive to women.

However, it is important to appreciate the difficulty under which women comedians in the club tradition have had to work. In this context it may be helpful to look at a review of Phyllis Diller written in 1970 by Charles Marowitz for *The Village Voice*:

> I believe she shares some of Hope's writers; I guessed as much because behind her endless stream of abuse against ugly women, fat women, horrid in-laws, there is something mechanistically routine. Like some oddly chosen go-between, she conveys what the committee intellect has conceived. . . . There is more to standup comedy than a manic commitment to anatomical derision. I suppose she would say that's her 'thing'. But she pushes unloveliness so far it almost conjures up a need for the opposite. We want her to say something funny about being pretty or wanted or sympathetic . . . she is a true pro, and her professionalism is clearly seen. But I felt all through the evening her material was preventing me from touching her, from knowing her.[8]

This is interesting for what it does and doesn't say. Marowitz offers a reasonable criticism of the lack of 'fit' between Diller as woman performer and the club style. However, he doesn't attempt to relate this to its political context: he might, by 1970, have borrowed some of the vocabulary of the newly burgeoning Women's Movement to suggest that Diller needed a routine to identify her as a unique and female voice, not to borrow male jokewriters; he might have inquired whether the string-of-gags style perpetrated by Hope wasn't too closely associated with misogynist humour to be appropriate for a woman. Instead Marowitz critiques Diller in terms of the old Aphra Behn bargain; he wants to 'touch' her, to 'know' her; the way in which the two words are used as virtual synonyms suggests a latent eroticism. One could imagine Marowitz wanting to 'know' a male comedian whose material didn't seem adequately to convey a personality, but 'touch'? The word 'know' here is not fully divorced from its biblical sense. In turn this suggests that when Marowitz asks for 'something funny about being pretty' what he wants is not a joke about prettiness, but an acknowledgement from Diller that she secretly longs to be 'pretty or wanted or sympathetic'. What he wants, in fact, is a vulnerable and sexually available figure, a pretty

Diller rather than one who is focusing her plain and middle-aged self away from the task of satisfying the male ego; in short, a Diller who is an even stronger supporter of the status quo.

The club convention of aggression also permits another strategy for women – an exploitation of their sexuality so overt it teeters on the edge of parody. One of the most successful in recent years is Ellie Laine. Laine says 'There are lots of male comics out there who are doing lots and lots of anti-woman jokes . . . I'm evening it up.'[9] Laine specialises in sexual put-downs which are carefully packaged into an apparently spontaneous and good-humoured relationship with the men in the audience, partly conducted through their womenfolk – 'You girls who don't know what I'm talking about, have you ever tried pushing a marshmallow in a money box'?'. Laine's persona is grounded in an apparent sexual availability: the fact that it is only apparent is part of the joke. Many of her stories feature her as insatiable, the man as useless: 'He said, "Look at that, darling, that is twelve stone of dynamite." I said, "Yeah, with a two inch fuse."' She stalks the room energetically in an outfit carefully chosen to be 'outrageous – no other woman would have the bad taste'. Because it is so outrageous – both in terms of the amount of flesh exposed and in its use of flashy, bedroomy fabrics – its message is, again, double-edged. It signals availability, but it also parodies the idea of 'sexy' clothing, so that a man who acted simply on the 'available' signal would look a fool. Laine interacts vigorously with the audience and sometimes finds herself physically entangled – 'I think me left tit's just fallen out,' she grunts to a man, stretched across his lap, 'Can you catch it before it hits the floor?' The effect is to give the man what he ostensibly wants, physical contact, but to do so in a way that embarrasses him a little rather than offering direct gratification. It is a potentially risky scenario: Laine has faced drunken catcalls, maulers and flashers during her sets but is now sufficiently well established to choose her clubs with care. 'I don't want staggy . . . I want family audiences . . . I need the women to get the laughs.' Granted, it is the women in the audience who lead the laughter as she homes in on a boy with fuzzy curls and teases 'Is it the same down there? . . . how do you know when you're right way up?' On the other hand, Laine's persona doesn't really undermine the sexual status quo; while the fact that her 'availability' is a game may send up male pretension, it also signals a willingness to negotiate on familiar patriarchal territory: her neat riposte to a man in the audience she has been larking with, who says mock-reproachfully 'I am fifty-eight', is 'I wish it was inches'. While it's slick, it also buys into the classic dualist image of women – madonna versus insatiable slut. Though she isn't directly available, she none the less uses a seductive charm to claw back the potential aggression of the anti-male jokes.

Again, though, it is worth considering the odds against which Laine has to work to establish even this relatively uncontroversial persona in a male-dominated comic world. Interviewed by Peter Watson on a programme that was at pains to show the careful rehearsal that goes into apparent ad-libs, she was still asked, 'Do you really hate men?' and 'You try to make out you're a really sexy person with lots of suitors and lovers – but you're not really, are you?' Laine's act is evidently disturbing enough for these questions to be a live issue for the male interviewer – and implied male audience; so much so that they take precedence over more detailed questioning from a feminist position.

New comedy, new chances?

The last fifteen years have brought a number of changes to the large provincial town I live in. Many of them – the unemployment, the crowded schools, the urban decay as public spending is cut – are unwelcome. But the face of entertainment has also changed, in ways not altogether unconnected with these social shifts. In the seventies, to hear a 'comedian' meant to go to a working men's club and listen to jokes emerging from a dinner-jacketed man over the chatter and clinking glasses. Today, there are venues where the comedian is the focus of attention, not the verbal wallpaper of the club or part of a variety bill; these venues are not purpose-built – the most popular is a gloomy bit of Edwardiana inspiringly named the Memorial Hall – but they are packed out. A good number of the comedians are women. And the jokes are different.

The change reflects a shift in the nature of comic performance. In America it began in the sixties; Britain combined aspects of the new American comedy with its own existing strains at the end of the seventies to develop what became known – although many performers reject the label – as 'alternative comedy'. There are clear differences in tone and emphasis, but a major part of the attraction of the new comedy on both sides of the Atlantic is its intimacy. The new comedian is an individual, with a personal point of view and a personal story to tell, not a joke machine. There is a relationship between performer and audience that is close, involved, and visibly flows between the two. Richard Fields, who owns one of the pioneer New York venues for the new style,

Catch a Rising Star, suggested that young audiences sought in the new comedy what they once got from rock'n'roll:

> What happened is that rock and roll became the way to sell Pepsi and blue jeans – it became a multi million dollar business, and people got fed up . . .The comic comes in with a little manila envelope, no heavy equipment, and he [sic] goes everywhere, including Raleigh and Buffalo . . . Rock goes in with six semi-trailers, the break point is one hundred thousand dollars just to put the act on, the act is surrounded by bodyguards so people don't kill them . . . Then you have a little comic coming on . . . it's real, it's touchable – it's not automated or push-button. Comedy is the rock and roll of the future, and that's why.[10]

The impulse behind the new comedy was not primarily feminist, and women performers have not been free from the problems inherent in other comic fields. It was, however, the first new form of entertainment to grow up alongside the women's movement, and therefore held possibilities for women to influence and shape its growth. A short history may help to clarify both the limitations and the promises which it still holds.

In 1963 Budd and Silver Friedman opened the New York Improv. It was not a paying venue; the idea was to provide a kind of school or studio for comedians new to the business. The same convention was adopted by Mitzi Shore when she opened the Los Angeles Comedy Store in 1972; Shore wanted to create an 'art colony', a place where comedy would be more than 'something you did to warm up a crowd for a stripper'.[11] Both began to generate 'stars' who went on to TV success. The rise of the new comedy coincided with the arrival of cable television in the USA. Standup gave cable what it needed – a form of entertainment that was cheap to produce and coincided with a clear trend in public taste. It provided the comedians with the opportunity to work not only in five minute slots but in hour-long 'specials', a demanding format which sorted out many of the most talented and inventive. The process drew more audiences to watch the comedians live. Cable was also free from the self-imposed censorship of network television: a cable audience had, in effect, paid for its ticket; it didn't have to buy more cornflakes to keep the show on the air. Two network shows did profile comedians – *The Tonight Show* with Johnny Carson and *Late Night with David Letterman* (Letterman himself was a product of the Comedy Store) – although, as we shall see, both were sometimes circumspect in their choice of comics.

By the late seventies, the owners of the new clubs were prospering – Shore grossed two and a half million dollars a year – and the comedians began to agitate for pay. The row as long and bitter and the result was a new situation which both sides view as something of a mixed blessing. While for some burgeoning talents standup became, for the first time, a possible way of earning a living, the increasing commercialism resulting from the new deal led, some felt, to less adventurous work and also to less adventurous audiences; they now arrived with the same expectations as the old nightclub patrons – aggressive jokes with a predictable structure. By the mid-eighties there were at least 300 new comedy venues, but many had abandoned the showcase format, and with it much experimental material.

The pattern of experimentation, professionalisation and commercialisation is one that can also be detected in the alternative comedy boom in the UK. Its most frequently cited watershed date came in 1979 with the opening of Peter Rosengard's Comedy Store in London. Rosengard had seen the Los Angeles Store and was attempting to duplicate the American phenomenon: at this stage Rosengard's Store had no kind of political ethos and some of the comedians who appeared were very much of the old working men's club school. However, the Store also coincided with some shifts in the left-wing Fringe Theatre groups, such as 7.84, CAST and Belts and Braces, which had grown up in the sixties and seventies – often making use of techniques from variety and standup. There was a severe funding crisis as Arts Council grants were axed; in addition there was a developing dissatisfaction with agit-prop as a theatre form, both in terms of its popular appeal and of the opportunities it offered the artists for personal expression. Roland Muldoon of CAST subsequently became artistic director of the New Hackney Empire in 1986 with a commitment to revitalise Variety. Tony Allen, who had long opposed subsidies for political alternative theatre, founded Alternative Cabaret to tour London venues with Alexei Sayle, Pauline Melville and Andy de la Tour. Most of the Alternative Cabaret comedians, who had a strong left-wing identity and a commitment to comedy that was non-racist and non-sexist, appeared at the Comedy Store, and eventually (after what Tony Allen has described as a 'civil war')[12] the old-style performers left them the field.

As with the American clubs, professionalisation and then commercialisation entered the alternative comedy arena. A new club, the Comic Strip, used many of the same comedians as the Comedy Store but the format changed: the Strip show was a fixed format rather than the freewheeling structure of the Store, where comics tried out new material every time. Then television entered the picture. While some alternative comedians were profoundly hostile to the idea of television, feeling that their material would pass out of their own control and be re-packaged as a commodity, others welcomed the chance of exposure. Shows like *Book 'em and Risk It* (Channel 4, 1983), *Stomping on the Cat* (1984), *Friday Night Live* (Channel 4, 1986–9) broadcast material from the cabaret in showcase format. Narrative comedy written and performed by artistes from the alternative circuit also boomed: under the Comic Strip umbrella French and Saunders, Rik Mayall and Ade Edmondson wrote and performed in a series of films such as *Five Go Mad In Dorset* and subsequently in sitcoms like *The Young Ones* and *Girls on Top*.

This pattern interacted both positively and negatively with the energies of women empowered by the impact of the women's movement to try new fields of work. Few people have ever tried to stop women working hard for little or no pay, and the pre-professional stage at least allowed them a chance to learn the craft. Some venues actively encouraged them. 'They were *desperate* for women', said Jennifer Saunders of both the London Comedy Store and the Comic Strip.[13] Mitzi Shore opened an annexe to the Los Angeles Store, the Belly Room, to provide a sympathetic environment for first-time comedians, and found it extensively used by women. When the first moves towards professionalisation were made, however, women often fared worse. Rick Newman describes the refusal of managers watching acts try out to accept that the lines of demarcation had shifted:

> Sometimes I'd put a female singer between comedians . . . and she would do humorous patter between her songs . . . well, some of these old-school managers and producers – the typical cigar-smoking characters – would holler from the audience rudely, 'Just sing!'[14]

Johnny Carson shrugged off the low proportion of women comedians featured on his show, a key slot in terms of a comic's career, with '[Women comedians] are sometimes a little aggressive for my taste. I'll take it from a guy, but from women, sometimes, it just doesn't fit too well.'[15] While all comedians on the networks encountered some degree of censorship, women tended to find producers expressing the same kind· of reservations Marti Caine discovered in club audiences. French and Saunders, for instance, found the episode of the 1983 Channel Four showcase series *The Entertainers* in which they appeared shifted from 8.30 to 11.15 pm because one sketch contained the word 'clitoris'. Jo Brand, a popular comedian on the live circuit, has appeared only fleetingly on television, cracking jokes about menstruation in a Channel Four arts programme – hedged about with warnings of 'shocking material' – designed specifically to show what the medium felt it could *not* normally allow on the air.[16]

Women comedians who do get the wider exposure of television often find they do not do so on the same terms as men. While the artists of the Comic Strip films broke up to work in single-sex sitcoms, *Girls on Top* had far more problems with the censor and had its transmission delayed by two years, only to find itself labelled less 'original' than *The Young Ones*, the all-male show with which it should have shown contemporaneously. Women who achieve their own shows, like Josie Lawrence and Emma Thompson, have found that if they do not instantly attract highly favourable reviews and high ratings, there are no second chances, while male comic talent is allowed to develop at a more leisurely pace.

The comedian–audience relationship, too, has often presented women with specifically gender problems. All comedians attest to the difficulties of learning the craft – the squalid backstage conditions ('I dream of a toilet that flushes' is a remark I've heard more than once), the humiliation of failure, the apparently inexplicable way that a routine will work brilliantly one night and 'die' the next. All of them, too, talk with mixed feelings about hecklers. Heckling is a part of the relationship with the audience; it is the guarantee that the communication process is alive and two-way; it can be a source of energy, generating ad-libs and laughter; it can also be profoundly hostile. The hostility may spring from personal dislike of a comedian's style; it may be overtly racist or homophobic. But while male comedians may be shouted down and told they're not funny, the audience rarely challenges their right to be a comedian at all. While a male comedian who is overtly gay may receive appalling insults, he is rarely treated as a sexual object. Few women comedians haven't had to deal with the cry 'Show us yer tits!' (to which Dawn French would politely respond, 'Why don't you show us your knob, sir?'). If a male comedian does not mention his sexual orientation, he will rarely find it questioned, while almost every woman hears, several times a week, 'Are you a lesbian?' (The classic riposte is 'Are you the alternative?') A male comedian who is physically distinctive in some way may get comments on his appearance, which he may or may not choose to exploit, but a woman's appearance is always judged. If she is conventionally attractive and chooses to dress to emphasise it, she may find she has to work for a hearing. (Jenny Jones, who wears low-cut dresses and sequins, estimates that she throws away the opening minutes of her act while the audience works out for itself that she has something to say.) If she is not conventionally pretty, she will find hecklers commenting on her looks. If she alludes to her own body without vanity or self-deprecation, she offers the heckler a cue. Jenny Lecoat once began an anecdote with the words 'I'm not particularly fat, but –' only to find herself shouted down. (Her response was to incorporate into her act both the anecdote and the story of the heckler.) For a woman comedian, heckling frequently results in specifically sexual banter. Jenny Jones once admonished a heckler, 'If you're going to heckle, it's important you have good timing. You were a little premature – but then, you're probably used to it.' This kind of exchange can be read by the audience in different ways: a woman wittily putting down a male nuisance; a bit of sexual banter between equals, a substitute, perhaps, for physical interaction; or a man sexually harrassing a woman and getting away with no more than a telling-off. However this relationship with the audience is read, the woman cannot avoid foregrounding her gender. She still finds herself negotiating Aphra Behn's bargain; and, while the word 'actress' has ceased to be a euphemism, too many women comedians find that men in the audience attempt to continue negotiations offstage. As one succinctly put it, 'It's as if he thinks I'm included in the price of the ticket.'

But the performer's gender is also important to the women in the audience. While women rarely come alone to watch club comedy, they go for the new comedy both to the more established venues and to those designed specifically for them, like the Cave of Harmony in London, or Black Orchid Productions in Denver. Women managers, rare in the earlier life of standup comedy, have responded both to the pressure to create this kind of space for performers to develop in a sympathetic environment, and to the needs of women audiences in single sex and mixed venues. Maria Kempinska says of her plan for Jongleurs in London, 'I wanted a place that everyone could feel relaxed in – that women could go in by themselves – I thought, if a woman could come in and not feel intimidated, and talk to people without feeling any pressure, then that would be my criterion for a good atmosphere.'[17]

The relationship of women comedians with feminism – and especially with the word 'feminist' – is not a simple one, nor can it be in an art form which is commercially based. The choice of whether or not to adopt the label springs from specific circumstances as much as from the performer's material. Jenny Lecoat, for instance, styled herself 'feminist comedian' when working the alternative circuit in London in the early eighties. It was a period in which comics often spelled out their exact left-wing allegiance – Jim Barclay, for instance, referred to himself as 'the wacky, zany Marxist–Leninist'. She was conscious of filling a precise gap – 'It was my market, wasn't it?'[18] Subsequently, however, she found that the label tended to set up expectations in the audience of a certain earnestness and stolidity, a style she satirises as 'Hey, look, women menstruate and that's *Really Important*.'[19] Others found that the label suggested tokenism; Linda Smith describes it as 'reactionary . . . until you get away from that ghettoizing, women are never going to get a fair crack of the whip'.[20] Helen Lederer felt that adopting a clearly labelled political stance also pressurised performers into self-censorship and crippled spontaneity. 'I think the battle is not focusing on the difference but trying to get into being female.'[21]

In the early days in the USA, some performers violently repudiated the label. 'Talking about the things [feminists] want me to is just as bad as doing pots and pans. And it's not even as funny,' said Elaine Boosler in interview in 1976. 'I'm a woman who's a comic, not a woman's comic.'[22] This kind of response, however, was almost inevitable, given the extreme caution with which the networks treated self-proclaimed radical feminists like Robin Tyler; with the interview itself going out under the by-line *Funny girl: New, Hot and Hip*, it would be hard for Boosler to claim the label even if she wanted to. But, whether or not they accepted the label, the specific activity women comedians are substantially engaged in is, I would argue, one that has also preoccupied feminist scholars of their generation – that of re-defining autobiography.

Until recently, when you picked up the autobiography of a public figure you could take certain things for granted. The figure would probably be male, and would see his task as narrating the impact of his unique self on the world. This would involve describing the development of that self – his conflict with his parents, the evolution of his difference from the community – and the ways in which he identified and achieved highly specific goals. As such, autobiography was a form for the privileged ruling class. It has much in common with the favourite literary form of that class, the naturalistic novel. It selects events, it shapes them into a pattern, and presents this pattern as if it were 'truth'.

It is far less easy for those on the margins – women, gays, people of colour – to dismiss their relationship to the culture at large, because that culture denies them individuality and defines them as the generalised Other. They 'play themselves' as a backdrop against which the privileged individual can assert his difference. Increasingly, however, the concept of unified and stable 'selfhood' has been perceived as untenable and the 'self' re-defined as fluid and shifting. Part of the autobiographer's task is to recognise the fundamental impossibility of pinning down this fluid entity – which, indeed, is changed by the very process of writing the autobiography. Feminist writers of their own lives, however, have drawn strength from this idea precisely because it disrupts the rigidities of traditional hierarchy; the act of writing helps them to shape a new identity, one that refuses the definitions imposed on it by the ruling élite, but draws strength from sharing the experience of that imposition with others similarly disempowered. As Susan Stanford Friedman puts it, 'Writing shatters the cultural hall of mirrors and breaks the silence imposed by male speech.'[23]

The female comedian does this quite literally. She stands up to be counted. Her task is to devise, develop and project a self in a process of dialogue with an audience. In doing so she transforms the autobiographical process itself into a public event. She dramatises the relationship between the personal and the political. She tells stories and jokes which are grounded in her own feelings and her own insights. But for the audience to find them funny they must, first of all, share her values, and, equally important, share in the process of constructing her onstage 'self'. An opener by Linda Smith sums up the process. 'My name is Linda Smith. All right, you've guessed it. That's my stage name. My real name is Wanda Starbright.' Linda Smith is Linda Smith, but not the *same* Linda Smith as the one we see on stage. Her stage presence is simultaneously a guarantee that her experience is personal and that it will be framed in a way that others can share.

The process of developing this presence is not an easy one; more than one comedian has described it as a birth process. Jack Rollins, one of the most powerful agents for nightclub comedy, described Joan Rivers in an apparent paradox that is as true in the world of new comedy: 'You're naturally funny. You'll make it in three years.'[24] The apparently natural expression of the comic self often depends on adjustments in timing and inflection so small that an observer cannot define them but merely notes the difference in their reception. Joy Behar, who has her own show on cable TV in the USA, talks about her early experience after a major success at the Improv:

> I said to myself, 'Hey, you can do this, babe!' Then I go back to the Improv, in a 2am spot, with the exact same material, and I died. A thousand deaths. Into the *toilette*. And I said 'I can't do this,' and went back into the closet for five years.[25]

If the differences in performance are small, however, they are crucial and their effect is measurable. Several times, I have seen new comedians performing the same set over a period of months. Two in particular used scatty, neurotic personae; in the early stages the audience seemed embarrassed by this; they seemed to feel confusion, even pity, for the women; then, although the changes within each set were imperceptible, both women seemed to reach an understanding with the audience. It was established somehow that these personae were constructs inviting our laughter, not problems with which we had somehow to deal.

Once the persona has been established, the comedian is free to examine all aspects of women's lives and to change our perception of them. Some, for instance, concentrate on the material that male autobiography tends to omit – dailiness and domesticity. For women to write about this is nothing new. There is a tradition of humorous journalism about the realities of living with a husband and family; often it shows considerable wit and craft – for instance Shirley Jackson's *Raising Savages* or Betty MacDonald's *The Egg and I*. But while these books were witty and vital, their tone was conciliatory: they didn't offer a challenge to the status quo but suggested a woman of spirit could cope within it – as long as she could escape for five minutes from the dirty dishes to dash off front-line dispatches before going back to change a few nappies. The subtext was 'ho hum'. It is still a live tradition: most of the weekly women's magazines have a column devoted to 'a look at life' from a humorous angle, geared to suggesting that life is indeed a funny old business. These are always understood to proceed from the domestic space, so that the writer herself remains domesticated in our imagination; she is not a 'public woman'. To stand on a stage, however, and perform material like Shirley Jackson's (or Sylvia Plath's), is to transform its meaning and significance. Instead of expressing humorous acceptance or individual anger, it insists on the whole audience, including males, adopting, briefly, a female perspective; it demands a public laugh at the incongruities inherent in the idea of the family rather than a straightforward acceptance of them.

Roseanne Arnold (formerly Roseanne Barr) made a conscious decision to package her act into a domestic–autobiographical framework, which she felt made it possible for her to articulate feminist ideas in a way that could be acceptable to a wide audience and provide her with an entrée into the mainstream. 'I figured out I could say everything I wanted to say by being a housewife.'[26] Her starting point was the old woman's-magazine ideal of the perfect wife and homemaker, the 'Domestic Goddess': 'What if I say "Domestic Goddess" as a term of self-definition, rebellion, truth-telling?' From this evolved her housewife-from-hell persona. Its substance is not so different from the 'humorous look at life' projected in *Woman* or *Redbook* – troublesome children, husbands who can't find things, day-to-day stresses and strains – but the presentation is different. For the domestic journalists, cheerful acceptance of one's own limitations is the only acceptable kind of humour. The only way of discussing the family in terms that are not rosy, terms which may draw attention to feelings of irritation and dislike, is to problematise the situation, to depict it in terms of a failure to 'cope' – material which can only exist on the fringe of 'comic' material, in anecdotes relating not to the narrator herself but a 'friend' we might be invited to pity. Arnold's persona, however, is that of a blue-collar woman who gives voice to genuine exasperation – 'brought to you by Fem-rage – for that one time of the month you're allowed to be yourself'.[27] She chews gum, her voice rises frequently to a shriek as if yelling over factory machinery; she doesn't sentimentalise the joys of motherhood. 'I love my kids, but I need something more – like perhaps a life . . . don't never read none of these books by those experts – "Never hit your kids in anger" – when *is* a good time to hit 'em?' Her husband's irritating habits are the stuff of classic ho-hum column material, but she presents them as a Stephen King fantasy 'about a husband with a mind of his own – don't worry ladies, it could never happen – it's called *Barbecue Starter*'. It isn't surprising that she has subsequently channelled this persona into a popular family sitcom; her overall effect is not to undermine the family as a unit but to establish the female voice, demanding changes, demanding recognition of her needs and desires, as a crucial part of that unit. It is the voice of a raucous woman who seizes her right to dramatise her life in lurid colours, and to parody the middle class *Woman* image. It pushes to the foreground the fact that she is usurping male territory – literally, in her HBO special, where her screen family kept trying to erupt into the action and were sent firmly back home. The anger latent in the lines is contained by the fact that she *is* the centre of attention; what remains is her enjoyment of the space she has seized.

Domestic comedy can go further than asserting the importance of the quotidian. It can also engage in a process crucial to feminism, that of naming. It breaks silences; it acknowledges problems society has preferred to confine to the private space. It can be shocking and also exhilarating to hear Brett Butler's opener – 'Hi, I'm Brett and I'm an alcoholic – oh God, wrong meeting!' – and her admission that 'I got married young. I thought a battered wife was the kind you dip in breadcrumbs and deep-fry.' It is important to see why: we are not laughing because we feel superior to Butler, despite the fact that she is in a sense lowering her status in front of us; we are not really laughing at the linguistic incongruities in the jokes. Rather the laughter springs from relief that a familiar situation has been named in a particular context – a context in which many of the ideas generally used to obfuscate the real problem of male violence and women's response to it cannot be used. The short, snappy joke forbids us to wonder whether it was her 'fault' – its structure precludes psychology. It also provides a frame which allows us not to feel compassion and concern – Butler is here, a survivor, narrating a past life; so our attention is squarely focused on the act of naming, the saying of the unsayable, which is the precondition for change.

Much of this 'naming' of course took place in the area of sexuality. In the early days this could be relatively simplistic – although it didn't lack entertainment value on that account. Take this extract from Jenny Lecoat's set in 1982:

> The problem is, right, they're all completely obsessed with their willies. Willy, willy, willy, willy, willy – that's all sex is to them. I mean, when those missiles go launching off Greenham Common, it won't be 200-foot clitorises flying up there. How many times have the straight women here had one of those men that parades round the bedroom for about five minutes before he gets into bed? Boinggg . . . that's my willy! What *are* you supposed to say? The next thing you know he's on top of you – the great white whale – going at it. And what's the next thing you hear? 'Oh . . . sorry.' We all know what that means, don't we? That means 'Thank you very much, love, it's the end of the show, can all fuck off and have a cup of tea'. That's what 'sorry' means – there's no conception of fingers or tongues, or anything that might give us a good time. Oh no, 'sorry, love, it's all over with my willy'. Then he fucks off into the kitchen and puts the kettle on! Of course, what they don't realise is that when they're in the kitchen making the tea . . . we're in bed, having a quiet wank.[28]

This is a fairly straightforward bit of 'naming', in that it identifies an aspect of patriarchy – phallocentricity – and attacks it from a female-superior viewpoint; women become the in-group, men the out-group whose beheviour is ridiculed. This very basic kind of aggression tended to give way to a more complex reading of sexual politics as acts developed. A later routine from Lecoat, for instance, also focuses on phallocentricity, taking as its premise the unwillingness of men to use a condom despite the AIDS crisis. Wryly, she comments, 'I end up feeling like a mother trying to make her little boy put on his thermal vest', and launches into a physical and verbal routine to elaborate. The joke this time involves recognition that heterosexual relationships are not simple transactions between inadequate male and frustrated female. This, however, is not the most important shift. By writing herself into the story in a less aggressive way, Lecoat shifts into a more positive frame: she is asserting her right to set the tone of discourse about sexuality rather than simply describing male intransigence.

Many female comedians have subsequently dealt with sexuality in terms of language; their target is not the individual male but the language that shapes phallocentricity. Pat Rosborough makes a direct and comic attack on the language of sex manuals and the way in which they have shaped our understanding of orgasm – of the female 'mature' vaginal orgasm as opposed to the 'immature' clitoral orgasm; for men, on the other hand 'a woman, a goat or a sock, right, it's all mature'.[29] Elaine Boosler parodies the macho image inherent in brand names, dwelling satirically on condoms. 'Trojans, Rameses, Pharaohs – you wanna get laid or you wanna conquer Egypt?' She sends up male mythology about penis size. 'If it reaches us it's long enough. . . . You never hear a woman say "Another inch and I'd have married him."' This allows her to make a more specifically feminist point about the direct consequence of this myth for women – the way in which women's bodies in male discourse are fragmented and treated as sexual objects rather than as parts of a whole being. 'I'll just get me a piece of ass' – 'Why don't you get a whole girl?' 'No, I'm full.'[30]

Given Boosler's success in the mainstream and her specific rejection of the 'feminist' label, it is perhaps worth looking at the stage presence through which these lines are mediated. Boosler moves with a grace that reflects her ballet training and dresses in striking, sometimes revealing, clothes, but her demeanour does not offer her as a sexual object. She prowls the stage athletically, almost a marching step that suggests the appropriation of territory rather than an attempt at seduction; sometimes she jumps with a high spirited yell; she can launch into a grotesque impression of a male sportsman – 'A guy cannot throw a ball without touching himself in fifty places first' – or a male swimmer coming out of the sea making extraordinary hawking noises ('What'd make *me* do that?'). She is willing to look grotesque and to clown; she is prepared to charm and to be vulnerable; but she is not willing to be conciliatory. Her analysis of language may be a feminist one; she does not apologise for this, nor does she stress it; rather, she presents it as a bit of entertaining incongruity that is part and parcel of heterosexual female life. Thirty years ago, such material would have been taboo. Twenty years ago, it would have made sense to a group of women skilled in consciousness raising. That it can get laughs in prime time is a measure of the change that has come over comedy.

Lesbian comedians have further widened the frame of sexual reference. Pioneers like Robin Tyler and Rachel Harrison used their sexuality as a platform from which to attack the opposite sex without concessions. Tyler's rationale for the aggression was that 'we mustn't be afraid of our own power'.[31] Or, as they put it in their act, 'If anyone gets insecure, just do a crotch check. It's still there.' They attacked patriarchy from an avowedly marginal position:

> *Tyler*   Women do not have penis envy.
> *Harrison*   Men have mammary envy.
> *Tyler*   That's because America is built on sucking. If you guys are gonna judge us by the size of our breasts, we're gonna judge you by the size of your wee wees.
> *Harrison*   And we all know all men aren't created equal, don't we?

Later performers were more concerned with their own sexuality than with using it as a place outside heterosexual society from which to attack. Claire Dowie, for instance, had a routine that depended on an audience not only willing to adopt a lesbian perspective for the duration of her set, but sufficiently at ease with that perspective to enjoy some of its paradoxes:

> The Gay Pride march – march, I mean it's walking . . . I had to walk everywhere – with a banner – aren't I persecuted enough? Why can't I sit in a pub and be proud? Occasionally march to the bar, perhaps . . . And then, I slept with a man. I didn't know – I thought it was OK, I thought he was right-on radical . . . cos he was gay as well . . . it's true, he's one of my best friends, and he's lovely, he's so camp . . . but anyway, I ended up in bed with him . . . don't try it. If you're a butch dyke, and you go to bed with a very camp man, don't try it. Don't. I thought it would be a giggle . . . I thought, oh this'll be a laugh . . . I was a bit drunk . . . I'd been being proud . . . I ended up on Valium for three weeks . . . it was awful . . . we're in bed together and it's like . . . I can't explain it . . . it was like there was a penis running round the bed and we weren't too sure who it belonged to. It was like . . . 'Is that yours?' No, that's not mine, mine's bigger than that.[32]

This allows straights in the audience into her world, honorary members as it were, and draws them into a comic variation on the 'some of my best friends are gay' line of the classic liberal. You can laugh as a gay at a bit of observation; as a straight, you have the option of laughing at yourself

– although Dowie is not setting you up as a figure of fun, as Tyler clearly is setting up the straight male. The gay woman comic who works in mixed clubs is almost inevitably going to find herself doubly vulnerable to the male gaze – as sexual object by virtue of her gender, and also as a lesbian in a theatrical frame often constructed to make her lesbianism part of a male fantasy; this can make the task of naturalising her perspective extremely daunting. As Julia McNamara, a young gay comic who works with mixed audiences, puts it:

> Why is it so difficult to celebrate being women in mixed audiences? The very fact that we stand before them, female, is an exotic experience for some audiences. They sit there, gobsmacked, and ignore every bloody word while you struggle through your thirty minutes. And that's never more true than when you're a lesbian, using blatantly lesbian material in a heterosexual audience that's still shocked to its tiny core at the idea of a woman coming to a nightclub unaccompanied, let alone gettin' down there and struttin' her stuff on stage.[33]

It is not surprising that many lesbian comedians choose to find other outlets. Both Claire Dowie and Robin Tyler, for instance, now work in different areas. Tyler lectures on comedy and Dowie has had considerable success with one-woman shows which are not primarily comic, and make different demands on her audience.

As well as naming and naturalising their own sexuality for an audience, women comedians have also dealt with issues more specific to female biology, like menstruation and childbirth. At one point, the former seemed to be almost obligatory, a fact that many women comedians now parody. As Jo Brand puts it, 'It's in my contract.' Childbirth issues have become popular as younger women comedians have become mothers. Helen Lederer has a routine about attempting to breast-feed in peace. 'We drew quite a crowd – at least no-one shouted "show us your tits!" Jenny Eclair, pop-eyed with fury at becoming an anatomical side-show for students, boggles at the hospital sister who 'referred to *my vagina* as "the birth *canal*"'. While patriarchy has romanticised birth, it is refreshing to hear women articulate their ambivalent feelings about it. Carole Montgomery deliberates on 'The thought of a little head coming out there . . . no no no . . . maybe a little head going in there . . .'[34]

This kind of humour is, in a very literal way, 'writing the body'. By virtue of that literalness – by performing this material in a public place for a mixed audience – women comedians have played an important part in the widening of the whole comic agenda. Bobcat Goldthwait talks about watching the birth of his child; Ben Elton has a routine which derives from an article by Gloria Steinem, a fantasy about the way men, if they menstruated, would make it a subject for macho boasting. Sexual politics were an important part of Tony Allen's material as early as 1980. The point is not that these men were influenced by women comedians – or vice versa – but that the presence of both women and men dealing with the same material highlighted the fact that sexuality was a much bigger area of human experience than the sexual act itself, and that different perspectives were both possible and necessary. Sex ceased to be something men did to women and became a complex area of experience yielding a rich variety of comic paradoxes.

Women have also begun to articulate a range of positions around the complex areas of food and body image. There are large women who talk about their size in different ways. Americans often take a fat power approach. Marsha Warfield, for instance, launches into aggressive anti-anorexic jokes and advises 'Never do laundry with skinny women – this'll really piss you off. They take their little Barbie underwear out of the drier . . .' Roseanne Arnold, too, takes the offensive: 'If you're fat, like, be fat and shut up. And if you're not, well, fuck you.' British comedians tend to be more self-deprecating, but this is rarely as simple a process as it was for club comics. Jo Brand, for instance, has described herself as 'the size of a modest Barratt house' but in the context of an act concerned with ideas of image and reality: at a time when British universities are reduced to selling themselves like competing soap powders, she describes her alma mater, Brunel, as 'the Arthur Mullard of higher education', and muses on the way advertisements push feminine hygiene products like panty liners, suggesting a 'nicer' name – 'fairy hammocks, for example'. Brand tends less and less to put down her appearance, and more and more to stress the fact that she is real and that the world of the advertisements is not. 'I fall into that group of women euphemistically labelled by the fashion industry as 'revolting obese lepers.'[35] The focus is on the pressures on women to look a certain way rather than on Brand's failure to do so. 'Women's knickers come in two kinds – black lace, the size of an atom, and grey, the size of Buckinghamshire, and you have to spray an awful lot of Charlie on them first.' Indeed, the keynote of Brand's appearance – as opposed to the glamour favoured by Warfield or Barr – is comfort. She wears loose tops and leggings, easygoing street clothes which connote freedom of movement, a person doing a real job. She often refers to her past as a psychiatric nurse, which underlines the sense of a real person as opposed to a carefully constructed glamour figure.

Sometimes the focus shifts away from body image and on to women's relationship with food. Elaine Boosler, for instance, draws yells of recognition with a routine asserting that 'a single woman cannot go to sleep if there is anything edible in the home', and with a set in which she pretends to be snacking M and Ms while on the phone, reaching the end of the packet with a wail of 'That's it? *I was gonna suck that one.*'[36] Many women recognise the situation; the fact that Boosler herself is fit and slender underlines the complexity of the relationship between women and food. On the whole, this kind of comedy does not specifically examine attitudes underlying that relationship – the connections between eating and anger, between sexual attractiveness and vulnerability, between capitalism and consumption. It tends rather to present women's conflicting desires – to eat and to conform to stereotypes of desirability – as a fact of life. Arguably, this is hardly conducive to social change. And yet it does at least seem a healthy step onwards from 'take my wife, she's so fat' jokes. It acknowledges the relationship, and by doing so undermines an assumption all too prevalent – that conditions like anorexia and bulimia are 'problems' in themselves rather than symptoms of a more complex social malaise. By naturalising the fact that women can have real psychic struggles over the last sweet in the bag, by eliciting the laughter of recognition, Boosler is going some way to naming the larger problem: that society loads women with conflicting and crippling expectations about their bodies. If Boosler – and the many others who deal in this kind of joke – fails to spell the problem, at least she is undermining false solutions. Certainly there are more radical approaches to the situation in more directly political contexts – the British theatre company Spare Tyre, for instance, perform cabaret sketches and songs which address these questions more directly; but these are preaching, if not to the converted, then to those with a specific interest, whereas Boosler is reaching people whose consciousness might be described as still unraised. There seems no reason, however, why this topic may eventually not be attacked within the personal, autobiographical style of standup.

Not all female humour is about specifically female topics. Many women ground their humour in non-gendered material and use a stage persona and jokes which could also be used by a man. The effect, however, is often coloured by the fact of their gender in interesting ways. The deadpan approach – a lugubrious monotone that seems to defy you to find it funny – has been favoured by men since Buster Keaton began to symbolise the human condition for Samuel Beckett. A woman using it is actively countering expectation in the audience that she will charm or use her sexuality. Margaret Smith, for instance, glumly opens with

'How 'bout that Kennedy Assassination, huh? . . . Yeah, I've been meaning to write some new material.' Hattie Hayridge looks like Alice in Wonderland, with blonde hair in a snood, wide eyes and a sailor dress, but counterpoints it with worldweariness edging into surrealism, telling stories of her childhood in which her parents confuse her with a spaniel and in which 'I was so lonely I invented six imaginary brothers and sisters . . . hated 'em.'[37] Deborah Margolin goes further into surrealist territory with fantasias on language, in which she asserts that 'the word misogynist is just like a Chekhov play – all the letters stand round wondering how to relate to each other', and describes living with a silent G: 'When he's lower case he's so well hung.'

Others seize and use the aggression permitted a male comedian. Judy Tenuta, for instance, is one of the most aggressive and surrealist standups in the US, using the soubriquet 'petite Fleur' as a contrast to an act in which she storms on, persuades the audience to clap along with her accordion, and then comments 'And they wonder how Hitler came to power.' She barely disguises her contempt for us, spitting out her chewing gum and demanding 'Crawl for it.' She sings a country and western song, but, typically, it's about the Pope:

> I just wanna cowboy to whom I can confess
> I just wanna cowboy in a long white silk dress.

All these personae, in fact, are about seizing the right not to be 'feminine'. Others explode the concept of 'femininity' by using conventionally 'feminine' mannerisms to counterpoint their satire. Rita Rudner, for instance, has a cooing voice and dresses prettily; her material is often explicitly sexual. For several women, self-deprecation and hesitancy provides a different kind of frame from that used by Joan Rivers and Phyllis Diller. Here, instead of addressing the audience with apparent confidence while describing their own failures and inadequacies, they are deliberately hesistant and awkward while asserting their own power. Lois Bromfield punctuates an account of a cruel joke she played on a member of the audience who didn't laugh with little shy lines like 'this is very sad but not really'. Comedians of this kind make conscious use of linguistic devices once simplistically assumed to be characteristic of women's language:[38] tag questions like 'isn't it?'; qualifications which hedge around a statement as if to placate the addressee for one's presumption in speaking with any certainty about the matter in hand. More recent studies have come to define this kind of language more precisely, as the language of the powerless, used by men as well as women in situations where they are ill at ease and perhaps threatened.[39] A woman comedian can play the language for contrast and incongruity against the fact that she is holding the stage alone, and against a use of swearing and sexual terms traditionally associated with men. It is a way of empowering the language of the powerless.

For British women comedians, apparent self-deprecation is often, too, a way of satirising their own relationship with the Left, with their own class position, and hence with the new comedy. Helen Lederer, for instance, plays on an upper-middle-class persona; she sends herself up with accounts of her parents' well-meaning celebration of her first period, or by shyly enquiring whether it's all right, at the Montreal Festival, to sneak a word like 'masturbation' through Customs. Pauline Melville developed a character called Edie, who was 'in the Woman's Movement, you know. I am. I mean, I'm not in the most militant branch – I'm just in the branch that pulls faces behind men's backs'. Linda Smith describes her right-on boyfriend, with whom she falls in love at first sight, 'a vision' in Peruvian knitwear, woolly hat, woolly jumper, woolly gloves and woolly socks; so right-on is he that he reads books like 'The Socialised Penis', which to Smith evokes images of wandering organs at parties murmuring 'Hello Dick', 'Hello Willy'. These frameworks allow for hard-edged socialist satire on almost any topic. Edie's naiveté didn't prevent her from observing that

> I heard there were two Afghanistani MPs come over here because they wanted to look at our system. They wanted to have a look at it for themselves, to see what actually happens. Mind you, of course, their skin's a bit darker than ours, so they actually got stopped at the airport, didn't they? They're actually in the detention compound at Heathrow. I think that's a shame, really, because now they'll never know what our system's like.[40]

Smith's comedy has covered everything from the Gulf War to the death of the Duchess of Windsor, of whose burial she grimly pointed out 'You can't be too rich or too thin.' However, she, like many others, feels that the political edge has softened on the alternative comedy circuit and that women in particular have a hard time of it. Melville, for instance, is now working as an actress and writer. In her early work – especially during the miners' strike of 1984 – she felt that she made real points of connection between socialism and the oppression of minorities:

> It was magic. I did some material that made the connection between black people being beaten up and the miners being beaten up. I heard a gasp of recognition – although it was a joke – that at last they realised what had been

happening. It was hilarious and everybody fell about, but you knew that your humour was binding a community together.[41]

She didn't draw an analogy between miners and battered women. This is perhaps significant when one looks at the relative lack of female political comedians in Britain. For many women on the Left, commit- ments to socialism and to feminism tend to interact rather than to blend. You cannot take for granted that all male colleagues will have feminist sympathies and where there is a perceived clash between the interests of women and the interests of the working class (assumed to be male) it is the former that will go to the wall. While many socialist–feminist come- dians are reluctant to ghettoise their humour and restrict themselves to feminism, in practice they may need to negotiate their right to the stage, just as Aphra Behn did.

6

Other selves: character comedy and the one-woman show

The single, consistent, comic 'self' presented on stage is often deployed in other ways. The comedian may make use of her persona in other kinds of enterprise. Victoria Wood and Rita Rudner have made TV commercials. Dawn French fronts a book of knitting patterns, Helen Lederer has published a book, *Coping*, which parodies the self-help manuals of the seventies and eighties. In each case the comedian herself acts as a sign which we must interpret in the light of her comic persona – but also a sign which carries more than comic meaning. To watch Wood or Rudner endorsing instant tea or coffee may involve laughter at the jokes within the text but it also means that we respond to them as successful women. To buy a book of patterns for colourful clothes for large women with Dawn French on the cover involves seeing French not simply as a popular comic figure but as an attractive, well-dressed woman at ease with her size. The persona, in other words, is a construct more durable than the performer's set, and I should like now to turn to the way in which it operates when the comedian assumes a role. I am not concerned here with specifically dramatic performance; many women comedians do interpret pre-existing texts, and these sometimes impinge upon their standup persona: for example, when Marti Caine played Fanny Brice in *Funny Girl* at the Crucible theatre in Sheffield she was marketed as a specifically local girl made good and a familiar comic personality. Some comedians have had film or television roles created with specific reference to the 'self' projected in standup. Hattie Hayridge, for example, plays a computer – a development of her stonefaced stage persona – in the science fiction series *Red Dwarf* (BBC2, 1988). I am chiefly inter-

161

ested here, however, in women who construct characters other than their comic 'selves' over which they have complete control – comedians not always physically 'out on their own' but who have set their own stamp upon their work, so that we always understand it in relation to the comedian herself.

It is difficult to define the precise relationship between character, performer and audience at work here, but it is instantly recognisable, and it is well illustrated by an extract from a routine for *BBC Music Hall* by Beryl Reid; the subject is 'how to tell a joke' and it plays with a character for which she is famous, Marlene the schoolgirl:

> Now I like say 'Any road up! like, a sign that I'm going to say another joke. Any road up – you know I said my mother's not very well – it's making her very irritable, 'cos just before I came here she hit me on the head with an oak leaf. The one out the centre of the dining room table. Didn't 'arf 'urt my head. (I like rub my head, see – acting like she hit me. She never touched me. Nice woman, my mother.)[1]

Reid is undercutting the mimetic convention that she and Marlene are one and the same; but the character who is performing that process is also a theatrical construct, 'Beryl Reid' the gossipy northern comedian chattily spelling out the obvious, rather than Beryl Reid as offstage self. Much of the audience's laughter at Marlene is shaped by their awareness of the 'Beryl Reid' who acts as her mouthpiece, who brings her on to entertain us; there is no attempt to 'lose herself' in the character, for this would undercut the pleasure. We are enjoying both the comic and her creation simultaneously. It is a formula which permits considerable flexibility – the performer's identification with the character can move towards naturalism or further into the distanced view shown here; it can allow the performer to show off a skill or to involve us closely in the fate of a character we come to care about. In fact it can walk on the edge of drama while ensuring that we do not lose sight of the comedian-as-author. This framework makes it possible for a performer to wield unusual power. It emphasizes woman as controller: she does not 'play herself' but creates a multiplicity of selves before the audience – selves which more conventional theatre practices might deny her. In this context she can be old or young, or black or white, male or female.

In this section I intend to examine two kinds of performance which make extensive use of character comedy. One is the television show, a relatively unstructured form which relies on the central performer to give it coherence. The other is the one-woman show, essentially a series of character monologues. I see these apparently dissimilar forms as linked, in that in both of them women have developed a complex and subtle relationship between standup and drama, a relationship which is perhaps their single greatest contribution to comic form.

In England the TV comedy show, whether headed by a man or a woman, includes a mixture of elements from variety, standup and revue: performers talk to the audience, act in sketches of varying lengths in which they may display various characters, display other aspects of their skill – such as singing – and interact with 'guest stars' who also perform solo spots. There may also be acts unconnected with them. The illusion the medium seeks to give is that we are having a 'night out' at a club or a variety theatre or a revue, and the presence of a studio audience is important. We are always made aware of them; they, in a sense, stand for us. On the other hand, it is also characteristic of television comedy shows of this kind to foreground the medium itself; parodies of various television conventions – the interview, the chat show, the soap opera – are a staple, as are in-jokes within standup routines about the upper echelons of the TV world.

Of the few women on British television to be given their own comedy show, Victoria Wood is the most successful – and in some ways the most traditional. Although of an age with the first wave of comedians from the alternative circuit to achieve media prominence, she has little to do with either alternative comedy or the clubs. Her career developed through television – she was engaged to do topical songs on a local BBCTV show at Birmingham's Pebble Mill – through revue, and through her work as a playwright – two plays, *Talent* and *Good Fun*, led to a commission from Granada TV and subsequently to the show *Wood and Walters* in 1982. Meanwhile she developed a one woman show, *Lucky Bag*, which opened at the King's Head in 1983 and featured songs, standup and character monologues.

Wood is one of the very few comedians, male or female, to win audiences right across the political and social spectrum. She has won BAFTA awards and retains the respect of performers who see many of the alternative first wave as having sold out to the media. In some ways she is the last exponent of the Variety tradition of strong northern women like Gracie Fields and Hylda Baker. Her strength, however, lies in the fact that she has retained a tight control over her work: while most performers use a number of sketch-, gag-, or song-writers, she writes all her own material, and draws on a relatively small circle of performers for both her shows and the one-off comic plays that have lately replaced them. Wood, unlike most of the northern comics she resembles, took a drama degree with strong textual emphasis; she developed the skill of writing plays sustained over hours alongside that of writing sketches, and the two skills nourish each other. As a result she has established an unmistakable voice, a clearly identifiable world that we are able to enter through all the forms she may choose.

The 'world' springs from a highly distinctive treatment of language. Like the young Harold Pinter and Joe Orton, Wood exploits a particular comic incongruity throughout her work – the complexity and sophistication of everyday speech when it is dealing with trivia like the planning of a kitchen or the ordering of food, and the emotion that lies unexpressed beneath it. With both Orton and Pinter, the emotion was that of violence, dragged to the surface by a plot which seemed to resonate beyond itself to point to some wider corruption in society. In Wood's work, we are reminded not of violence but of social pressures that can be equally damaging. A more overtly political sketch than usual makes this plain:

> *Corin* I hear you've introduced some revolutionary schemes to help the hospital pay for itself?
>
> *Kevin* Oh, you heard about that? Yes, I'm glad to say, half of our morgue is now a very successful freezer centre.
>
> *Corin* Really.
>
> *Kevin* Tremendous. You can pop down there, pay your last respects and pick up a very competitive shoulder of lamb at the same time.[2]

There are two levels of comedy here: the sheer linguistic incongruity of that eighties' consumerist middle-class jargon, 'a very competitive shoulder of lamb', in the midst of a serious discussion about National Health cuts, and a biting anger at a deeper incongruity: that the media and the people who have the power to make this kind of decision and justify it on television see no kind of anomaly in using such language.

There are in fact two kinds of character in Wood's comedy: one is the figure of relative power – often, as here, power in terms of the media. Many comedians have chosen to send up the world of television in their shows, casting 'the BBC', or the management, or, as Frankie Howerd called the controller of Light Entertainment, 'Thing', as top dog to their own underdog; Wood prefers to seize on the linguistic features that show up class prejudice and materialism in the control of the medium. A running feature of the mid-eighties shows was a pair of daytime TV presenters, Margery and Joan (Wood and Julie Walters), who looked at the typical daytime programme mix of gadgets, holidays and social problems:

Joan	Of course one thing about being in a crowd of people is that we can't always be sure of personal daintiness.
Margery	That's right, Joan. Now I don't mind jamming a hand into my armpit and sniffing it in public, but some people do; and for them these musical dress shields are going to be a real boon.
Joan	How do they work, Margery?
Margery:	Well, I'm pretty whiffy today, so this should show you. Just pop it under my arm here, wait a moment – and if there's any pong at all, this happens. (*It plays a computerized version of 'Eidelweiss'.*) And a lovely melody to boot.
Joan	And finally and very quickly, Margery?
Margery	Finally and very quickly Joan – redundancy.
Joan	What about it, Margery?
Margery	It's upsetting, it's traumatic, but above all, it's embarrassing.
Joan	So how do we keep it a secret, and stop people recognising us in the queue at the social security?
Margery	Not easy, Joan – at least it wasn't – until this little hoohah popped up on general release. (*She stands up and picks up a kind of shortened Punch and Judy booth.*) Light, portable, you can wear this in the dole queue and friends and neighbours will pass you by, none the wiser. (*She puts it on over her head, it comes down to waist level.*) And when your number's called and you reach the window – (*rolls up a little blind in front of her face*) hey poncho – you can be seen and heard in perfect privacy. (*Lights and music.*) – You'd probably need a bigger size, Joan.[3]

This is a comedy more diffuse in its focus than alternative standup. It hits accurately at the way in which television reduces all experience to programme fodder, and at the tunnel vision of a class which reduces it to etiquette. At the same time there is a dimension of sheer surrealism – the musical dress shields are comic because they are only a little more bizarre than the kind of items you see advertised every day, totally pointless and yet trading on a kind of anxiety about body image that is again recognisable. There is also a comic duality in the relationship between Margery and Joan – the surface constructed by the linguistic formalities of the chat show, which expects both courtesy and mutual rapport, and the genuine loathing underneath. The sketch works as satire but also as a bit of nonsense, a delight in the incongruities of language for their own sake.

Within a more conventionally dramatic framework, such as the thirty-minute plays in her 1989 BBC series, Wood treats the figures of power in much the same fashion, a sharp accuracy placing them in a few lines. 'You don't talk to Philippinos', remarks a well-heeled friend at a party, 'you hand them your used cutlery.'[4] The remark is made to 'Victoria Wood'. In the whole series, Wood appears as 'herself' – shy, spiky, sympathetic, a little overweight, on the side of the underdog and easily roused to flights of irony. It's identical to the persona she uses in the standup routines that open her sketch-based shows. She chats to us confidently, about her past, about her adventures on the way to the theatre, but the jokes are habitually against herself and her entrance and exit are always rapid, as if she doesn't want to outstay her welcome. Her clothes are colourful but concealing, with big pockets into which she can thrust her hands; invariably she wears trousers. The effect is not so much masculine as tomboyish, playful. The stress is not on glamour but on her 'ordinariness'; she has no formal power and does not care for it; she is content as an observer; she will even cast herself as victim, although we are invited not so much to laugh at her as to share her experience and laugh with her at the power figures. There are shop assistants who carry to a natural conclusion both the pressures of the fashion industry on female body shape and their understandable loathing of the job. 'I don't think we're actually supposed to serve people – just shoot them if they do something suspicious', remarks a snooty girl to Wood as customer, adding, 'We don't usually let obese people in the cubicles in case they sweat on the wallpaper.'[5] The incongruity lies not in the fact salespeople are supposed to behave as if the customer is always right, but in the fact that they are speaking aloud a subtext we all recognise: insecurity of a customer feeling her own body image threatened by her posh surroundings, versus resentment of a harrassed worker who can't afford the goods.

But there is yet another kind of Wood character: 'ordinary' like Wood herself in the sense of lacking formal power but with enormous individuality. Her typical activities are boringly normal: waiting for buses, shopping, organising her local dramatic society, serving in a shop. She talks about furniture or food or the neighbours. And yet it is clear that she is barely contained by the ordinary, that the tissue of trivia making up her day is always on the verge of being shattered. This is, perhaps, what gives Wood's characters their vitality. They are not so much caricatures as portraits drawn in sharp bold strokes. It is not necessary to like someone who introduces herself 'Good evening. My name's Kitty. I've had a boob off and I can't stomach whelks, so that's me for you.'[6] On the other hand it is difficult to patronise her or treat her as a figure of fun to whom we can feel superior. Kitty inhabits a world in which things predominate but in which ideas are never quite crushed out of sight:

> 'I don't know why I've been asked to interrupt your viewing like this, but I'm apparently something of a celebrity since I walked the Pennine Way in slingbacks in an attempt to publicise Mental Health. They've asked me to talk about aspects of life in general, nuclear war, peg-bags . . .'

Wood's language sounds like parody, but it's not. The incongruity of jamming together nuclear war and peg-bags does not work only on the surface. The real incongruity is that this is how we see life, through a haze of trivia, and especially a haze of consumer goods, and that television in particular encourages us to do so. The comedy lies in the condensation of life into the space of a few lines, much as Oscar Wilde condensed sexual passion, jealousy and desire into a scene with some muffins. The muffins, in the end, are as important as the issues to the characters, because they have to go on living in the world, no matter what happens. And Kitty will go on. The fact that she can jam so much energy into a quick chat, leaping from topic to topic, indicates the vitality that enables her to do so.

Wood's 'ordinary' characters are not 'eccentric', and this differentiates them from most of the characters used by male comedians in sketches. Like their counterparts in sitcom, they are often at odds with society. But women like Kitty, or the self-assured Kelly Louise Tunstall ('I said I'll have a pint of Babycham, some pork scratchings and if I'm not here when you get back I'll be in 't toilet putting Hide and Heal on me love bites') are centred, at peace with themselves and their world. If we find them funny, it's our privilege.

French and Saunders, like Wood, trained in drama, and like Wood have worked over a wide range: in standup, in which they debuted at the Comic Strip in 1980; in the Channel Four films involving the Comic Strip team, one-offs that allowed them to play a wide range of characters from Blyton's Famous Five to Saunder's creation of Meryl Streep in *Strike!*, a Hollywood version of the miners' strike; and in *Girls on Top*. As with Wood, their show *French and Saunders* (BBC2, 1987, 1988 and 1990) has benefited from this breadth of experience. Firstly, they have been able to acquire a high degree of control over their material: Saunders recalled that many of the Comic Strip film producers were women, and that they were willing for them not just to write and act but to help direct and edit, to discuss lighting. Second, and associated with this, is the basis of the show in drama as well as standup; their sketches pay the kind of attention to detail more often found in full-length plays. A running gag in one show had them disguised as two old men, leering over Page Three ('You know who wants to ban it, don't you – only queers and Lebanons'), avowing that their favourite TV presenters were 'begging for it', and slumping over the Royal Christmas broadcast with a pint that dribbled on to beer guts wobbling with unfulfilled desire. The makeup for the sketch took about four hours and was elaborate and precise. The effect was to distance it from the standard Dirty Old Man sketch in the programmes like *The Benny Hill Show*, in which the man is constructed as anarchic-but-endearing as he charges after a mock-terrified beauty. Instead it allowed French and Saunders to explore and ridicule the assumption that a woman's 'no' really means 'yes'. But it also distanced the sketch from the quickie impression of a pestering male that might appear fleetingly in a female standup set. It allowed time, not just for mocking laughter at the characters, but for shared pleasure as the performers sustained and enjoyed their outrageous transformation. The more barbed the parody, the more entertainingly inventive it became, as the dreams of the gross pair moved ever further from reality – 'Queen or no queen – she's got a woman's needs.'[7]

This concern with detail means that many French and Saunders sketches come close to dramatic form; rather than driving relentlessly towards a simple punchline they make telling incidental points that locate the comedy in the real world rather than that of light entertainment. One sketch, for instance, shows two chambermaids seizing the chance to use the hotel facilities. It's a comic idea that has been used to make a single point – perhaps a rather reactionary joke about servants and their 'betters'. French and Saunders expand it into a small comic play about power. The chambermaids fix with a steely glare a guest who doesn't want them to clean her room, and her reply that it's only eight o'clock cuts no ice: they snap that it helps if the guests are PROMPT. When they finally get into a room, they order breakfast, try on the guest's lipstick and play with her Polaroid camera; at the same time they clean with resentful efficiency – Saunders vigorously cleaning the toilet and then applying the same cloth to the bath with equal energy. It borders on caricature, and yet the genuine pleasure on their faces as they settle on the bed to watch *Neighbours* conveys a real sense of a hard life drudging in the service of the better-off.

Much of their material is about power. Both trained teachers, they have a devilishly accurate sense of the way in which children can undermine the morale of their staff by manipulating the liberal clichés –

'You don't just demand respect, miss, you earn it.' In an extended schoolgirl sketch the teenage brats are comically wise to this, reproaching the teacher who complains about their white stilettos with 'My parents can't afford new hiking boots, miss', sneaking fags and displaying a crudely drawn picture of breasts as 'a glacial valley'. But when they chat in a service station about their future and plan a job dancing on a cruise ship where you earn 'Almost two and a half thousand a year', it's hard simply to laugh at them.

This precision in terms of power play is counterpointed by the dynamics of their standup material. 'French and Saunders' are, more clearly than most double acts in the mainstream, a comic construct; they do not pretend to be their 'real selves'. While many double acts work with the structure 'top dog and underdog', most have moments of sentiment, as if spontaneously allowing 'real' and affectionate 'selves' to have their momentary say. Even now, the old variety trick of top dog and underdog uniting in a sentimental song like 'You Are the Wind Beneath My Wings' or 'Side by Side' remains a staple ending. With French and Saunders, affection never breaks through. In a *Radio Times* interview about the 1987 series, Saunders clearly separated her identity from the onstage persona. 'I *play* Jennifer Saunders, the person who has got all the money together to make the show. She loves the entertainment and variety world. She's a bit of a failed entertainer really . . . a horrible woman.'[8] 'Saunders' has Saunders' cool, remote beauty to which is added a dimension of spoiled arrogance and total stupidity. She bullies 'French' mercilessly. 'French', however, is belligerent rather than downtrodden, obedient only in the most irritating fashion. While Saunders lounges on a settee ('The bones in my legs have disappeared'), too lazy to answer the door, French dynamites it down and enters in Burger Girl gear. 'Have you brought the hamburgers?' sneers Saunders. 'I didn't want to, Jennifer', pouts French, 'I had to.' The 1987 series set the relationship in a fictional context: the premise was that Saunders ran a tacky show and, like many a cheap firm, had got French on a YOPS scheme. When Saunders' attempts to run the show ended in disaster – she failed as an acrobat, an escapologist, and a host – French would take over, once locking Saunders in a toilet in order to finish. While the carefully tacky format – elderly dancers, cheap costumes, naff band – could come close to making it a one-joke show, it did serve to underline the fictional nature of 'French and Saunders'. This in turn added an extra punch to the sketches; in most of these the power relationships were quite different. The two of them, especially in the schoolgirl act, were often aggressors together. This added to the sense of the sketch as a self-contained entity, and kept the audience aware that it was making its own point, rather than simply acting as a further demonstration of double act conventions.

Like other double acts, French and Saunders made use of parody; they drew extensively on TV documentary and cinema. Their parodies were, however, often more barbed than those by performers like Morecambe and Wise: while these got their laughs from placing the act in an unlikely context, French and Saunders concentrated on absurdities in the traditions of TV and cinema normally disguised by gloss. Sometimes these were funny by virtue of the sheer accuracy of observation. There is a parody of *Gone With The Wind* in which Saunders, as Scarlett, puts on her dress for the picnic; like Vivien Leigh, she throws it on anyhow, and like Vivien Leigh's dress in the movie, its complicated frills fall perfectly into shape. But Saunders clearly isn't Vivien Leigh; she's an ordinary woman, not a star shot behind a filter, and her ordinariness makes us realise just how many takes that spontaneous tumble of frills really needed. A resentful French plays Mammy, loaded with pinnies and petticoats but making no attempt to look black. Her evident dislike of the part underlines the racism of the film without further comment. The 'ordinariness' of this parody is typical of their approach. Often a film parody sets up the contrast between a comic personality and a glamorous or heroic part: Eric Morecambe as Mark Antony, complete with his glasses and an occasional, irrepressible cry of 'Arsenal!', is the classic of the genre. The laughter it invites is purely benevolent. French and Saunders, however, sink themselves into the parts with apparent seriousness; the incongruity springs not from their unfitness for their roles but from the unreality of those roles. Their comedy is often physical, but we are not invited to laugh at their bodies – rather at the ludicrous expectations of show business glamour. So, for example, they do a ballet routine in which they earnestly chirrup 'I do feel naughty' while nibbling a single raisin, and lecture the camera about the relentless discipline of the dance, while their bodies look totally out of place among the greyhound-sleek dancers who surround them. It is clear, however, that they are ordinary bodies, not grotesque, and that their shape is not being mocked. French, who is quite a large woman, refuses to play 'fat parts'. When they do their version of 'A Girl's Best Friend' dolled up to look like Marilyn Monroe and Jane Russell, they look attractive and almost convincing; when they turn round and waggle bunny-rabbit scuts attached to their sequined rumps, it's the film that seems ludicrous: the idea of grown women acting the Bunnygirl becomes absurd when defamiliarised by putting the scut on the body of a normal human being rather than a model carved into shape by Hugh Heffner's plastic surgeons.

Both Victoria Wood and French and Saunders use material that is familiar, even conventional, and they rarely find themselves in dispute with television companies; to some degree, of course, this is owing to self-censorship, and there is little on their shows as overtly radical as the material common in comedy clubs. However, this should not disguise the fact that they are innovative within this form: they have taken over TV formulae and transformed them. In their work – and latterly in that of Emma Thompson and Josie Lawrence, who have not yet been given second chances by the networks – it has been possible to see subjects male comics have avoided. Body images have been challenged; 'take my wife' jokes have been replaced by routines that acknowledge the real stresses of housework (I think especially of Saunders as an increasingly manic hostess and Thompson crouching in despair in an enormous frying pan as she recalls the domestic disasters of the week). There are sketches and songs that assert female sexuality – Victoria Wood's ballad of Barry and Freda closes with her cry 'Beat me on the bottom with a Woman's Weekly'. While they may avoid sustained and direct political comment, they have provided visible, popular assertions that women are not objects of humour but the makers of it; and by their refusal to fall into physical stereotypes of Brainless Beauty or Mean-Mouthed Dragon they have made it clear that female comedians work on their own terms, not those of patriarchy.

One woman, many faces

'Ruth Draper are now at the height of their career', wrote Kenneth Tynan in 1952.[9] Draper died in 1956. She never called herself a comedian. She has, however, a claim to be called the founder of a durable comic tradition among women, and her name is cited by many exponents of the comic form in which women are arguably pre-eminent, the one-person show. Draper was born in 1884: she was thus a contemporary of Marie Lloyd in Music Hall, Sophie Tucker in Vaudeville, and Moms Mabley at the Apollo, but as a New York aristocrat a career like theirs would have been impossible for her; for half her life she did not even contemplate working in the legitimate theatre. She did, however, cherish an ambition to write, and performed monologues to entertain her friends. It was Henry James who – rather patronisingly – urged her to turn professional, and her theatrical career was far more successful than his. She wrote, staged and performed characters she knew – the gushing society hostess, the intellectual snob reading Dante with a thick New York accent, the exotic foreign actress throwing a tantrum in furious pseudo-Slavic gibberish – and drew capacity crowds in locations from Fiji to Mussolini's palace. Lily Tomlin describes her art thus: 'She did women and she did them with humanity.'[10]

Draper was fortunate in that the only form convention opened to her was the best vehicle for her talent. Other women have valued it as the only way of 'doing women with humanity', in that it offers them total control – of the text, of their performance, and of the way that their sex is understood by the audience. It offers a rare opportunity to engage with the audience over a sustained period – and to vary the terms of that engagement. Often it occupies a territory midway between standup and drama. Liz Lochhead's poetry readings, for instance, are part storytelling, part monologue, sometimes in character, sometimes wryly standing outside the action. Miriam Margolyes presents *Dickens' Women* – characters who in a conventional dramatisation might be 'cameo roles'; here they allow her to flesh them out, not simply as a way of demonstrating her versatility, but to give her control over the audiences' laughter as she moves from comic object to sharing her satirical insight into their author. Claire Dowie in *Adult Child, Dead Child* explores the pain of adolescent breakdown: the story is not comic, but she preserves the conventions of standup, sometimes moving out of character to talk with the audience, making no attempt to change her own appearance. This sense of frontiers being pushed back, boundaries eroded, is one of the features that makes the form so exciting for women. Another, equally important, is the sheer breadth of vision it makes possible; it is a chance for a woman to bring onstage a whole society, and to express her own view of it.

Joyce Grenfell, a friend of Draper's, was the first to translate her art into specifically comic terms. She ranged over what might be called a whole parish of characters: children and old women, countesses and cleaners, rich American tourists and dim young debutantes. Her presentation reflected her own upper-middle-class Englishness: she wore formal evening dress, to which she added the odd prop or scarf, and behaved to the audience like a party hostess, both gracious and charming but with a steely eye for bad manners. Clive James recalls a performance in Australia at which her treatment of a chocolate-crunching audience had the authority of a tough comic in a rowdy club:

Joyce advanced regally to the footlights and told the audience that if the eating of the chocolates could be delayed until the end of the performance it might be possible to enjoy both her and them, but if the chocolates had to be eaten now then she would be obliged to withdraw. The audience sat stunned, a freshly unwrapped strawberry cream half-way between lap and gaping mouth.[11]

This particular kind of audience control was possible because it was wholly consistent with the style of the show itself. Good manners were, in a sense, the subject as well as the condition of performance, and it's important to bear this in mind. Grenfell invites laughter at the way people use language: a bouncy woman in her forties galumphs round her school reunion dinner introducing herself as 'Lumpy Latimer', in ringing tones cultivated on the hockey field and as unchanged by time as her intellect; a lady strangulates her provincial vowels to elocutionary daintiness as she holds forth on flower arranging: 'Now, when you are making beech-nut husk flowers do not confine yourself to *boutonnieres*. Be *bold* about it! You can make great sprays of lupes, or delphs';[12] an old countrywoman sucks her teeth and ponders a new concept after a lecture at the Women's Institute 'On hormones . . . Well, they're not very nice, hormones. But did you know we was all supposed to have them?'[13] She has sometimes been labelled as patronising in her treatment of working-class women. It may well be true that her ear for regional speech is less sharp than for the oddities of the pretentious and the social climber. Grenfell learned her craft in revue during the nineteen forties and fifties; for much of this period the English stage was riddled with class prejudice; to be eligible at all for dramatic treatment it was essential to have a private income and a house with a tennis court; all other characters were functionaries showing the detective into the library and mouthing a crude *patois* laced with phrases like 'Beggin' yer pardon, mum.' But Grenfell gave these figures real dramatic space, and the dignity of her demeanour precluded the assumption that they were automatically figures of fun. She created a territory on which all her 'parish' could meet, that of good manners. We never meet her characters at times of major crisis; issues of class or sexual politics are never foregrounded. But we do meet them at moments of relaxation, at parties and jumble sales and over cups of tea – at moments when good and evil are not at stake, but when small social dilemmas arise. A lady gulps in mid-hymn as she realises that she has left the gas on under the soup and sings of the disasters that may befall; the more pious her intonation, the greater the dawning panic in her eyes. 'A Terrible Worrier' is at first terrified that she may have won a cruise in the church raffle – where would she put her dentures on an ocean liner? Then she has a more concrete problem – what can she do with the very dead rabbit she *has* won? And when she finds her answer – she dumps it in a parked car – she wonders if she's liable to prosecution. This shared anxiety over trivia unites her characters of all classes, and it makes them comic; but it's also a genuine concern to do the right thing, to show good manners, and this demands our respect. At times, a character with a satirical manner will spell this out. 'Do lie down if that's how you fell', coos the Vice Chancellor's wife to a young anarchist, 'but could you perhaps keep your feet off that little cushion? . . . Oh, did your cigarette quite make the fireplace?' And, occasionally, the very absence of malice in a speaker forces us to feel the indignation she – and her imaginary interviewer – does not: 'It is a nice little room', agrees a toothless old lady in her bedsit. 'I've got the use of a cold tap halfway down the stairs and the other thing is just down the bottom of the stairs and across the yard. Yes, it is, very convenient.'[14]

A contemporary of Grenfell's, Athene Seyler, was one of the few women to discuss the process of comic performance in print, and defined it as 'inextricably bound up with kindliness'.[15] This sums up the good manners at the heart of Grenfell's work. 'Kindliness' allows each of her characters to express themselves. It does not permit the audience to concentrate on their social situation, even when it is painful, and thus precludes judgement; it is not a laughter that will prompt change. But it does celebrate women who have rarely been permitted centre stage, and invites affection for figures which the drama of the time too often reduced to stereotypes.

Grenfell's 'parish' came together from individual monologues featured in revues and radio programmes and private entertainments, and the strength of her own show derived from its resemblance to a social event at which characters and audience mingled freely – a garden party, perhaps, or a church fête; it was certainly, in the fragmented and complex England of the post-war period, an anachronistic event, and there was an element of nostalgia at a Grenfell evening, as well as laughter. As she sang in 1965:

> I wouldn't go back to the world I knew
> It was selfish, small and tame
> It had to go – the world I knew
> But it was fun then, just the same![16]

For Lily Tomlin in the late seventies and eighties, the one-woman show was a more consciously crafted overview of American society, the logical conclusion of earlier struggles to keep control over her own work. She came to prominence as the eccentric telephonist Ernestine on *Rowan and Martin's Laugh-In* in 1969; her success, however, led to disputes about the nature of her material and she eventually sued for sole rights over characters she felt were being cheapened and exploited. With her writer Jane Wagner she developed two shows, *Appearing Nitely* in 1977 and *The Search For Signs of Intelligent Life in the Universe* in 1985. The latter went into print and became the first play in twenty years to reach the best-seller list.

In *Search* a bored hairdresser remarks

> I get sick of being the victim
> of trends I reflect
> but don't even understand.[17]

This mixture of wisdom and naiveté is crucial to Tomlin's relationship with the audience. *Search* focuses on the experience of being an individual in a society which exalts the individual and the development of individual potential. The characters, like many of Tomlin's audience, are highly conscious of the fact and many are attempting to work with the process, to expand their own possibilities. Some are actively involved with aspects of the Human Potential Movement – ESP, transcendental meditation and the alternative therapies; others are involved in the Women's Movement; others have small, highly specific goals: Edith Beesley wanted an orgasm, discovered vibrators, and promotes them with all the energy she once reserved for Tupperware. All, in different ways, are trying to shape themselves, and all are being shaped by the social forces around them, forces varying in power from fashion trends to the increasing materialism of the Reagan years. Tomlin imparts to them all the slight puzzlement of someone not quite in control, like the pantomime character who can't understand the audience's yell of 'She's right behind you!' This comedy of bewilderment is enhanced by the consistent presence of Tomlin; although she makes extensive use of lighting and music, characterisation is achieved through her facial and physical mobility; we are aware of her *becoming* each figure in turn, and this underlines the extent to which they are largely constructed by language. One group of characters – active in the Women's Movement for years – makes this plain. In the seventies we find them preoccupied with images of the female body:

Edie is becoming more radical by the minute, Marge. Today we had lunch at this restaurant. She had on a tank top, she leaned back, and I saw one armpit as smooth-shaven as a bathing-suit model, and in the other armpit, this *shock* of hair. I'm not sure *what* it meant politically, but it *did* have visual impact.[18]

Tomlin lets us enjoy the image and the extreme earnestness of the character, Lyn; she follows her into the world of psychotherapy, flotation tanks, whole food and the search for the New Man, with her marriage to 'The only man I've ever known who can remember where he was when Sylvia Plath died.'[19] It's sketched in with a light touch; Tomlin remains clearly aware of her audience and shares her enjoyment of this surface trivia, rather as if she were inviting us to look at an old photograph album with pictures of ourselves in dated clothes. At the same time, however, her portrayal of the later career of her feminist characters calls for a more complex response. Lyn's marriage to the New Man, who in the eighties aspires to be a 'holistic capitalist', runs into trouble; Tomlin portrays her naturalistically as careworn and exhausted, but also as seriously self-deluded by the new economics:

We import ethnic clothing, mostly from South America. And no, don't say it; I don't think we're exploiting cheap labour, so much as I think we're giving work to people who would be out of work – if we weren't exploiting cheap labour.[20]

Marge, one of the most energetic figures of the little group, is raped; she tells us with bitter irony that the thief stole her rape alarm whistle. Later she will hang herself in a macramé plant holder. It is comically incongruous that these symbols of the alternative culture feature in a violent episode; it is not a dignified death, yet this does not diminish the fact that society has failed Marge, failed to protect her from a violence that, with all her absurdities, she was committed to ending. It has colluded with her when she ceases to value herself.

Tomlin's working style functions particularly well with these characters so consciously constructing themselves. While a work is gestating, she and Wagner tour for a long period; Tomlin in performance moves in and out of character, explaining to the audience what changes she and Wagner might make in the script, asking for feedback. Her audience clearly feel that some characters are their property: she was expected to discuss at some length, for instance, the changes Edith Beesley had undergone since her Tupperware parties in *Appearing Nitely*, and pointed out that while Edith may be a prude, she might well end up peddling

vibrators out of a sense of civic duty: 'She would never suppress information', she remarked to one Edith fan. This sense of shared creativity
between performer and audience, of shared language and shared sympathies, is symbolised by Tomlin's own 'presence' in the show. Although
we never lose sight of Tomlin behind the characters, she is not the
mistress of ceremonies *in propria persona*. The story-teller, or chorus
figure, is a bag lady named Trudy. Trudy has had electro-shock treat-
ments and now claims to be in touch with aliens who are seeking other
life forms. Tomlin plays her with a jutting jaw, an expression of intense
pugnacity and a suggestion of great physical strength. Trudy presents the
other characters to us – including a dark-haired comedian, Tomlin herself, who will eventually entertain Trudy and the aliens (though the
aliens prefer to look at the audience). Trudy is the only character who
knows she is a comic figure. She rejoices in her funny walk, her hat that
doubles as umbrella and satellite dish; they represent the fact that she has
chosen to see life as a comedian sees it. She has formerly placed her
understanding of language at the service of consumerism in her life as a
'creative consultant' – 'Who do you think had the idea to package panty
hose in a plastic goose egg?'; her commitment is now to eccentricity,
after her own road to Damascus:

> I said, 'Mr Nabisco, sir! You could be the first to sell the concept of munching
> to the Third World. We got an untapped market here! These countries got
> millions and millions of people don't even know where their next meal is
> coming from. So the idea of eatin' between meals is somethin' just never
> occurred to 'em!
> I heard myself sayin' this!
> Must've been when I went off the deep end.[21]

Trudy has taken for herself the wise-fool role normally given to a man.
She is fully aware of her own roots in comic and literary tradition and
articulates ideas usually left beneath the surface in comic dialogue:
continually, she struggles to explain to the aliens what 'art' is, a difficult
task when confronted by a can of soup and an Andy Warhol can of soup:
'This is soup, and this is art.' It is this self-awareness that makes us trust
Trudy, and helps us to perceive the central paradox of the show: that all
these characters, filtered through a single actress, all desperate to define
themselves as individuals, are in fact profoundly interconnected. A vain
man in a locker-room whinges that his pregnant wife fails to appreciate
his honesty in telling her about his casual pick-ups; but he also fantasises
about the possibility of a 'secret kid' from an encounter with a lesbian

longing for motherhood. Later, some casual talk among the women's consciousness raising group reveals that the 'kid' is alive and the embodiment of his father's dreams, but he will never know this. A teenage punk, Agnus Angst, leaves her family in a comic, cathartic rage, that nevertheless reveals a real concern for social justice; by the end of the show we learn that she is lost, a tragic statistic in the city she has judged with teenage self-righteousness. The bored lady who feels herself a trend victim meets Trudy. At the end, she is wearing the umbrella hat.

Tomlin wanted to change the parameters of standup. 'The comic who stands up there telling mother-in-law jokes is being himself. . . . I'd rather be the mother-in-law.'[22] This does more than assert the female perspective over the male: it also stresses the fact that man and mother-in-law are inextricably connected. This is not to sentimentalise her characters, but to redefine the idea of individualism that drives them all. There is little direct political comment. Statements like Edie's barbed joke about Kissinger's definition of power as aphrodisiac – 'The bombing in Vietnam shows what it takes for him to get it up'[23] – are part of the language patterns of the more politically conscious characters rather than original insights. But we are implicitly asked to recognise that materialism is not an integral part of the development of self. The wealthier characters become burdened with things – leaky flotation tanks, Batacas, the works of Gordon Liddy – that turn them into style victims, while the poorer ones struggle against the material world to change themselves: a prostitute funds her friend to become a hairdresser; the bored lady he shampoos has a long way to go before she realises that he too has a story. The implicit pulling-apart of capitalism and the idea of the self makes *Search* as a whole far more subversive than its individual jokes suggest.

For Whoopi Goldberg the issue of control over her material is as central as for Tomlin. As a stage actress she complained of 'people in dinner theatres saying "We can't put you and a white guy together, because the folks from Texas can't handle it."'[24] In Hollywood her only major film success was in *The Color Purple*, which had an all-black cast. Subsequent movies have cast her as the lone black character and then treated her relationships within the plot with a queasy racism. *Fatal Beauty*, for instance, had a romantic subplot to its detective interest which was originally designed for Cher. When Goldberg took over the part, some vicious cutting resulted. Her bedroom scene with the white actor Sam Elliot was deleted, making nonsense of the rest of the story, and Goldberg vented her anger publicly, telling *Jet* magazine 'If Sam

Elliot had put some money on the table after the lovemaking scene it would still have been there.'[25] It is in her standup, in particular what she called her 'Spook Show', that Goldberg is able to articulate black experience and to show her own comic range. The show has a harder edge than *Search*. The characters inspire affection but they also move us to anger on their behalf, an anger they never express – because they have their dreams intact, because they are busy getting on with their lives, or because they can't be bothered. A little girl tells us that she has decided to be white; it's funny when she dresses up, covering her cornrows with a white sheet which she flaunts as 'long, luxurious blonde hair' – but it's a bitter fact that a world of white power will not help her to see her own beauty. We laugh at her dreams, because they are childish. She wants to appear on *Love Boat* and live with Barbie and Ken in a 'dream house'. But there is a second and more angry dimension to this laughter, because we realise that her desires are constructed by a social system that also precludes their fulfilment.

Many of her 'spooks' are comic precisely because they are constructs, mouthing sentiments foisted on them in a style dictated by the media; but Goldberg never permits us a simple laughter. 'Surfer Chick', for instance, is a deadly accurate parody of a mall-cruising airhead: she flutters her hands and preens her hair and lards her conversation with pseudo-profundities culled from New Age fads – 'Like, before there was the mall there was the Ocean, right?' It's the more comic because it contrasts with sexual and social ignorance. But Goldberg is in control of this laughter. As the girl describes her attempts to come to terms with her pregnancy in the same Valley-girl jargon, we are aware that her absorption in the tacky Californian culture is both a source of strength and a crippling limitation. She is bouncy, not defeated, when she describes how her mother threw her out of the house, and when her church does not want to listen to her. ('She said "Blasphemer!" I said, "No, surfer"'.) The audience is beginning to acquire respect for this survivor, and to laugh with her rather than at her. Then the laughter is stopped. The girl describes her attempt to abort herself with a coat hanger, and the failure which wrecks her reproductive system for good. But she is still an optimist: 'I really love my life, you know, so much I really wanna do, you know, I mean I'm turnin' fourteen next week, I mean if you're on the beach, I mean if you come by the sea wall, look me up.'[26] Traditionally comedy finds a lack of self-knowledge a source of laughter, tragedy sees it as the instrument which brings about a character's downfall. Here the clichés are a survival tool: she can convince herself that she is happy. But they also move us to anger, at a culture that exploits sexuality and youth and offers her so little.

Like Tomlin, Goldberg makes use of one character who has the intelligence to articulate his experience for himself, the junkie, Fontaine. But while Trudy has stepped out of the rat race, Fontaine has never been admitted to it. 'I weren't always a joke', he assures us after a shambling entrance, 'I got a PhD I can't do shit with – so I stay high so I don't get mad.' He lopes through the audience, singing tunelessly, and patronisingly remarks to one well-heeled lady 'I'm glad you cool enough not to clutch your pocket-book.' Through Fontaine the audience confronts its own preconceptions, and finds them comic. Fontaine moves from making us find white prejudice comic, to observational comedy grounded in shared experience: he talks about day-to-day trivia, hassles with airlines, and the peculiar horrors of airline food, throwing in an impression of a badly cooked string bean on an in-flight meal. He goes on to exploit the unity he has achieved with the audience: he invites laughter as he lands in Europe and reveals his ignorance of its culture – but his audience, too, are aware of lacking the information he gives them, and it's America's relationship with Europe rather than Fontaine that is the focus of laughter. His cultural innocence allows him to throw his own experience into a new light: he links the sufferings of the Jews with that of black Americans, but he is also aware that there *is* a difference. For him, he explains, 'going into hiding' means that all your friends know where you are; for Anne Frank it was not like that. Beside her suffering, his own ('Like why can't I get an American Express Card?') is ludicrous; but while we laugh at the incongruity of this instance, we are aware that his experience has been genuinely painful. This is underlined when the laughter dies. Fontaine finds himself alone in the Anne Frank House, reading the inscription over the door which is taken from Anne's diary, her affirmation that despite all she has seen she knows that 'People are really good at heart'. Only a child could say that, Fontaine tells us, and this accounts for the fact that 'I'm in that room crying.'

He, and the scene, are no longer funny. Goldberg has taken to herself the right, not simply to perform her own comedy, but the right traditionally denied women, to decide what is funny; by definition she must also define what is not. Through moments like this comes a heartening sense not just of specific achievements by one woman, but of the female reconstruction of humour that is gaining momentum.

Snapshots, 1987–92: not really a conclusion

I

I am walking by the Thames with a clown. It has taken a great deal of effort to find her. Having turned up at the clown Mecca, the annual Clown Convention at Bognor Regis, I find very few women behind the red noses. Finally, with the help of the Tourist Board, I track down a bare half-dozen, several of whom work as 'straights' to a male clown. Fizzie Lizzie, however, is the real thing, and can make my son laugh even today when she's in mufti. Lizzie is knowledgeable about her trade, she's writing a thesis. The knowledge seems to ground her: despite the over-poweringly male presence in the clown world, she has tapped in to a piece of women's history lost to most of us. She describes female clowns in pictures by Toulouse-Lautrec. I look them up, afterwards, and find figures at once grotesque and wrapped in a disturbing haze of sexual ambivalence. Lizzie sees her own clown as a mischief-maker, an anarchist, and the possessor of skills – juggling, unicycling; she's happy to make a fool of herself, feels it's untrue that women cannot or will not do this, but she also feels strongly that 'you've got to have somewhere to come down from' – that no clown, least of all a female one, should be a comic victim. Like several female clowns I talked to, she likes the sense of power, what she calls the 'watch me' element, the sense of dominating the party or the ring or the stage. The makeup is a liberation: she can do things behind the greasepaint she wouldn't do barefaced – it makes her feel 'protected'.

Nevertheless, she shares with several other women clowns I have talked to an attitude to her makeup I have not heard men express: she is eager to de-mystify herself. When entertaining children she puts on her makeup in full view; for many of them, the whiteface is frightening, but 'they've all seen mum doing her face'. Women clowns have, she feels, a special kind of accessibility, and she has sometimes invited children into the act. This is not, she stresses, an easy or sentimental option. Clowns who work in the sad-faced-victim mode can bring out a cruel streak in the audience, a desire to destroy the act, 'like sparrows will peck a budgerigar to death'. It needs an authoritative persona. The brew that might result from this mixture of tradition and accessibility seems to me a heady one: anarchy and honesty; respect for the feelings of an audience and an energy to create change; 'playing yourself', rather than selfishly hugging the power of your mask, but claiming nonetheless the magic of transformation. Clowns, Lizzie says, pass on their skills through the family line, but they can also act as mentors. I would like to see what happens if female clowns begin networking. I would have liked to find a movement strong enough for a whole chapter. 'I want', says Lizzie of her act, 'not so much to make people laugh as to change the situation, to cause laughter to happen.'

II

'A true joke, a comedian's joke, has to do more than release tension, it has to liberate the will and the desire, it has to *change the situation*.'[1]

Lizzie's words find an echo in Trevor Griffith's play, *Comedians*. I am watching a performance at the Liverpool Everyman, twelve years after it debuted in 1975. All the comedians in the originally all-male play about aspiring club comics at an evening class, preparing and performing their first engagement, are now played by women, and Griffiths has reworked it with material provided by the performers, themselves professional comics: Jenny Lecoat, Pauline Daniels, Eileen Pollock, Lynda Rooke, and Christine Moore.

For me this occasion crystallises much of my thinking about both comedy and feminism. As I talk to the director, Kate Rowland, it is clear that this is an important play for both of us, for what it says and also for what it fails to say. Kate rightly describes it as 'classic . . . beautifully constructed'. The fierce clarity with which Griffiths presents comedy as ideological battlefield has rarely been surpassed. The original text draws clear lines: on one side, the saleable comedy of sexual and racial disparagement, symbolised by the agent, Challenor; on the other, comedy as a force for social change. But this latter camp houses a powerful internal struggle. Eddie Waters, once a major comic on the northern circuit, preaches a carnivalesque humanism. He makes his students ground their acts in observation, detail, experience; when these are present destructive stereotypes cannot exist, the audience can confront its own fears and desires, and heal itself through laughter. Some of Eddie's pupils hold to this ideal; others sell out and produce Challenor's commercial poison. But Eddie is also engaged in ideological and Oedipal struggle with his prize pupil, Gethin Price. Gethin makes his own act, a surreal whiteface performance, part skinhead, part clown, an overt expression of class anger which culminates in an address to two dummies in immaculate evening dress. He pins a flower on the woman dummy's breast, and blood oozes out. In the aftermath Eddie accuses Gethin of 'drowning in hate': Gethin counters that Eddie has gone soft. 'Nobody hit harder than Eddie Waters. . . . Truth was a fist you hit with. Now it's like cowflop, a day old, hard till it's underfoot and then it's . . . green, soft. Shitten.'[2] Eddie's career ended when he saw Buchenwald in 1945. The laughter ended, not just because of the enormity of what had happened, but because 'I got an erection in that . . . place . . . something in me loved it, too.' Gethin has no time for this liberal–humanist pain. 'The Jews still stayed in line, even when they knew, Eddie! What's that about? I stand in no line. I refuse my consent.'[3]

John Bull writes, 'What is at stake is no longer a debate about rival theories of comedy but the conflict between reformism and revolution.'[4] I would agree with this, but as a feminist I find my interest lies precisely in the way that this displacement is not fully accomplished. It is on specifically comic territory that the question of sexuality is first raised. Gethin provocatively recites an obscene limerick, which Eddie deconstructs, pointing out that it is 'a joke that hates women'. Gethin later responds with a parody of this analysis, and we never actually hear him disown his limerick. Throughout the play, the comics closest to Challenor's position make overtly sexist jokes and those close to Eddie eschew them – but Gethin's enshrine some of the most violent sexual images of all. Griffiths never faces this fact within the text: while he implicitly degrades the figure of Eddie through the concentration camp story, his stage directions stress the 'perfection', 'effortlessness', the 'grace' of Gethin's art, so much so that Gethin seems to have captivated his creator as well as his teacher; the stabbing of the dummy may be a statement of class aggression but it is also an act of rape and this aspect of its 'perfection' is ignored. By doing so the play fails to face the question of the relationship between feminism and revolutionary socialism.

Kate Rowland's production went some way to filling that gap. The sexual shift complicated our relationship with all of the student comedians. The male performers who capitulated to Challenor were motivated by a desire for *more* than they have – money, fame, prestige, a better life; the women, as Kate put it, were driven by hunger: they wanted a voice, struggling to forge for themselves a confidence that even the well-to-do were denied in their lives. This in turn transformed the laughter: watching the original you had in many ways pre-judged the men and the jokes – your laughter was measured, unspontaneous. Listening to the women, you were sometimes caught on the hop by a racist or sexist gag, your response qualified by the joy in seeing a woman hold her own in a male world; you were moved by the failure even of those whose position you despised. The struggle between Gethin and Eddie, now Glenys and Ella, ceased to be an Oedipal battle for the moral high ground and became more complex: a mother confronted a daughter figure, rebellious, articulate, and with energies the older woman had lost – but still warped and distorted by sexist conditioning. Cheryl Maiker as Glenys had none of Gethin's sexual menace: when she pinned a flower to the male dummy, and he bled, it was a class gesture, an angry flower-girl killing a toff; her limerick was not a provocative gesture but an indication of a still limited understanding of the way she herself might be made an object through language. When Gethin walked off into an unknown future, it was clear he would fight, but he did not seem personally vulnerable; when Glenys rejected Ella's teaching she also threw over an understanding of sexual politics without which she seemed profoundly endangered, a woman offering heself to a cause that might itself misunderstand, exploit or betray her.

Ella retained a dignity that Eddie did not. This was partly due to Griffiths' understandable reluctance to attempt an equivalent of Eddie's description of his arousal in Belsen.There is still a debate to be had about the relationship between oppression and desire, and feminists – especially lesbian feminists – have been the first to attempt to structure it. The point at which laughter intersects with these relationships has not been investigated. The structure of Griffiths' play is a possible framework for such an investigation, and the Liverpool version offers it a valuable focus.

III

It is the evening after the General Election of 1992. Labour's defeat, though narrower than last time, has nonetheless been crushing. I go to a comedy club, Route 52. Tonight as usual the host is Linda Smith, a comedian well known on the London circuit but based in Sheffield. She was a student here when it was known as the Socialist Republic of South Yorkshire, and retains a commitment to popular entertainment in the area as organiser as well as comic.

The club is packed. Before the acts begin there is a buzz in the air: anger, disappointment. Everyone, clearly, is shattered by the news. And for many of them – me included – coming to the club is connected to it. A good time, tonight, has become not just desirable, but important, an act of defiance. The comedians' sets themselves touch lightly on what has happened; it seems too soon to come to terms with it. Linda's patter cheerfully takes for granted that the government are a walking disaster. ('The Monster Raving Loony Party did well, didn't they? Never thought they'd win'), sides wipes the Labour party as a bunch of overgrown schoolboys. She puts gut responses into words, tonight, rather than offering sharpness of insight. The evening's about comradeship, mostly.

The mixed audience seems to welcome the fact that a woman's in charge. Route 52 is a club which uses CIU premises; I've brought a friend, but can't sign her in because I count as a 'lady member'. I'm told that this situation will change, is being renegotiated, but tonight's rules set up an odd tension with the entertainment. Despite Linda Smith's evident control of the evening and the audience, we're on Challenor territory. The fact disturbs me. As this book has progressed, I have found it impossible to keep pace with the new female talent pouring into the market. Comics I went miles to see have brought out videos, women I watched in small tatty venues are filling the big spaces. The Liverpool Festival of Comedy, which first moved Kate Rowland to transform *Comedians*, is now run by a woman.

But women's hold is still precarious. Laughter is as fluid as any social force, and the right to control any mode of discourse can never be captured on a permanent basis. Women's major contribution to comic theory is, perhaps, to have stressed the importance of a laughter that does not stop, that works ceaselessly to steal the language, rebuild it and fly with it. The law ceaselessly re-establishes itself; but women have begun to suggest, to hope, that it can ceaselessly be blown up again with laughter. If that possibility is to be realized, we must maintain our presence on that bridge that marks the move from sorrow to joy.

Notes

Introduction: or, Why this book does not exist

1. Congreve, *A Letter to John Dennis Concerning Humour In Comedy*, 10 July 1695. Reproduced in John Hodges, *William Congreve: Letters and Documents* (Macmillan: 1964).
2. John Fisher, *Funny Way to Be a Hero* (Frederick Muller for Granada: 1973) p. 197.
3. Cited in Dyan Machin, *Forbes* magazine (November 1987).
4. *Bylines* (BBC1 31 Sept. 1989).
5. *The Stage* (14 Sept. 1989).
6. Tertullian, *De Culta Feminarum* (c. AD 225).
7. Cited Gilbert and C. Roche, *A Women's History of Sex* (Pandora: 1989) p. 143.
8. Quoted in Fidelis Morgan, *A Misogynist's Sourcebook* (Jonathan Cape: 1989) p. 126.
9. Translated by David Rosenberg, *The Book of J* (Faber & Faber: 1991) p. 71.
10. Reginald Blyth, *Humour in English Literature: A Chronological Anthology* (Folcroft: 1959) pp. 14–15. Also exhumed by Regina Barreca (see below). Two readers this decade is more than Blyth deserves.
11. See Jennifer Coates, *Women, Men and Language* (Longman: 1986) p. 103.
12. Liz Lochhead, *True Confessions* (Polygon: 1985) p. 134.
13. Lesley Ferris, *Acting Women* (Macmillan: 1990) p. 29.
14. Debbie Reynolds, *My Life* (Pan: 1989) p. 259.
15. Barbara Windsor, *Barbara* (Arrow: 1991) p. 70.
16. Interview with Richard Merryman, 3 August 1962. Printed in Carl E. Rollyson Jnr, *Marilyn Monroe: A life of the Actress* (UMI Research Press: 1986) p. 208.
17. Cited in Graham McCann, *Marilyn Monroe* (Rutgers University Press: 1988) p. 87.
18. Merryman interview, op. cit., p. 211.
19. Ferris, op. cit., p. 46.
20. Quoted in Barreca, *Last Laughs: Perspectives on Women and Comedy* (Gordon and Breach: 1988) p. 4. Her detailed reading of Priestley makes clear how powerful the 'small potatoes' technique can be.
21. Linda Woodbridge, *Women and the English Renaissance; Literature and the Nature of Womankind 1540–1620* (University of Illinois Press: 1984) p. 319.

22. Hélène Cixous, *The Newly Born Woman*, translated by Betsy Wing (Manchester University Press: 1986) p. 89.
23. See her interview in *Taxi* magazine July 1988.

Ch. 1: Theoretical perspectives

1. R. Barreca, *Last Laughs: Perspectives on Women and Comedy* (Gordon & Breach: 1988) p. 4.
2. Michael Godkewitsch, *The Relationship Between Arousal Potential and the Funniness of Jokes*, in J. Goldstein and P. McGhee, *The Psychology of Humour* (Academic Press: 1972) p. 150.
3. J. Suls, *Cognitive Process in Humor Appreciation*, in P. McGhee and J. Goldstein, (eds), *Handbook of Humor Research*, Vol. I (Springer-Verlag: 1983).
4. P. Chapman, J. Smith and H. Foot, *Humor, Laughter and Social Interaction*, in P. McGhee and A. Chapman (eds), *Children's Humor* (Wiley & Sons: 1980) p. 166 (my italics).
5. John Strickland, 'The Effect of Motivation Arousal on Humor Preferences', *Journal of Abnormal and Social Psychology*, Vol. 59, 1959, pp. 278–81.
6. R. Young and M. Frye, 'Some Are Laughing, Some Are Not – Why?', *Psychological Reports*, Vol. 18, 1966, pp. 747–54.
7. J. M. Davis and A. Farina, 'Humour Appreciation as Social Communication', *Journal of Personality and Social Psychology*, 15, 1970, pp. 175–8.
8. G. Wilson and A. H. Brazendale, 'Sexual Attractiveness and Response to Risque Humour', *European Journal of Social Psychology*, Vol. 3, 1973, p. 95.
9. G. Wilson and A. H. Brazendale, 'Vital Statistics: Perceived Sexual Attractiveness and Response to Risque Humour', *Journal of Social Psychology*, 95, 1975, pp. 201–5.
10. G. Wilson, *The Psychology of Performing Arts* (Croom Helm: 1985).
11. A. Chapman and C. Gadfield, 'Is Sexual Humour Sexist?', *Journal of Communication*, Summer 1976, pp. 141–53.
12. D. Zillman and J. Cantor, 'A Disposition Theory of Humour and Mirth', in A. Chapman (ed.), *Humour and Laughter: Theory, Research and Application* (Wiley, 1976) p. 167.
13. J. Cantor, 'What is Funny to Whom?', *Journal of Communication*, Summer 1975, p. 164–70.
14. Aristotle, *Poetics*, translated by T. S. Dorsch, *Classical Literary Criticism* (Penguin: 1965) p. 37.
15. Ibid., p. 51.
16. T. Hobbes, *On Human Nature*, in W. Molesworth (ed.), *The English Works of Thomas Hobbes*, Vol. IV (Bohn: 1840) p. 46.
17. A. Koestler, *Act of Creation* (Danube: 1960).
18. K. Lorenz, *On Aggression* (Bantam: 1967) p. 253.
19. See John Sweeney, 'Buttons Unbuttoned', *The Independent Magazine*, 17 Dec. 1988, p. 40.
20. Interview, *Open Door*, BBC2, 9 June 1990. As I have been writing this book a new style of comedy has come to prominence in the US, most

notably associated with 'The Dice Man' (Andrew Dice Clay), whose act is grounded in extreme racism, misogyny and homophobia. While his material makes Davidson and Manning look positively benign, it's a moot point whether their hypocrisy or his aggression is the more dangerous.

21. Ben Jonson, *Timber; or, Discoveries Made Upon Men and Matter*, in C. H. Hereford and P. and E. Simpson (eds), *Works*, Vol. VIII (QUP: 1947) p. 643.
22. Philip Sidney, *Apologie for Poetry*, in D. J. Enright and E. de Chickera *English Critical Texts* (OUP: 1962) p. 43.
23. Northrop Frye, *The Argument of Comedy* (English Institute Essays: 1949) p. 63.
24. Immanuel Kant, *Critique on Judgement*, translated by J. H. Bernard (Macmillan: 1914).
25. Herbert Spencer, *On the Physiology of Laughter: Essays on Education and Kindred Subjects* (Dent: 1911).
26. Sigmund Freud, *Jokes and their Relation to the Unconscious*, translated by Strachy (Penguin: 1976) p. 189.
27. Ibid., p. 141.
28. Ibid., p. 142.
29. Ibid., p. 176.
30. F. Cornford, *The Origin of Attic Comedy* (CUP: 1934) p. 3.
31. Ibid., p. 59.
32. Rosalind Miles, *The Woman's History of the World* (Paladin, 1990) p. 53.
33. M. Bakhtin, Introduction to *Rabelais and His World*, translated by H. Iwolsky (MIT Press: 1971) p. 9.
34. A. Koestler, op. cit., p. 40.
35. A. Schopenhauer, *The World as Will and Idea*, translated by R. B. Haldane and J. Kemp, Vol. II (RKP: 1886) p. 279.
36. S. A. Kierkegaard, *Concluding Unscientific Postscript*, in J. R, Morreall (ed.), *The Philosophy of Laughter and Humour* (State University of New York Press: 1986) p. 83.
37. M. Douglas, *Jokes, Implicit Meanings* (Routledge & Kegan Paul: 1975) p. 98.
38. A. Zijderveld, 'Jokes and their Relation to Social Reality', *Social Research*, Vol. 35, 1968, p. 302.
39. Sarah Daniels, *Masterpieces* (Methuen: 1984).
40. Estelle Philips, 'On Becoming A Mother-in-law', *Abstracts of the British Psychological Society*: 1991.
41. *Guardian*, 13 April 1991.
42. Norma J. Gravely, 'Sexist Humour As a Form of Social Control – or, Unfortunately – the Joke is Usually On Us', in R. Winegarten (ed.), *Selections on the Status of Women in American Society* (University of Texas Press: 1978).
43. Ibid.
44. Julia Kristeva, *About Chinese Women*, translated by H. Ranous (Boyars: 1977) p. 28–9.
45. Mary Daly, *Beyond God the Father* (Beacon Press: 1985) p. xxv.
46. Ibid.

47. Hélène Cixous, *The Laugh of the Medusa*, in E. Marks and T. de Courtivron (trs and eds), *New French Feminisms* (Harvester: 1981) p. 249.
48. Ibid., p. 249.
49. Ibid., p. 255.
50. Ibid., p. 258.

Ch. 2: Born in the USA: a story of money and angels

1. See Gaye Tuchman, 'The Symbolic Annihilation of Women by the Mass Media' in G. Tuchman, A. Daniels and J. Benet (eds), *Hearth and Home: Images of Women in the Mass Media* (OUP: 1978) pp. 11–13.
2. Quoted in M. Edmondson and D. Rounds, *From Mary Noble to Mary Hartman: the Complete Soap Opera Book* (Stein and Day: 1973) p. 33.
3. Bart Andrews, *The I Love Lucy Book* (Doubleday: 1973) p. 33. This quotation and subsequent citations of titles and transmission dates for *I Love Lucy* are taken from this book.
4. Todd Gitlin, *Inside Prime Time* (Pantheon: 1983) p. 72.
5. Ibid., pp. 73–4.
6. Erica Jong, *Parachutes and Kisses* (NAL: 1984) p. 17.
7. This process is entertainingly documented in Julie D'Acci, 'The Case of Cagney and Lacey', in H. Baehr and G. Dyer (eds), *Boxed in: Women and Television* (Pandora: 1987).
8. S. Bathrick, 'The Mary Tyler Moore Show: Women at Home and at Work', in J. Feuer, P. Kerr and T. Vahimagi (eds), *MTM: Quality Television*, (BFI: 1984) p. 99.
9. *Ricky's Life Story*, TX 5 Oct 1953.
10. Quoted in B. Friedan, *The Feminine Mystique* (Penguin: 1976) p. 53–4.
11. The Christian Broadcast Network is still running this; the most recent broadcast was on 22 December 1987 and I imagine it will not be the last.
12. Friedan, op. cit. chapter 1, *passim*.
13. *The Girls Want to Go to a Nightclub*, TX 15 Oct. 1951.
14. Bart Andrews, op. cit., p. 34.
15. Ibid., p. 128.
16. *LA At Last!* TX 7 Feb. 1955.
17. P. Mellencamp, 'Situation Comedy, Feminism and Freud: Discourses of Gracie and Lucy' in T. Modleski (ed.), *Studies in Entertainment* (University of Indiana Press: 1986).
18. *Job Switching*, TX 15 Sept. 1952.
19. George Burns, *Gracie: A Love Story* (Hodder & Stoughton: 1989) pp. 44–5.
20. Ibid., p. 72.
21. Ibid., pp. 256–7.
22. Ibid., p. 249.
23. Mellencamp, op. cit., p. 87.
24. *Love is All Around*, Episode 1 (Burns & Brooks) TX 19 Sept. 1970. All details of MTM productions are taken from J. Feuer, P. Kerr and T. Vahimagi (eds), *MTM: Quality Television* (BFI: 1984).
25. Tom Carson, 'The Even Couple', *The Village Voice*, 8 May 1983.

26. J. Feuer, *The MTM Style*, op. cit. Feuer, Kerr, Vahimagi, p. 36. The working conditions carefully documented in this book now seem both idyllic and remote.
27. Episode 6, *Support Your Local Mother*.
28. *Rhoda, The Separation*.
29. Episode 23, *The Birds . . . And . . . Um . . . Bees* (Treva Silverman).
30. *Love Is All Around*.
31. Gitlin, op. cit., p. 214.
32. Episode 28, *Room 223* (Susan Silver).
33. Episode 4, *Divorce Isn't Everything* (Treva Silverman).
34. Serafina Bathrick, op. cit., p. 119.
35. *TV Guide*, 19 Sept. 1970, p. 34.
36. Episode 40, *Fire One, Fire Two*.
37. Episode 168, *The Last Show*.
38. Pat Dowell, 'Ladies Night', *American Film*, Jan/Feb 1985, p. 47.

Ch. 3: British sitcom: a rather sad story

1. Barry Curtis, *Situation Comedy*, BFI Dossier No. 17 (BFI: 1982) p. 4.
2. *The Media Show*, Channel 4, 12 Nov. 1989.
3. See *Guardian*, 13 March 1991.
4. Jill Hyem, 'Entering the Arena' in H. Baehr and G. Dyer (eds), *Boxed In: Women and Television* (Pandora: 1987) p. 161.
5. Quoted in Hyem, ibid., p. 161.
6. *Guardian*, 5 April 1989.
7. *The Media Show*, Channel 4, 12 Nov. 1989.
8. G. Brandt (ed.), *TV Drama* (CUP: 1981) p. 170.
9. Roy Clarke, *The Great Boarding House Caper*, TX BBC1, 10 Nov. 1976. Published in D. Self (ed.), *Situation Comedy* (Hutchinson: 1980).
10. Gaye Tuchman, op. cit. p. 5.
11. Eric Chappell, *Great Expectations*, TX YTV, 18 April 1978. Published in D. Self, op cit.
12. John Cleese and Connie Booth, *The Psychiatrist*, TX BBC2, 26 Feb. 1970. Published in *The Complete Fawlty Towers* (Methuen: 1988) p. 214.
13. See *Guardian*, 10 April 1991, and several interviews in *Woman*.
14. *Radio Times* 10 Nov. 1978.
15. Carla Lane, *The Never-Ending End*, TX BBC1, 5 March 1976, in Self, op. cit., p. 46.
16. M. Eaton, 'Television Situation Comedy', in T. Bennett, S. Bowman, C. Mercer and J. Woollacott (eds), *Popular Television and Film* (BFI/Open University: 1981) p. 34.
17. Terry Lovell, *A Genre of Social Disruption*, BFI Dossier No. 17 (BFI: 1982) p. 24.
18. *Guardian*, 26 Feb. 1991.
19. *Pebble Mill At One* interview, 24 Jan. 1987.
20. *Equal Opportunities in the Mechanical Media*, Equity report, March 1992.
21. *The Stage*, 23 March 1991.
22. Sue Teddern, *Baby Come Back*, TX BBC1, 14 Sept. 1991.

23. Tom Shone, 'No Laughing Matter', *Sunday Times*, 29 March 1992.
24. Mellencamp, op. cit. p. 81.

Ch. 4: On the Halls: Ms/Readings and Negotiations

1. Sylvia Plath, *The Bell Jar* (Faber: 1974) pp. 70–1. Compare also Victoria Wood on turkey necks in *Sold Out* (Methuen: 1991).
2. Quoted by C. Gallagher, *Who Was That Masked Woman? The Prostitute and the Playwright in the Plays of Aphra Behn*, in R. Barrecca, *Last Laughs* (Gordon & Breach: 1988).
3. Aphra Behn, *The Forced Marriage*, quoted in ibid., p. 25. While specific to Restoration comedy, Gallagher's analysis of this play provides a valuable framework for the study of gender-in-performance.
4. Quoted in W. Willeford, *The Fool and his Sceptre* (Arnold: 1969) p. 28.
5. Ibid.
6. Helene Cixous, *The Newly Born Woman*, translated by B. Wing (Manchester University Press: 1987) p. 32.
7. Quoted in H. Scott, *The Early Doors* (Nicholson & Watson: 1946) p. 140.
8. *Does the Theatre Make For Good?*, interview with M. Clement Scott, A. W. Hall, 1898, p. 3.
9. Jerome K. Jerome, *The Idler*, March 1892.
10. Cited in J. S. Bratton, 'Jenny Hill; Sex and Sexism in the Victorian Music Hall', in J. S. Bratton (ed.), *Music Hall: Performance and Style* (Open University: 1986) p. 95.
11. Quoted in H. Chance Newton, *Idols of the Halls* (EP (reprint): 1975), p. 111.
12. Ibid.
13. Quoted in Bratton, op. cit., p. 104.
14. Ibid., p. 104.
15. T. S. Eliot, *Selected Essays* (Faber & Faber: 1941) p. 456.
16. Ibid., p. 458.
17. Quoted (with some indignation) by Naomi Jacob, *Our Marie* (Hutchinson: 1936) p. 199.
18. See, for example, P. Bailey (ed.), *Music Hall: The Business of Pleasure* (Open University: 1986) p. xii. Also M. Banks and A. Swift, *The Joke's On Us* (Pandora: 1987) p. 44.
19. Cited in Tracy C. Davis, *Actresses As Working Women* (Routledge: 1991) p. 119. This usefully investigates the relationship between comic and erotic material.
20. Sheila Jeffreys, *The Spinster and Her Enemies* (Pandora: 1985).
21. Cited in Jacob, op. cit.
22. Ibid., p. 198.
23. H. Willson Disher, *Winkles and Champagne* (Collins: 1938) p. 120.
24. Quoted in Banks and Swift, op. cit., p. 90.
25. Alec Guinness, *Blessings in Disguise* (Hamish Hamilton: 1985) p. 10.
26. Played by Harry Thompson, *Radio Lives*, BBC Radio 4, 26 July 1990.
27. By Haines, Harper and Forrester, BBC Sound Archives.
28. BBC Sound Archives.

29. Cited in L. Martin and K. Segrave, *Women in Comedy* (Citadel: 1986) p. 291.
30. Cited in Lande Smith, *The Stars of Standup Comedy* (Garland: 1986) p. 131.
31. *New York Times*, 24 May 1975, p. 26.

Ch. 5: Making it on your own: women in the new comic traditions

1. B. T. Hall, cited in J. Taylor, *From Self-Help to Glamour*, History Workshop Pamphlet no. 7, Oxford 1972.
2. Les Dawson, *A Card for the Clubs* (Star: 1977) p. 37.
3. See 'CIU Decision Leaves Women out of the Clubs', *The Stage*, 12 April 1990.
4. Interview, M. Banks and A. Swift, *The Joke's On Us* (Pandora: 1987) p. 20.
5. Marti Caine, *A Coward's Chronicles* (Hutchinson: 1990) p. 15.
6. Central Independent TV 1989.
7. Quoted material from Joan Rivers, *What Becomes A Semi-legend Most?*, Geffen Records.
8. Cited L. Martin and K. Segrave, *Women in Comedy* (Citadel: 1986), p. 343.
9. Material from *A Day in the Life*, BBC2, 31 July 1989.
10. Quoted in Betsy Borns, *Comic Lives* (Simon & Schuster: 1987) p. 55.
11. Ibid., p. 32.
12. See Oliver Double, 'An Approach to Traditions of British Standup Comedy', PhD thesis, University of Sheffield, 1991, ch. 5.
13. *Elle*, Feb. 1989.
14. *New York Times*, 29 July 1987.
15. Ibid.
16. *Signals*, Channel Four, 10 Jan. 1990.
17. Interviewed in R. Wilmut and P. Rosengard, *Didn't You Kill My Mother-in-law?* (Methuen: 1989) p. 148.
18. Banks and Swift, op. cit., p. 128.
19. *Open Space*, BBC2, 1986 (New Variety).
20. Oliver Double, op. cit., appendix, p. 68.
21. Banks and Swift, op. cit., p. 32.
22. Interviewed by Mark Jacobson, *Funny Girl: New, Hot and Hip* (New York, 22 March 1976).
23. S. Friedman, *Women's Autobiographical Selves*, in Shari Benstock (ed.), *The Private Self: Theories and Practice of Women's Autobiographical Writings* (Routledge: 1988) p. 41.
24. Joan Rivers, *Enter Talking* (Dell: 1986) p. 126.
25. *Taxi*, July 1988, p. 18.
26. Roseanne Arnold, *My Life As A Woman* (Collins: 1990) p. 172.
27. Arnold's HBO Special 23 Sept 1987.
28. Wilmut and Rosengard, op. cit., p. 134.
29. *Women Tell The Dirtiest Jokes* (Vestron Video: 1985).
30. Showtime Special, *Party of One*, TX 6 March 1988.
31. Martin and Segrave, op. cit., p. 420.
32. Quoted in Wilmut and Rosengard, op. cit., p. 203.
33. 'Laughing Loudest', *Spare Rib*, no. 217, Oct. 1990.

34. *Women Tell The Dirtiest Jokes* (Vestron Video: 1985).
35. See her set for *Paramount City*, Channel 4, 8 April 1990.
36. *Party of One*, 6 March 1988.
37. *Friday Night Live*, Channel 4, 8 April 1988.
38. See Robin Lakoff, *Language and Woman's Place* (Harper & Row: 1975).
39. For example, O'Barr and B. Atkins, cited in J. Coates, *Women, Men and Language* (Longman: 1986) p. 112.
40. Wilmut and Rosengard, op. cit., p. 44.
41. Banks and Swift, op. cit., p. 48.

Ch. 6: Other selves: character comedy and the one-woman show

1. BBC Music Hall, 3 May 1951 (BBC Sound Archives).
2. Victoria Wood, *Barmy* (Methuen: 1987) p. 26.
3. Ibid, p. 44.
4. V. Wood, 'Staying In', in *Mens Sana In Thingummy Doodah* (Methuen: 1990) p. 156.
5. V. Wood, *Up To You, Porky* (Methuen: 1985) p. 87.
6. Ibid. p. 69.
7. D. French and J. Saunders, *The French and Saunders Video*, BBC Video.
8. *Radio Times*, 7 March 1987 (my italics).
9. K. Tynan, *Tynan on Theatre* (Penguin: 1964) p. 297.
10. L. Martin and K. Segrave, *Women in Comedy* (Citadel: 1986) p. 374.
11. *Joyce by Herself and Her Friends*, ed. Reggie Grenfell and Richard Garnett (Futura: 1981) p. 126.
12. Joyce Grenfell, *Turn Back the Clock* (Futura: 1984) p. 18.
13. Ibid. p. 235.
14. Ibid. p. 263.
15. Athene Seyler, *The Craft of Comedy* (reissued Nick Hern Books: 1990) p. 5.
16. J. Grenfell, *Turn Back the Clock*, p. 223.
17. Jane Wagner for Lily Tomlin, *The Search for Signs of Intelligent Life in the Universe* (Harper & Row: 1989) p. 53.
18. Ibid., p. 147.
19. Ibid., p. 153.
20. Ibid., p. 193.
21. Ibid., p. 21.
22. Martin and Segrave, op. cit. p. 37.
23. Wagner, *The Search . . .*, p. 140.
24. Martin and Segrave, op. cit. p. 417.
25. Kathy Maio, *Feminist in the Dark* (Crossing Press: 1989) p. 84.
26. *Whoopi Goldberg Direct from Broadway*, Vestron Video 1987.

Snapshots, 1987–1992: not really a conclusion

1. Trevor Griffiths, *Comedians* (Faber & Faber: 1976) p. 20.
2. Ibid., p. 65.
3. Ibid., pp. 67–8.
4. John Bull, *New British Political Dramatists* (Macmillan: 1984) p. 149.

Suggestions for further reading

Theory

Aristotle, *Poetics*, in *Classical Literary Criticism*, tr. Dorsch, London 1965.
Mikhail Bakhtin, *Rabelais and his World*, tr. Iwolsky, Cambridge, Mass. 1968.
Hélène Cixous, *The Laugh of the Medusa*, in *New French Feminisms*, tr. Marks and de Courtivron, Brighton 1991.
Mary Douglas, *Implicit Meanings*, Boston 1975.
Sigmund Freud, *Jokes and their Relation to the Unconscious*, tr. J. Strachey, London 1966.
Northrop Frye, *The Argument of Comedy*, in *English Institute Essays 1948*, New York 1949.
Goldstein and McGhee, *The Psychology of Humour*, New York 1972.
Arthur Koestler, *The Act of Creation*, London 1964.
Athene Seyler, *The Craft of Comedy*, London 1990.
R. Winegarten (ed.), *Selections on the Status of Women in Society*, Dallas 1978.

A useful sampler of male comic theory can be found in D. Palmer, *Comedy: Developments in Criticism: A Casebook*, London 1984.

Although not all the essays are specifically theoretical, I have found the volume edited by Regina Barreca, *Last Laughs: Perspectives on Women and Comedy* (New York: 1988) invaluable in shaping my own theoretical thinking, and would also recommend the second volume, *New Perspectives on Women and Comedy* (Philadelphia: 1992), which appeared after the completion of this book and contains valuable material on Roseanne Arnold.

Television

H. Baehr and G. Dyer (eds), *Boxed In: Women and Television*, London 1987.
T. Bennett (ed.), *Popular Television and Film*, London 1981.
J. Cook (ed.), BFI Dossier 17, *Television Sitcom*, London 1984.
J. Feuer, P. Kerr, T. Vahimagi (eds), *MTM: Quality Television*, London 1984.
Todd Gitlin, *Inside Prime Time*, New York 1983.
P. Mellencamp, *High Anxiety*, Indiana 1992.
S. Neale and F. Krutnik, *Popular Film and Television Comedy*, London 1990.

Performance

Lisa Appignanesi, *Cabaret*, London 1984.
M. Banks and A. Swift, *The Joke's on Us*, London 1987.
Betsy Borns, *Comic Lives*, New York 1987.
J. Bratton (ed.), *Music Hall: Performance and Style*, London 1986.
R. Busby, *British Music Hall*, London 1976.
Tracy Davis, *Actresses as Working Women*, London 1991.
Lesley Ferris, *Acting Women*, London 1990.
John Fisher, *Funny Way to be a Hero*, London 1973.
John Hind, *The Comic Inquisition*, London 1991.
L. Martin and K. Segrave, *Women in Comedy*, New Jersey 1986.
H. Chance Newton, *Idols of the Halls*, London 1928.
Allardyce Nicoll, *The World of Harlequin*, Cambridge 1963.
Ronald Lande Smith, *The Stars of Standup Comedy*, New York 1986.
R. Wilmut and P. Rosengard, *Didn't You Kill My Mother-in-law?*, London 1989.

Performers

Bart Andrews, *The 'I Love Lucy' Book*, New York 1985.
Roseanne Arnold, *Roseanne: My Life As a Woman*, New York 1989.
Carol Burnett, *Once More Time*, New York 1987.
George Burns, *Gracie: A Love Story*, London 1988.
Eleanor Bron, *The Pillow Book of Eleanor Bron*, London 1985.
Marti Caine, *A Coward's Chronicles*, London 1990.
Fascinating Aida, *Fascinating Who?* London 1986.
Graham McCann, *Marilyn Monroe*, New Brunswick NJ 1987.
Sarah Maitland, *Vesta Tilley*, London 1986.
Carl Rollyson, *Marilyn Monroe: A Life of the Actress*, Ann Arbor, Michigan 1986.
Joan Rivers, *Enter Talking*, New York 1986.

Scripts

R. Blatchford (ed.), *Television Comedy Scripts*, London 1983.
John Cleese and Connie Booth, *The Complete Fawlty Towers*, London 1988.
Dawn French and Jennifer Saunders, *A Feast of French and Saunders*, London 1991.
Joyce Grenfell, *George – Don't Do That. . .* , London 1980.
        Turn Back the Clock, London 1984.
        Stately As a Galleon, London 1984.
        Joyce Grenfell Requests the Pleasure, London 1987.
D. Self (ed.), *Situation Comedy*, London 1980.

Jane Wagner, *The Search For Signs of Intelligent Life in the Universe*, New York 1989.

Victoria Wood, *Up to You*, London 1985.
        Barmy, London 1987.
        Mens Sana in Thingummy Doodah, London 1990.

Videos

Lucille Ball, *I Love Lucy*, CBS/Fox (4 volumes at present released).

Cleese and Booth, *Fawlty Towers*, BBC Video (4 volumes).

French and Saunders, *French and Saunders: The Video*, BBC Video.

Whoopi Goldberg, *Direct From Broadway*, Vestron.

Whoopi Goldberg, *Live in Concert (Fontaine . . . Why Am I Straight?)* (Comedy Club).

Joyce Grenfell, *Joyce Grenfell Entertains*, BBC Video.

Carla Lane,   *Bread*, BBC Video
          Butterflies, BBC Video.

Marks & Gran *Birds of a Feather*, BBC, Palace Video.

Victoria Wood, *Victoria Wood as Seen on TV*, BBC Video.
        More Victoria Wood as Seen on TV, BBC Video.
        An Audience With Victoria Wood, LWT/Parkfield Entertainment.
        Sold Out, MCEG/Virgin.

Index